UNIVERSITY OF NORTH CAROLINA AT CHAPEL HILL
DEPARTMENT OF ROMANCE LANGUAGES

NORTH CAROLINA STUDIES
IN THE ROMANCE LANGUAGES AND LITERATURES

Founder: URBAN TIGNER HOLMES
Editor: FRANK A. DOMÍNGUEZ

Distributed by:

UNIVERSITY OF NORTH CAROLINA PRESS

CHAPEL HILL
North Carolina 27515-2288
U.S.A.

NORTH CAROLINA STUDIES IN THE
ROMANCE LANGUAGES AND LITERATURES
Number 292

ESCAPE FROM THE PRISON OF LOVE:
CALORIC IDENTITIES AND WRITING
SUBJECTS IN FIFTEENTH-CENTURY SPAIN

ESCAPE FROM THE PRISON OF LOVE:
CALORIC IDENTITIES AND WRITING SUBJECTS IN FIFTEENTH-CENTURY SPAIN

ROBERT FOLGER

CHAPEL HILL

NORTH CAROLINA STUDIES IN THE ROMANCE
LANGUAGES AND LITERATURES
U.N.C. DEPARTMENT OF ROMANCE LANGUAGES

2009

Library of Congress Cataloging-in-Publication Data

Folger, Robert.
  Escape from the prison of love : caloric identities and writing subjects in fifteenth-century Spain / Robert Folger.
    p. cm. – (North Carolina studies in the Romance languages and literatures ; no. 292).
  Includes bibliographical references and index.
  ISBN 978-0-8078-9296-1 (hardcover)
    1. Spanish fiction – To 1500 – History and criticism. 2. Spanish fiction – Classical period, 1500-1700 – History and criticism. 3. San Pedro, Diego de, fl. 1500 – Cárcel de amor. 4. Courtly love in literature. 5. Subjectivity in literature. 6. Self in literature. 7. Gender identity in literature. I. Title.
PQ6147.S44F64 2009
863'.095353–dc22   2009006465

Cover design: Heidi Perov

© 2009. Department of Romance Languages. The University of North Carolina at Chapel Hill.

ISBN 978-0-8078-9296-1

DEPÓSITO LEGAL: V. 2.689 - 2009

ARTES GRÁFICAS SOLER, S. L. - LA OLIVERETA, 28 - 46018 VALENCIA
www.graficas-soler.com

anima autem cum sit pars corporis hominis, non est totus homo, et anima mea non est ego.

Thomas Aquinas, *Commentary on I Corinthians* [15, lect. 2, 924, page 780]

["but the soul, although it is part of man's body, is not an entire man, and my soul is not I." (197)]

TABLE OF CONTENTS

	Page
1. INTRODUCTION	13
2. THE PREMODERN SELF	22
2.1. SUBJECTIVITY	27
2.2. FACULTY PSYCHOLOGY AND THE FOLD OF THE SELF	42
2.3. *AMOR HEREOS* AND THE CONSTITUTION OF THE SUBJECT	62
2.4. ONE SEX, MUCH (GENDER) TROUBLE	71
2.4.1. Caloric identities	71
2.4.2. Juan de Flores and gender anxiety	92
2.4.3. Juan Huarte de San Juan's *Examen de ingenios para las ciencias*: a naturalist approach to the problem of gender	104
3. *CÁRCEL DE AMOR: L'ÉCRITURE DE SOI*	112
3.1. FROM PERFORMANCE TO IDENTIFICATION	112
3.2. EL AUCTOR AND HIS FOREBEARS IN *SÁTIRA DE INFELICE E FELICE VIDA* AND *SIERVO LIBRE DE AMOR*	132
CONCLUSION: "VUESTRA MERCED ESCRIBE SE LE ESCRIBA [...]"	154
TEXTS CITED	165
GENERAL INDEX	187

LIST OF ILLUSTRATIONS

	Page
1. Diego de San Pedro. *Lo carcer d'amor.* Barcelona: Johan Rosenbach, 1493	14
2. Gregor Reisch, *Margarita philosophica.* Freiburg im Breisgau: Schott, 1503	47
3. Wild Man, Cathedral of Ávila (16th century)	75
4. Leriano/Deseo, two aspects of the courtly lover	80
5. Fold Leriano/(Laureola)Deseo	81
6. El Auctor as an identificatory stage and subject, constituted through 'imaginary gazes'; fold El Auctor/Leriano (/(Laureola)Deseo)	123

CHAPTER 1

INTRODUCTION

There is certainly no image I have given more thought to than the famous woodcut in Diego de San Pedro's *Cárcel de amor* [*Prison of Love*], that is, the illustration of the encounter between the narrator, Leriano, and the Wild Man, Deseo. This image has been and is both a screen of sorts for my thoughts on premodern subjectivity and gender, and at the same time, a *machina mentis* which actually helped me to formulate these thoughts.[1] At different stages of my research I turned back to *Cárcel* and this image in order to fine tune my interpretation of the text, propelling my argument on subjectivity and gender. This movement is reflected in the text that follows.

My starting point was the issue of gender in *Cárcel de amor* and Spanish sentimental fiction. I soon realized that it was necessary to tackle the even more comprehensive issue of subjectivity, a vexing question for medievalists in general. Since there are so few studies on subjectivity in Iberian medieval literatures – let alone on sentimental romance and *Cárcel de amor* – I had to draw on studies from other provinces of medievalism and early modern studies. Consequently, I hope that I will be able not only to provide a new reading of *Cárcel de amor*, but also to make a contribution to the discussion of premodern subjectivity in gen-

---

[1] Regarding medieval "mind machines", structures that function as gathering and compositional tools, see Mary Carruthers (*The Craft of Thought* 22-24), who explains that thinking is "built upon remembered structures 'located' in one's mind as patterns, edifices, grids, and – most basically – association-fabricated networks of 'bits' in one's memory that must be 'gathered' into an idea" (23).

Diego de San Pedro. *Lo carcer d'amor*. Barcelona: Johan Rosenbach, 1493[2]

---

[2] The history of the fascimile editions is somewhat blurry. In 1906, apparently for the Societat Catalana de Bibliofils (see Alminyana i Vallés 156), Lambert Mata prepared a "photographic" reproduction of the London exemplar. There are two more "mechanic" facsimile editions (1907 and 1912) by the director of the Society, Ramón Miquel y Planas. This reproduction is taken from Miquel y Planas's 1907 edition (7).

eral. In order to facilitate the dialogue with colleagues from other fields, I will provide translations for quotes in any language other than English.[3]

In the first part of the present study, I develop my understanding of the premodern self, establishing a dialogue between premodern texts and specialized literature on gender and subjectivity. First, I critically review studies on premodern subjectivity, supplementing them with my reading of 'postmodern' notions of the subject (1.1.). I will then show how so-called faculty psychology provided a model for the gradual build-up of structures of the self in the form of *hexis* or *habitus* through the 'deconstructive' assimilation of images. This model also accounts for a courtly mode of performative self-fashioning through amatory 'identification' with a mental image (1.2.).[4] I argue that the premodern subject was a 'dispersed,' 'weak' subject constituted by a fold (in the Deleuzian sense) in the choric phantasmatic field. Against the backdrop of this epistemic order, I argue that courtly love, seen in relation to pathological passionate love (*amor hereos* or lovesickness), is a mode of subject constitution reserved for a courtly elite (1.3.). In the next chapter my aim is to tease out the precarious nature of gender inherent in subject constitution through passionate love (1.4.). The courtly technology of the self, based on performance and the ostentation of passionate love, involves a gendered process which leads to the establishment of a masculine speaking 'I'; this gendered subject is not grounded in two distinct naturalized sexes but in a caloric economy that sexes the body (1.4.1.). Analyzing *Cárcel de amor*, again with a particular focus on the initial woodcut, I contend that this identity is threatened by the internal logic of courtly subjectivity. I show how the sentimental fictions of Juan de Flores, *Grimalte y Gradissa* and *Grisel y Mirabella*, articulate the gender anxiety which courtly subject constitution produced, displaying most radically

---

[3] If not otherwise indicated, all translations are mine.
[4] I use the notion of 'self-fashioning' as a *terminus technicus* and not as a catch-all for self-presentation. Apparently unaware of the psychoanalytical underpinning of Stephen Greenblatt's notion, a considerable share of studies make allusions to or even focus on the authors' 'self-fashioning,' meaning a 'disembodied' posturing-as in literature. I mean a becoming, grounded in a material practice.

the consequences of passionate love for the male subject (1.4.2.). I use a sixteenth-century 'medical' text, Juan Huarte de San Juan's famous *Examen de ingenios*, to explore the means (and limitations) that contemporary scientific discourse employed to 'fix' the gender trouble inherent in the premodern model of caloric identities (1.4.4.). Huarte's reformulation of the traditional "one-sex-model" attempts to rescue and restore the old model and, at the same time, unwittingly unsettles it. The *Examen* indicates that the scientific discourses could offer only a partial solution, explaining the need for other discourses to stabilize the patriarchal order. This brief chapter is also meant as a safeguard against reductionism, as a reminder of the complexity of gender issues and the unmanageable ramifications of epistemological changes. Thus it is a retarding element in my story which punctures the smooth narration of historical change. The reader aware of the pitfalls of literary history – or at ease with it – may skip this chapter.

The second part of this study turns back to focus on San Pedro's *Cárcel de amor* (2). While in the analysis of Flores's texts the emphasis was on showing how literary texts reflect (on) subjectivity and gender, my reading of *Cárcel* calls attention to the fact that texts were (or could be) instrumental in shaping subjectivity. I will show that this text is not only indicative of a crisis of courtly self-fashioning, but also exploited the possibilities of the new print medium: *Cárcel* models a new form of parasitic-identificatory constitution of the subject and novel writing and reading practices (2.1.). Printed texts physically separated the readers from text producers, separated performers and an actively participating audience, enabling the reading subject to identify imaginatively with a gender role. This reading subject eschewed the risk of being feminized, which was the nightmare of the courtly masculine subject in the premodern order of the sexes. Analyzing the truly complex figure of El Auctor and his forebears in the anonymous *Sátira de infelice e felice vida* and Juan Rodríguez del Padrón's *Siervo libre de amor* (2.2.), I will show that a new idea of authorship and authorial self-fashioning ("impresario, producer, *and* production"; Starn 217) was concomitant with and supplementary to readerly identificatory subject constitution.

The probing of new readerly and writing subjects in *Cárcel de amor*, in conjunction with the technical possibilities of print-publishing and its epistemological implications, foreshadows essential parameters of Golden Age literature. In the conclusion, I will sketch how *Cárcel de amor*'s configuration of authorship and subject constitution resonates in the first piece universally accepted as modern literature on the Spanish Peninsula: *La vida de Lazarillo de Tormes, y de sus fortunas y adversidades*. I am aware that concluding this study on sentimental fiction and *Cárcel de amor* with a necessarily sketchy analysis of this text may be strategically unwise – on several accounts. Why not follow the established paths of literary genealogy, for instance, having a look at Fernando de Rojas's radical dismantling of the sentimental lover in *Celestina*, or Leriano's descendants in the pastoral novel? Moreover, *Lazarillo* is one of the sacred texts of Spanish literary history; even basic issues like authorship, date of composition, generic status, influence and models are debated with nearly religious fervor. Postulating a new reading, in a few pages, will likely be met with skepticism. These few pages provide a summary of a monograph on the topic of subjectivity and "tactical writing" in early modern Spain.[5] The work on this study has convinced me that Lazarillo is the text best suited to highlight the transcendence of *Cárcel de amor* and San Pedro's monumental status in the history of Castilian letters. I do *not* claim, on any account, that *Cárcel de amor* was an influence on the unknown author of *Lazarillo*, that it was a model, or that it was known to him (although the latter claim is plausible); I hold, however, that Lázaro, the author-*persona*, realizes the potential for 'no-longer-medieval literature' that San Pedro probed in *Cárcel* with his El Auctor, and that this realization is related to the imbrication of literary discourse, media change, and the emerging state and its institutions in Early Modern Spain.

This brief outline shows that the basis of my study is *Cárcel de amor*, enriched (and perhaps complicated) by the analysis of historical texts and contexts, in conjunction with postmodern theory. The following synopsis of my findings on *Cárcel* is intended to provide the reader with an additional map:

> We will see that premodern epistemology (in particular natural philosophy and faculty psychology) regards the self, unlike the

---

[5] The title of this mongraph is *Writing as Poaching: Subject Constitution, Strategic Interpellation and Tactical Writing in Early Modern Spanish Culture*.

Cartesian self, not as a singular vantage point of knowledge, but as the result of a continuous 'folding in' of images (*species*). These images are either generated by imagination on the basis of templates or emanated from objects. The weak or dispersed subject is constituted by a gradual build-up of mental structures in the form of *hexis* or *habitus* through the 'deconstructive' assimilation of images. In the visual and aural choric field, gazes (of people and 'things') are of particular importance because they bestow value (*existimatio*) upon the subject. Since the dispersed subject is predicated on 'seeing' and 'being seen,' he is essentially a product of performance, particularly in the courtly sphere. For the noble self, the game of courtly love has the function of ostentating noble breeding and soliciting benevolent gazes that ratify the projected self. Moreover, seen from the angle of faculty psychology, passionate love implies an assimilation (of the beloved's species and by it) which promises a near-instant transformation into an-other which is fantasized as perfect in body and soul. With this amatory transformation, however, the male lover runs the risk of being emasculated: In terms of gender, his masculinity is threatened because lovesickness makes it impossible to fulfill his obligations as nobleman, and in terms of sex, because the incessant mental contemplation of the beloved woman consumes vital heat (*pneuma* or *spiritus*), the decisive factor in the premodern notion of sexual difference. In *Cárcel de amor*, Diego de San Pedro narrates an exemplary story of the disastrous effects of passionate love for the male noble (courtly/chivalric) subject. The protagonist, Leriano, ultimately fails to accrue *existimatio* as a peer and lover, and dies of lovesickness – effeminated.

In *Cárcel*, this somber story is essentially the vehicle for other forms of self-constitution which are parasitic in relation to courtly love. The first-person eyewitness narrator, El Auctor, is a double of Leriano. El Auctor provides the reader with a locus of identification. Identification, the totalizing assumption of an image in the psychoanalytic sense, is a mode of subject constitution incompatible with the gradual build-up of *hexis*. In the premodern period, identification is unique to passionate love and passion devotion, that is, the identification with the man of sorrows. With the creation of Leriano (who is passionately in love with Laureola, and whose death is modeled on the passion of Christ) and of his double El Auctor, San Pedro enabled the readers to identify with Leriano, dodging the danger of 'real' amatory service and passionate love. The disassociation of the face-to-face situation is pivotal in this readerly identification. It is related to the transition from manuscript culture to print culture which tends to make reading a 'private' process (shielded from the others' gazes).

This introduction requires two terminological clarifications which involve broader issues that I will not be able to discuss at length. First, I have eschewed, as far as possible, the always vexing question of periodization. Researching and particularly writing this book has intensified my qualms about labelling 15th-century texts medieval or late-medieval. There are good reasons to see the supposed historical break around 1492 as merely the culmination of processes which gained momentum in the second half of the 14th century (the unification of the Spanish Kingdoms under the house Trastámara, new forms of government, 'ethnic cleansing,' the beginnings of colonialism and overseas expansion, etc.). From my particular perspective, focused on Castilian letters and the emergence of new forms of subjectivity and literature, two authors may be used to delineate the waning of the Middle Ages: Juan Ruiz and Pero López de Ayala. Juan Ruiz's *Libro de buen amor* (*Book of Good Love*), written in the first half of the 14th century, is a scintillating display of the possibilities of medieval writing and hermeneutics – and what I will describe as the 'dispersed' subject. In the chronicles of the chancellor López de Ayala, written only a few decades after the *Libro de buen amor*, we find a strikingly different authorial subject, who shows a fascination for the opaque personality of King Pedro I.[6] A considerable share of the texts written after Ayala's chronicles, sentimental fictions among them, have more in common with the literature of the Spanish Golden Age than with the texts epitomized by the *Libro de buen amor*. A central claim of this book is that the Isabeline era marks a watershed, implying that the current is uninterrupted. Hence I will use the term 'Early Modern' to refer to a time period that spans from 1350 to the end of the 17th century. In instances where I want to emphasize the continuities between the Middle Ages and the Early Modern Period (and occasionally Greco-Roman antiquity) I will use the adjective 'premodern,' meant as an

---

[6] See Gumbrecht (*'Eine' Geschichte der spanischen Literatur* 109-19). Due to the particularities of the MLA style, the italicization of "*Eine*" ("*A*") in the title regularly falls victim to editorial diligence.

equivalent to 'pre-enlightenment'; I am aware that the latter term brings further complications, particularly in the case of Spain, but it is a useful marker for historical alterity.

The second terminological note refers to my use of the very notion of 'subjectivity.' The reader of the following pages will notice that I associate premodern subjectivity with masculinity, sometimes even to the point of collapsing the two terms. In the following pages I will not explicitly address female subjectivity. This serious omission is, on one hand, due to the scarcity of evidence or sources that would allow the reconstruction of notions of the female self.[7] In the late sixteenth and seventeenth centuries, when writers like Teresa de Ávila,[8] Sor Juana Inés de la Cruz or María de Zayas assert their authorship and produce substantial texts, an analysis of female subjectivity becomes possible.[9] Much of what can be said on subjectivity and female identity before the sixteenth century has been said or can be inferred from Ronald E. Surtz's book, the "The Mothers of Saint Teresa of Avila," and Barbara F. Weissberger's recent monograph on Queen Isabel (*Isabel Rules: Constructing Queenship, Wielding Power*). In another recent book, Denise K. Filios traces female voices in lyric poetry, defining female performance as the locus for the unsettling of, or a resistance to, hegemonic models of female identity, particularly through "parodic mimicry" (3), a Butlerian excessive self-perfor-

---

[7] In two articles, Vicenta Blay Manzanera has catalogued female speech in *cancionero* poetry, documenting the scarcity of 'testimonies'; see also her contribution in the collection of essays *Cultural Contexts/ Female Voices*, edited by Louise M. Haywood. One possible avenue for addressing this issue would be an analysis of male projections of female subjectivity in works, like Rojas's *La Celestina* or Francisco Delicado's *La lozana andaluza*. A particularly interesting case is Juan de Flores's *Grimalte y Gradissa*; see chapter 2.4.2, and Louise M. Haywood's "Gradissa: A fictional female reader in/of a male author's text".

[8] Teresa de Ávila can be seen as an emblematic figure representing the genre of the female *vida espiritual*, which produced hundreds of female autobiographies in Spain and the Americas; see Kathryn Joy McKnight's study (particularly p. 17-59).

[9] Studies which point in this direction are, for instance, the articles by Edward Howells, Elisabeth Rhodes, and Ruth El Saffar ("The 'I' of the beholder"), in the case of Teresa de Ávila; Jacqueline Cruz and Yolanda Martínez-San Miguel in Sor Juana's case; and Lisa Vollendorf's and Marina S. Brownlee's analyses of María de Zayas's *Novelas ejemplares*. Referring to Paul Smith's notion of subjectivity, Martínez-San Miguel argues that female subjectivity can be conceptualized as a negotiation of male subject positions. The female subject, then, would be a *tactical* (Certeaudian) subject *par excellence* – although Martínez-San Miguel speaks of "estrategias"; see also Stephan Leopold and Rosilie Hernández-Pecoraro.

mance.[10] Nevertheless, Filios's study shows that the ventriloquism of female characters was instrumental in the performative construal of male identities, indicating that female voice and *place* is the voice and the place of the *other*.[11] I think that there is an intrinsic reason for the difficulty of describing medieval female subjectivity: similar to the construction of female sex as deficiency (of vital heat, physical strength, and intellectual capacity), female subjectivity was constructed as a lack of agency and 'voice';[12] Freud's and Lacan's perplexity about the peculiar nature of the female psyche and their desire to scrutinize it would have had no meaning for premodern men. Negating the particularity of the female subject produced the necessary blind spot for the affirmation of masculine subjectivity. Tracing the contours of this blind spot would go beyond the scope of the present study.

It is my pleasure to acknowledge the support I have received from E. Michael Gerli and Antonio Cortijo Ocaña. Their comments and constructive criticism as expert readers for the NCSRLL helped me to improve my text; more importantly, I am, like anybody else working in this field, indebted to their insightful work on Spanish sentimental fiction. Anna Larsson's editorial help and zeal for linguistic clarity has been invaluable. The deficiencies of this book are solely my responsibility. Many thanks also to Kelly Fowler for the graphic design of the illustrations. Finally, I am grateful to the general editor, Frank A. Domínguez, who made this publication possible, and to the Universiteit Utrecht for a publication grant, and to the Program for Cultural Cooperation Between Spain's Ministry of Culture and United States Universities for their support.

---

[10] Filios's study is complicated by the fact that we lack substantial evidence regarding medieval performance practices, particularly female performance. The reconstruction of these performance situations from lyric texts tends to be speculative.

[11] See Michel de Certeau's famous definition of the notion of 'tactics,' characterized by "l'absence d'un propre" (60) ["the absence of 'a proper'"]. Stephen Rendall translates here "proper locus" (36), which I think unduly reduces the complexity of the French text.

[12] Weissberger shows the complexity of the process of Isabel's appropriation of masculinity in her construction of 'queenship' (*Isabel Rules: Constructing Queenship, Wielding Power*).

Chapter 2

THE PREMODERN SELF

In Spanish cultural memory, the date 1492 is heavily overdetermined: it marks not only Columbus's first voyage to the 'Indies,' but also the conquest of Granada, the last Moorish stronghold in the Iberian Peninsula; the expulsion of the Jews from the Spanish Kingdoms; and, as a cultural highlight, the publication of Antonio de Nebrija's first grammar of the Spanish language. Diego de San Pedro's masterpiece *Cárcel de amor* is also related to this epoch-making year: the first extant edition of the text was printed in 1492 (Seville: Cuatro Compañeros Alemanes).[1] Textual evidence[2] – and the fact that a Catalan translation was published only a few months later, with elaborate illustrations including a banner with a Spanish title in the first woodcut of the allegorial prison – suggests that the actual *editio princeps* may have been printed slightly before 1492. However, the association of *Cárcel* with this year is apt. It is not my intention to argue that this brief text is monumental – although I think that it ranks among the most outstanding achievements in Spanish letters – I rather think that it is, due to its intriguingly liminal status, a perfect token for the *epoché* 1492. *Cárcel de amor* is a brilliant display of medieval "techniques or technology of the self" (Foucault, "About the Be-

---

[1] *Cárcel de amor* is certainly the best-studied text of sentimental romance. Regarding scholarship see Robert Folger (*Images in Mind* 194-227), and, for older studies, Keith Whinnom's still indispensable checklist (*The Spanish Sentimental Romance* 39-55). I will discuss pertinent scholarship in the course of this study.
[2] See Vicenzo Minervini (29-30).

ginning of the Hermeneutics of the Self" 203), which cancel themselves out on the road to a new form of subjectivity. *Cárcel* explores and models imaginary identification, interpellation and self-fashioning, commonly seen as the hallmark of the Renaissance.

Although it is uncertain when Diego de San Pedro actually wrote his *chef-d'œuvre*, there is no doubt that the plot he unfolds is situated in the Spanish Kingdoms on the verge of becoming a nation state and an imperial power. San Pedro, who figures in the text as El Auctor, tells us about a strange encounter he had on his way back to Peñafiel from a military campaign against the Nasrid Kingdom of Granada.

> *Comiença la obra*
> [...]
> [P]or unos valles hondos y escuros que se hazen en la Sierra Morena, vi salir a mi encuentro, por entre los robledales do mi camino se hazía, un cavallero assí feroz de presencia como espantoso de vista, cubierto todo de cabello a manera de salvaje; levava en la mano isquierda un escudo de azero muy fuerte, y en la derecha una imagen femenil entallada en una piedra muy clara, la qual era de tan estrema hermosura que me turbava la vista; salían della diversos rayos de fuego que levava encendido el cuerpo de un honbre que el cavallero forciblemente levava tras sí. (4)[3]
> [*Here begins the story.* (...) (J)ust as the sun was beginning to illuminate the earth, through some deep and shadowed valleys in the Sierra Morena, I espied coming towards me, from among some oak-groves through which my path led, a knight fierce in bearing and frightful to behold, covered all in hair, like a wild man. He bore in his left hand a shield of stout steel, and in his right the image of a woman, carved from shining stone, which was of such extreme beauty that it dazzled my eyes, and from which issued fiery rays which wreathed in flames the body of a man who was being drawn irresistibly along behind the knight. (4)][4]

---

[3] All quotes are taken from Carmen Parrilla's edition. In the 16th and 17th centuries *Cárcel de amor* was repeatedly reissued and translated into numerous European languages (Corfis 21-47; Whinnom, "Introduction" 7-9; Parrilla, "Prólogo", ed. *Cárcel* 73-79). Bilingual Spanish-French editions indicate that it was considered, as late as 1650, a model text of good Spanish (Corfis 39-47).

[4] All English quotes from *Cárcel* are taken from Whinnom's translation.

The observer soon learns that the savage knight is Deseo ('Desire,' 'Yearning'), who has enslaved the young nobleman, Leriano, with the help of an image of his unsympathetic beloved, the Macedonian princess Laureola. Obeying Leriano's plea, El Auctor accompanies the outlandish triangle of passion to a strange Prison of Love, which allegorically represents the phenomenology of passionate love.[5] Once he gains access to the prison he witnesses the bizarre torture of the passion-ridden captive. When El Auctor accepts a mission to deliver a letter to Laureola and convince her to write a response, Leriano succeeds in escaping from the Prison of Love.

At the Macedonian court, a jealous rival named Persio accuses them of having an illicit love affair. Although Leriano triumphs over his enemy in an ordeal, King Gaulo imprisons his daughter. After various attempts to appeal to the King's clemency and sense of justice fail, Leriano rebels against his sovereign, frees Laureola, and eventually proves her innocence. This leads to the princess's rehabilitation but, fearing for her reputation and honor, Laureola definitively rejects her importunate 'savior.'[6] Distraught, Leriano leaves the court. Henceforth he refuses food and lies down to wait for death. Shortly before he dies, he dissolves Laureola's letters in a cup of water, drinks it, and expires with the words: "Acabados son mis males" (79) ["My sufferings are ended" (82)]. El Auctor, who had supported Leriano all along as a go-between and partisan, departs, in tears, to Peñafiel, where he reports to his Lord, "besando las manos de vuestra merced" (79) ["kissing your lordship's hands"].[7]

Shortly after the first extant edition appeared, a Catalan translation was executed by Bernardí Vallmanya (Barcelona, 1493 [imp. Johan Rosenbach]).[8] This version contains a series of

---

[5] See Folger (*Images in Mind* 207-12).

[6] Elizabeth Teresa Howe, among others, argues that Laureola, not Leriano, is the actual victim in *Cárcel de amor*. This view is questioned by Weissberger, who sees in her a "victorious heroine" ("Role-Reversal and Festivity in the Romances of Juan de Flores" 208).

[7] Whinnom translates "where I remain your lordship's humble servant" (82). As I will explain in due course, the kiss is important because it indicates the libidinal dimension of this submission to 'power'.

[8] Regarding the translation see R. Miquel y Planas's introduction (*Lo carcer d'amor*) and Vicenzo Minervini. The wood-cuts were probably executed for a lost Castilian *editio princeps*; see María Rosa Fraxanet Sala (430).

wood-cuts – sixteen in total – which illustrate key scenes of San Pedro's text, including the initial encounter I described above (caption 1).⁹ This image is well-known and has been reproduced on numerous occasions. *Cárcel* criticism, however, has not paid due attention to its complexity.¹⁰ And, indeed, it deserves attention because this wood-cut is the work of a careful and ingenious reader who provided a fascinating supplement to the text. It is the nodal point of my reflection on subjectivity and the interplay between sex and gender in Early Modern Spain.

Cárcel is commonly grouped with the texts of so-called sentimental romance (*novela sentimental*) or sentimental fiction (*ficción sentimental*). It is a heterogeneous group of texts subsumed under a generic label whose definition is debated. Few, however, will deny that the basic feature of sentimental fiction is the in-depth exploration and presentation of emotional states and intimate thoughts associated with cases of passionate love.¹¹ In the earliest works of sentimental fiction, Juan Rodríguez del Padrón's *Siervo libre de amor*, Don Pedro's *Sátira de infelice e felice vida*, and the anonymous *Triste deleytaçión*,¹² this sentimental probing

---

⁹ Alan Deyermond has recently studied the editorial history of the woodcuts ("The Woodcuts of Diego de San Pedro's *Cárcel de Amor*").

¹⁰ Aside from Alan Deyermond's seminal analysis of "El hombre salvaje en la novela sentimental" and his recent "The Woodcuts of Diego de San Pedro's *Cárcel de Amor*, 1492-1496," the most notable exceptions are Erich von Richthofen and Harvey L. Sharrer's careful analysis. See also Fraxanet Sala and Timothy Husband (65-67).

¹¹ The lowest common denominator among critics is that the texts of sentimental fiction are, as Keith Whinnom laconically puts it, "short love-stories" (*Diego de San Pedro* 76). The question of the generic status of sentimental fiction is one of the 'traditional,' controversially discussed topics in scholarship. The debate was revived by Antonio Cortijo Ocaña ("La ficción sentimental: ¿un género imposible?") as a guest editor of a critical cluster on sentimental romance in *La corónica* (29:1 [2000]). See Rohland de Langbehn's critical comment ("Una lanza por el género sentimental ... ¿ficción o novela?") and the ensuing reactions in a forum of the same journal (31:2 [2002]). Notwithstanding the position in this debate, it is advisable to heed Patricia Grieve's warning and avoid the pitfall of seeing in *Cárcel* a paradigmatic or typical text (*Desire and Death in Spanish Sentimental Romance* 27).

¹² Unearthing texts predating the presumed 'prototype' *Siervo*, Antonio Cortijo Ocaña's monograph *La evolución genérica de la ficción sentimental de los siglos XV y XVI: género literario y contexto social* has considerably widened the spectrum of sentimental fiction.

is cast in terms of (pseudo-)autobiographical reports, missives sent from the patient-lover to a confidant.[13]

These few remarks suggest that sentimental fiction is essentially propelled by a "hermeneutics of desire" (Foucault, *The Use of Pleasure* 89).[14] The genre has its place in what Michel Foucault has called the "Beginning of the Hermeneutics of the Self." In the introduction to the English translation to Foucault's homonymous essay, Mark Blasius characterizes this hermeneutics of the self as a continuous analysis of one's thoughts "and the self's iteration and social reinforcement through an ongoing verbalization of this self-decipherment to others" (199). This self-decipherment is intimately related to the prominent role of epistolary discourse in sentimental romance (in the overall structure and/or in the intercalated letters).[15] Writing letters about oneself and one's condition could be

> un entraînement de soi-même par l'écriture, à travers les conseils et les avis qu'on donne à l'autre: elle constitue aussi une certaine manière de se manifester à soi-même et aux autres. [...] Écrire, c'est donc 'se montrer,' se faire voir, faire apparaître son propre visage auprès de l'autre. ("L'écriture de soi" 425).
> [a 'self-conditioning' through writing and the advice and admonitions given to somebody else: it constitutes a certain way to manifest oneself to oneself and to others. (...) Writing, then, is a 'showing oneself,' making oneself seen, making one's own face appear to the other.]

---

[13] The epistolary form (often traced back to the influence of Eneas Silvio Piccolomini's *Historia de duobus amantibus*) is commonly acknowledged as one of the defining characteristics of sentimental fiction; see the recent survey of César Besó Portalés, which unfortunately does not take into account studies written after 1995. Regarding the importance of medieval *ars dictaminis*, in particular Boncompagno da Silva's *Rota Veneris*, see Cortijo Ocaña ("Introducción"). Cortijo Ocaña has articulated his thesis of this influence in a detailed analysis of the foundational text of the 'genre,' *Siervo libre de amor* ("De amicitia, amore et rationis discretione").

[14] The prevalence of "interior action" over chivalric or amorous adventures is a commonplace in sentimental fiction scholarship; see, for instance, Rina Walthaus. José Luis Canet Vallés convincingly argues that the analysis of the process of falling in love (*enamoramiento*) is the *raison d'être* and structural principle of sentimental fiction. In my own approach to sentimental fiction I am indebted to his reasoning (Folger, *Images in Mind*).

[15] This does not mean, of course, that the letters did not have an essentially persuasive intention; see Miguel-Prendes's "Las cartas de la *Cárcel de amor*".

Though sentimental fiction grows, as I will show, out of traditional courtly modes of self-fashioning, it marks a beginning of new techniques of the self based on novel writing and reading practices. Within the corpus of sentimental fiction, particularly *Cárcel de amor* has a liminal status because it not only participates in sentimental fiction's hermeneutics of the self, but also explores new modes of writerly self-assertion that we commonly associate with Renaissance literature.

2.1. SUBJECTIVITY

We post-medievals tend to think of the self or 'I' in terms of 'subject' and 'subjectivity,' both loaded terms, gravitational centers of relentless discussions, if not polemics. Matters are further complicated if the focus is on premodern notions of subjectivity. Three main perspectives can be discerned in this discussion. There are those who associate subjectivity with modernity, some of them considering it a defining characteristic. From this perspective 'premodern subjectivity' is a contradiction in terms, and a study of this concept is at best a quixotic endeavor, at worst a distorting imposition of anachronistic terms in historical analysis. Others see in subjectivity an anthropological constant, assuming that it is, and was, constitutive of 'human nature' and man's psychic reality; a variation of that view, represented for instance by Anthony Low, is that subjectivity gradually gained prevalence over an "emphasis on community," in a historical process of alienation with "psychological pressures that thwart personal desires" (X and XVIII). Finally, subjectivity can be seen as a general term referring to configurations of the self that change over the centuries and hence require historicization. The last approach, which will be the basis of this study, demands a detailed discussion of the notion.

The unavoidable starting or reference point is René Descartes's postulate that "each individual has a unique or privileged access to his or her own inner discourse – an access that could not legitimately be contradicted by any collective process or external authority" (Heller and Wellbery 5). Opposed to an outside world (*res extensa*), the interiorized self (*res cogitans*) is the ground of knowledge and experience of the world. Descartes's subject is the centerpiece in what Roy Porter has called "our received great saga of the self" (8).[16] The 'invention' of the subject or individual is attributed to Renaissance humanism; after Descartes's foundational codification of subjectivity, the subject develops into Hume's "punctual self" (Taylor 159-76), Kant's transcendental subject and its aftermath in German 19th-century idealism's *Subjektphilosophie*, and the Enlightenment notion of the subject as a free, autonomous and rational being.[17] This 'humanist' subject is still hegemonic in our Western culture, despite the fact that it was philosophically assaulted by Friedrich Nietzsche and undermined by Freudian psychoanalysis more than a century ago. In the last few decades the (post-)Cartesian subject has come under attack from many sides: sociology, philosophy, psychoanalysis, feminism and gender studies, and lately, post-colonial theory. In the field of literary criticism French philosophy has been particularly influential; 'neo-structuralists' like Michel Foucault, Jacques Lacan, Louis Althusser, and Gilles Deleuze, to name only a few, have, more or less explicitly,[18] advocated the 'death of the subject,'[19] precisely referring to the subject as it presumably emerged in the Early Modern period.

I have no intention of taking sides in the ultimately ethical discussion of the preferability of one form of subjectivity or another, nor do I want to assess the sociological, philosophical or psychological validity of a particular notion of subjectivity. The

---

[16] Margareta de Grazia discusses the problems of teleological approaches to the history of subjectivity; see also Lee Patterson ("On the Margin") and David Aers.

[17] See Manfred Frank ("Subjekt, Person, Individuum").

[18] The case of Foucault, unquestionably the most influential thinker in historically oriented studies, is instructive: subjectivity was for him, as he makes clear in his late essay "The Subject and Power," the overarching topic of his prolific *œuvre*. However, it wasn't until his last project, the three-volume *History of Sexuality*, that he explicitly addressed individual techniques and the care of the Self (*souci de soi*). In spite of Foucault's anti-teleological impetus, the Middle Ages figure in his work in a rather traditional way as the blurry Other of antiquity and modernity. Unfortunately, the fourth volume of his *History of Sexuality*, which was supposed to shed light on Christian (medieval?) practices of the self, was never published.

[19] The question of subjectivity is the linchpin of Manfred Frank's detailed analysis and critique of what he labels as 'neo-structuralist' thinking (*Was ist Neo-Strukturalismus?*). It is impossible to provide an exhaustive review of the scholarship on subjectivity. Nick Mansfield provides an overview of important current trends; see also Paul Smith's monograph and his discussion of the meanings of 'subject' in different discourses.

value of (post-)modern critiques of the humanist subject resides in the fact that they question the teleological "saga of the self," and that they provide new ways of thinking about the self. Thinking about self after Descartes suggests asking, without bias, about the status of self before him. I am by no means advocating a flat correspondence between the pre- and the postmodern; as John Jeffries Martin cautions us, in projecting our 'postmodern' notion of the 'self' onto the early modern or medieval past, we risk a distortion similar to the one 19th-century scholars like Jacob Burckhardt committed in seeing Renaissance man as a mirror of their elitist bourgeois selves.[20] I am convinced, however, that recent anti-humanist notions of subjectivity provide conceptual alternatives to the (still) entrenched notion and implications of a 'standard' (autonomous, disembodied, interiorized) subjectivity. If adapted to a different historic epistemic regime and brought into accordance with contemporary ideas of selfhood, postmodern theory provides analytic tools to approach an adequate description of pre-modern subjectivity.

It is obvious that the question of selfhood is often implicitly and sometimes explicitly addressed in Early Modern writings, particularly in texts wherein the author or narrator presents or produces an image of his or her Self. I am, however, not primarily interested in showing how, and to which degree, literary or historiographical artifacts reflect philosophical notions of subjectivity. This approach tells us little about the texts in question and contributes even less to the history of *Subjektphilosophie*, which has been told by scholars like Charles Taylor, who has written the most comprehensive and elaborate history of subjectivity from the perspective of the history of ideas.

According to Taylor, the modern subject is characterized by a notion of inwardness and the affirmation of ordinary life. Since he screens philosophers' conceptions of the self, from Plato to the twentieth century, with these criteria in mind, his study is tainted with a certain teleological bent. More importantly, philosophy is not the only and arguably not the most significant discourse in which subjectivity is discussed or negotiated. Philosophy, theology, and medicine, among others, are discourses which must be seen as part and parcel of dispositives of subjectification. I use 'dis-

---

[20] See Martin (8-15).

positive' here in the Foucaultian sense, that is, as a heterogenous network of discursive and non-discursive elements (discourses, institutions, administrative measures, etc.) with the strategic rationale of responding to an 'urgency.'[21] We must not forget that discourses are related to non-discursive institutionalized and institution-based practices and rituals. My main interest resides in probing this intersection of subjectivity, 'ethopoetic' texts and institutions (bureaucracy, the court, 'literature,' historiography),[22] reconstructing the logic and fault-lines of Early Modern subjectivity and its unspoken implications and over-determinations.

Since I share the post-modern skepticism about an essentialized and universalized notion of subjectivity, characterized by reflectivity and 'self-possession' of thoughts and emotions,[23] it is all the more imperative to describe my own understanding of it. As a matter of fact, it is necessary to justify its general usefulness. Niklas Luhmann, for instance, proposes to discard the concept. Departing from the "traditional connotations" of 'subject' as "hypokeimenon/subiectum – something 'lying under' and supporting attributes," he asserts that "'subject' means something that underlies and carries the world, and, therefore, exists in its own right as a transcendental and not as an empirical phenomenon" (319). He concludes that the term should be dropped "if we are simply referring to a part of reality. How can we conceive of part of reality as underlying or supporting reality?" (320). Luhmann suggests supplanting 'subjectivity' with "psychic system," "consciousness," or "personal system," terms which betray systems theory's reductionism and Luhmann's unacknowledged bias toward the disembodied, autonomous subject.[24]

Another assault against the appropriateness of the "vocabulary of subjectivity" for "theorizing the distinction between pre-modern and the modern" (123) has recently been launched by

---

[21] See Foucault (*Dispositive der Macht* 119-125). Deleuze characterizes a dispositive as an interplay of discourses and "visibilities" (*Foucault* 56-60); see also Joseph Rouse (110).

[22] With "*éthopoiétique*" Foucault refers to writing practices which effect "la transformation de la vérité en *êthos*" ("L'écriture de soi" 418) ["the transformation of truth into ethos"].

[23] See Frank ("Subjekt, Person, Individuum" 9).

[24] Hans-Georg Pott argues (73-74) that Luhmann's system-environment dichotomy ultimately substitutes the traditional distinction between subject and object.

William Egginton in his *How the World Became a Stage: Presence, Theatricality and the Question of Modernity*.[25] This study argues that 'subjectivity' is neither a historically specific nor a theoretically coherent notion. According to Egginton, most studies on subjectivity conflate "philosophical," "political," and "aesthetic" subjectivity. Glossing on Heidegger, he rejects "philosophical" subjectivity – which he collapses with the Cartesian notion of the self-grounding subject – because it is a "mode of talking about experience" rather than a "mode of experience" (128). Egginton argues that 'real' experience is predicated on visual practices and an ensuing "spatiality." This spatiality characterizes a historically specific phenomenology. The peculiar modern form of spatiality is, according to Egginton, "theatricality," a concept he considers capable of accounting for all aspects of subjectivity and which should, according to the author, supplant the concept of subjectivity all together:

> Theatricality is the historically-specific description (i.e. mine) of the historically-specific form of mediation that structures the spatiality of Dasein's experience in the modern world (137).

While medieval spatiality was based on "presence," Early Modern theatricality was

> that form of spatiality in which viewers constantly confront pictures containing copies of their selves, and in which they are free to manipulate that world at a distance or be manipulated by in it [sic] as characters. (139)

Theatricality enables identification and thus provides a model for agency, which is situated in the terrain of "political subjectivity" or theories of subjectification. Egginton holds that with the development of modern forms of governance, the nation state, the traditional

> 'imaginary' bond, in that the lord's personal image was always present to the vassal and the vassal knew his lord by sight and

---

[25] Egginton's fundamental argument is also summarized in an earlier article (1996) with the title "An Epistemology of the Stage: Theatricality and Subjectivity in Early Modern Spain".

sound was substituted by a symbolically mediated relationship between sovereign and subject. (143)

The "change from personal to procedural forms of domination also involved a shift in the nature of the roles played by individuals within the system" (143). The main media of this transformation were literature and, above all, the theater (the realm of "aesthetic subjectivity"; 153-64). The theater established a 'screen,' the site of imaginary self-performance and the reconciliation of individual fantasies and ideology.

Important cues can be taken from Egginton's study: I agree that in the Early Modern Period, distancing between authorities and subjects made it necessary for the subject to be able to identify (in the psychoanalytic sense) with *images* as 'role models.' I am, however, not convinced that Early Modern theater was as central (and as pioneering) in this process as Egginton asserts. The purpose of this study is to show that nearly a century before the theater became theatrical and visually trained the masses, a new form of literature emerged which required and, at the same time, probed the identificatory potential of the *letter*.[26] We will see that these 'discourses of subjectivity' were part of a dispositive that emerged with the invention of the printing press and the rapid dissemination of related cultural practices (writerly and readerly ones).

Egginton fails to acknowledge the momentous impact of these developments because an essentialized notion of visuality determines his analysis of Early Modern visual culture. His account of "theatricality" is based on an understanding of vision which is exclusively ocular, while premodern epistemology paid equal if not greater attention to 'interior' visuality.[27] The exterior sense of vi-

---

[26] As the contributions in the collection of essays *Culture and Control in Counter-Reformation Spain* (edited by Anne J. Cruz and Mary Elizabeth Perry) indicate, we must posit, in my opinion even in the period before the Council of Trent, "varying forms of social control exerted by Spanish institutions" (Cruz and Perry 14), that is, instruments of subjection, such as religious ceremonies, the institutions of 'popular' cults of saints and religious oratory. In a book-length study of *Writing as Poaching* (currently under consideration) I argue that the very "procedural forms of domination" (Egginton, *How the World Became a Stage* 143), that is, bureaucracy, were of crucial importance for the emergence of new forms of subjectivity – and literature.

[27] Studies by Robert S. Nelson, Norman Bryson, David Summers, Suzannah Biernoff, and Cynthia Hahn, among others, illustrate various aspects of this alien concept of visuality.

sion was, as I will presently show, contiguous and subordinated to the visual powers of the interior senses. The prevalence of modern psychology in Egginton's argument is its major weak spot. Although he relies essentially on psychoanalytical, that is, Lacanian, categories in his attempt to historicize the constituents of modern forms of subjectification, he points out that psychoanalysis is not a historical model (150). This holds true for the Freudian model based on a historic family model and gender order. It is also a fact that Lacan's analyses are concerned with historical matters only in terms of illustrating his theory of the (post)modern subject. Yet the Lacanian Symbolic and Imaginary are, as we will see, potentially historical notions and can be historicized by integrating past conceptions of selfhood and identity.

Egginton's objections to the notions of "philosophical" and "political" subjectivity are not convincing either.[28] I have already pointed out that 'philosophy' does not provide a master-code of subjectivity, but relegating it to the status of a mere "linguistic or conceptual manifestation of the new spatiality" (*How the World Became a Stage* 137) is problematic. 'Philosophy' as Egginton understands it is in itself a historical notion which is not applicable to Early Modern scholarship.[29] Scholarship comprised a wide range of *practices* which were,[30] at any rate, indexical and integral of a Symbolic Order – at least if we focus on the learned elite. If 'Philosophy' is indeed a manifestation of a new form of subjectivity, it is necessary to take into account the hegemonic currencies of scholarship, that is – particularly in the 16th and 17th centuries, and particularly in Spain – Platonism and Aristotelian Natural Philosophy. Both schools of thought provided elaborate accounts for the description of subjectivity. The theoretical approaches to the question of the 'nature of man' (which had a practical application in medicine, for instance) also provided a model of agency. Hence Egginton's critique of the concept of subjectivity

---

[28] The third category, "aesthetic subjectivity," which Egginton labels as "correlates" of the other categories (*How the World Became a Stage* 153), is actually a subcategory which does not require further discussion in this context.

[29] As Ulrich Johannes Schneider shows, our notion of philosophy has its roots in the late 18th century.

[30] Glimpses of the practical aspects of Early Modern scholarship are provided, for example, by the contributions in *Die Praktiken der Gelehrsamkeit in der Frühen Neuzeit*, edited by Helmut Zedelmaier and Martin Mulsow.

– that it conflates a "philosophical" understanding and a "political" one – is, in my opinion, a point in its favor: the grounding and empowered subject is always subject to power. There is, then, no convincing reason to discard subjectivity as an analytic category and historic phenomenon which may or may not have undergone a change in the Early Modern Period.

There is, however, a viable alternative to the analytic concept of subjectivity, which is well-established in scholarship: the repeatedly mentioned *self*.[31] According to Stephen Greenblatt, 'self' can be understood as

> a sense of personal order, a characteristic mode of address to the world, a structure of bounded desires – and always some elements of deliberate shaping in the formation and expression of identity. (*Renaissance Self-Fashioning* 1)

This self is, according to Greenblatt, characterized by "a consistent mode of perceiving and behaving" (2). Although this definition is a useful one, it cannot supplant the term subjectivity. For, as Taylor points out, there is nothing natural about thinking

> that we 'have' selves as we have heads. [... T]he very idea that we have or are 'a self,' that human agency is essentially defined as 'the self,' is a linguistic reflection of our modern understanding and the radical reflexivity it involves. (177)

Subjectivity, on the other hand, is not essentially predicated upon reflexivity or self-knowledge. If we do not restrict our view, as Luhmann or Egginton do, to a canonical philosophical tradition, it becomes clear that the term 'subject' had other "traditional connotations" (Luhmann 319) in common usage,[32] and that the subject is not only and not necessarily an autonomous self-

---

[31] Unlike subjectivity, self is a term that is attested in the English Renaissance, having a boom in the 17th century, see Peter Burke. Jonathan Sawday speaks of the emergence of "vocabulary of ipseity around 1650" (30). The lack of psychological terminology comparable to ours, was the starting point for Anne Ferry's study of the "inward" language of poetry.

[32] Analyzing medieval scholastic authors, Theo Kobusch reminds us that the term 'subiectum' is not as unidimensional as Luhmann assumes: in Alexander of Hales *subiectum* means "human nature of Christ" (744), consisting of body and soul.

grounding vantage point. The human being, body and soul, as subject (*sujeto*) is subjected to a foreign power which rules over many similar subjects. In this sense the term subjectivity captures, in Mansfield's words, the "social and cultural entanglement" of the self, the fact that it is "always linked to something outside of it [...]. The word subject, therefore, proposes that the self is at the intersection of general truths and shared principles" (2-3). This is the reason why subjectivity always connotes both empowerment and submissiveness, individuation and normalization.

A broad definition of subjectivity which is not limited to notions of the self and not measured by Cartesian or Post-Cartesian subjectivity makes it possible to take into account that self-fashioning always implies submission and empowerment. Peter Haidu, in a recent study on subjectivity in the (French) Middle Ages, has coined a useful shorthand: he speaks of a "potentiality for action" (114).[33] Hence I understand subjectivity as an eminently "political" notion, to use Egginton's classification, as a model for agency which cannot, however, be separated from the "philosophical" subjectivity. Contemporary reflections on the nature of man must be taken into account. It is apparent that a sense of self is crucial in establishing subjectivity as agency, but it is equally clear that it cannot be reduced to it. An important supplement to Haidu's minimal definition is John Jeffries Martin's observation that notions of the self are essentially anchored in the

> relation between those dimensions of experience that people describe as internal (conscious or unconscious thoughts, feelings, beliefs, emotions, desires) and those they describe as external (speaking or writing, hating or loving, praying or blaspheming, laughing or crying, stealing or buying, and so on). (14)

A corollary of this view is that the subjectivity (self cum agency) is anchored in a bodily reality because it is the body and its functioning and boundaries that establish inside and outside. This bodily reality, too, must be historicized, since it is constituted by

---

[33] Pertinent in this respect is Paul Smith's notion of the 'agent,' which he defines as a "subjectivity where, by virtue of the contradictions and disturbances in and among subject-positions, the possibility (indeed, the actuality) of resistance to ideological pressure is allowed for [...]" (xxxv).

culturally specific discourses and dispositives. In other words, there is always a gender aspect to subjectivity. Moreover, the psychosomatic nature of subjectivity may be suppressed in some notions (the most prominent example is, of course, the Cartesian subject) but remains, nevertheless, a necessary frame of reference.

Under the umbrella of the sprawling debate on the nature of 'our subjectivity,' its desirability and alternative forms, a host of studies have addressed the question of the historical genesis of (modern) subjectivity and its (medieval) equivalents.[34] Debunking the widespread "saga of the self" which silhouettes the splendorous heroes of subjectivity (Augustine, Petrarch, the Humanists, Montaigne, Descartes, Locke, Rousseau...) against the dire background of non-self-conscious medieval intellectual currents, (the Church Fathers, Scholasticism, Natural Philosophy) recent scholarship has provided us with a much more nuanced picture, a demystification of the Renaissance and a reconstruction of the complexity of medieval poetics of the self.[35]

---

[34] Peter von Moos speaks of the "boundlessness" ("Uferlosigkeit") of the topic ("Persönliche Identität und Identifikation vor der Moderne" 2); see his useful bibliographical appendix, in which he focuses on studies from the angle of social history (25-42). The most comprehensive historical study of philosophically-framed ideas about selfhood is Charles Taylor's *Sources of the Self*. Important recent monographs centered on (or related to) subjectivity, 'identity,' 'individuality' in the formative period are, among others, the works by James F. Burke (*Vision, the Gaze, and the Function of the Senses*), Luiz Costa Lima, Susan A. Crane, William Egginton (*How the World Became a Stage*), Louise O. Fradenburg, Stephen Greenblatt (*Renaissance Self-Fashioning*), Valentin Groebner, Hans Ulrich Gumbrecht (*'Eine' Geschichte der spanischen Literatur*), Peter Haidu, Ruth Mazo Karras, Sarah Kay, Kenneth J. Knoespel, John Jeffries Martin, Lee Patterson (*Chaucer and the Subject of History*), Evelyn Birge Vitz, Caroline Bynum Walker (*Metamorphosis and Identity*) and Michel Zink (*La subjectivité littéraire*). Moreover, numerous collections of essays have been dedicated to the topic, for instance, the books edited by Peter von Moos (*Unverwechselbarkeit*), Thomas C. Heller/Morton Sosna/David E. Wellbery (*Reconstructing Individualism*), Manfred Frank/Anselm Haverkamp (*Individualität*), Roy Porter (*Rewriting the Self*), Wolfgang Matzat/Bernhard Teuber (*Welterfahrung – Selbsterfahrung*), Reto Luzius Fetz/Roland Hagenbüchle/Peter Schulz (*Geschichte und Vorgeschichte der Subjektivität*), Rudolf Suntrup/Jan R. Veenstra (*Self-Fashioning/Personendarstellung*). In Spring 2007, the search term 'subjectivity' yielded 2763 entries in the Modern Language Association International Bibliography. 'Self' and 'subjectivity' combines to roughly five hundred medievalist studies. Naturally, the figures more than double if we include the Renaissance period. Judging from the number of recent dissertations dedicated to the topic, more books are to be expected in the near future.

[35] See David Aers's polemic yet useful review of early modernists' sometimes

Subjectivity and historical notions of self have been the subject of numerous studies on the literatures of the major European languages. Although only a few critics have systematically addressed the issue in Spanish letters, it is not a marginal one – all the less since 16th- and 17th-century Spain was the avant-garde in Early Modern literature, a literature which is apparently characterized by stunningly 'modern,' or rather, 'non-medieval' forms of subjectivity. Landmarks of 'subjective literature' include Fernando de Rojas's *La Celestina*, the anonymous *Lazarillo de Tormes*, and Cervantes's *Don Quijote*, not to forget the Spanish *comedia*, which Egginton has identified, as it were, as the cradle of modern forms of Dasein. Accordingly, scholarship on subjectivity and Spanish literature tends to crystallize around the masterpieces and great writers of the Golden Age of Spanish Literature.[36] The emergence of new forms of subjectivity in Spain is mostly presented as a rupture marked by the discovery of the Americas, that is, by a widening of the horizons, or as being triggered by technological innovations like the printing press, or as a reaction to intellectual movements like humanism, which made forays into Spain.

Little has been said about the birth of the modern subject not as a rupture but as a gradual emergence, that is, a process of *longue durée*. One of the most notable exceptions is Hans Ulrich Gumbrecht, who sketches the picture of an 'organic' process rather than a rupture or violent imposition of epistemic regimes.[37]

---

blurred view of medieval conceptions of the self, in which he also points out the spheres in which subjectivity was established or negotiated (heresy, confession, the Augustinian tradition); see also Patterson ("On the margins"). Several medieval 'birth dates' of the individual and the subject have been postulated; see Bynum's critique of these approaches ("Did the Twelfth Century Discover the Individual?"); Gumbrecht suggests a change of perspective, focusing not on features of subjectivity in texts, but on a form of subjectivity that is predicated on the intervention of the recipients ("Lachen und Arbitrarität/Subjektivität und Ernst").

[36] See, for example, George Mariscal's *Contradictory Subjects: Quevedo, Cervantes, and Seventeenth Century Spanish Culture* and Marina S. Brownlee's *The Cultural Labyrinth of María de Zayas*.

[37] In his *Diskurs-Renovatio bei Lope de Vega und Calderón*, Joachim Küpper argues, based on sweeping generalizations, that nominalistic skepticism led to a breakdown of the medieval unified and universal discourse and the emergence of conflicting partial discourses in the early 16th century. He explains the particular nature of Spanish Golden Age literature and subjectivity as a result of an attempt at "restoration" of the medieval general discourse in the wake of the counter-reformation.

To Gumbrecht and his history of Spanish literature we owe the most comprehensive attempt to relate Spain's pioneering role in literary history to the emergence of modern subjectivity. Subjectivity is the leitmotiv of his *'Eine' Geschichte der spanischen Literatur*.[38] Gumbrecht argues that the co-presence, cohabitation and competition of three great cultures (Christian, Islamic, Jewish) made experiences of alterity possible. The breakdown of collective horizons of meaning in the 15th century cast the individual into the role of conveyor of meaning – earlier than in other parts of Europe. Subjectivity was a dispositive that helped people deal with the chaos of the traditional sense-conveying order.[39] In medieval and early modern Castilian texts, Gumbrecht recovers the traces of subjectivity whose 'developed' stage (beginning in the second half of the 15th century) involved the transformation of the body into the "primary object of perception," turning it into an instrument which could be used to conceal or feign intentions.[40]

I do not doubt that the features Gumbrecht describes eventually came to characterize Early Modern subjectivity. I am more reluctant, however, to subscribe to the notion that subjectivity is exclusively predicated upon the need to 'reduce complexity' in perception, which amounts to the claim that notions of the self are determined by historical contexts. In the present study I want to emphasize that premodern subjectivity had its own logic and coherence, and that this logic was crucial in the emergence of post-medieval, that is, Early Modern, notions of the self. This implies that it is necessary to reconstruct premodern notions of selfhood and the dispositives on which subjectivity was predicated.

---

[38] Jean Dangler's recent *Making Difference in Medieval and Early Modern Iberia* proposes a study of medieval and early modern "alterity", essentially focused on subjectivity. Unfortunately, her notion of subjectivity (blurred with the notion of "identity") is not sufficiently theorized; "medieval alterity" presupposes a form of subjectivity that did not exist in the Middle Ages. *Making Difference* establishes a stark contrast and abrupt break between the Middle Ages and the Early Modern Period, although the author mitigates this binarism in her own conclusion.

[39] See Gumbrecht (*'Eine' Geschichte der spanischen Literatur* 166).

[40] See Gumbrecht (*'Eine' Geschichte der spanischen Literatur* 97). Gumbrecht sees in Íñigo López de Mendoza (1388-1458), Marqués de Santillana, the beginning of a "new phase in the history of subjectivity" (*'Eine' Geschichte der spanischen Literatur* 159).

It is, indeed, a reconstruction because, as Lee Patterson has pointed out, selfhood is not a modern phenomenon but a modern problem.[41] This means that we approach selfhood with a set of questions that have never been articulated. My aim is to broaden the picture, shedding some light on some antecedents of Early Modern subjectivity which were theorized and practically shaped in premodern psychology.

In my description of premodern subjectivity, the 'potentiality for action,' I draw on psychoanalytic categories. This approach cannot, of course, claim novelty. In his pioneering 1977 study *Stanze: La parola e il fantasma nella cultura occidentale*, Giorgio Agamben revindicated the fundamental importance of "pneumophantasmology" in medieval culture and its manifestation in the *dolce stil novo*, 'translating' some of its intricacies into the idiom of Freudian psychoanalysis (and Heideggerian philosophy). Psychoanalysis of Lacanian provenance has lately received greater attention, although, as Suzannah Biernoff observes, it is

> not surprising that psychoanalytic theory encounters its historical limits in the pre-modern period, where subject-object relations (mediated by vision) are more indeterminate, and where bodies (or at least *fleshly* bodies) are more fluid (1).

On various occasions, well-nigh "uncanny" (Cynthia Hahn 175) parallels have been stated between Lacan's theories and premodern psychology and its epistemological foundations. In his Lacanian reading of Sor Juana Inés de la Cruz's *auto sacramental* "El divino Narciso" Matthew D. Stroud finds in premodern literature the perfect illustration of Lacan's split subject and proof that

> [t]he splitting of the human subject and its relationship to the Other is not just a fictional construct of twentieth-century psychoanalysis. [...] In their rejection of Cartesian certainty and the illusion of wholeness, pre-modern literature and post-modern theory converge in their study of the human subject. (210)

This presumed 'convergence' is likely to arouse the suspicions of every historically-minded critic. In her recent *Sight and Embodiment in the Middle Ages*, Biernoff has tackled the issue of the

---

[41] See Patterson (*Chaucer and the Subject of History* 12).

'applicability' of the Lacanian account of identity formation and libidinal economy. Based on a thorough analysis of premodern accounts of the self,[42] she emphasizes the alterity of medieval vision, its 'fleshly,' 'passionate' nature, discarding as inadequate the modern notion of the disembodied eye. Nevertheless, aware of the historical limitations of psychoanalysis, Biernoff succeeds in mobilizing important Lacanian insights for her own argument. In a similar vein, my main interest is not to critically engage with Lacan's psychology on the basis of historical material, nor to 'apply' his theory in my readings of premodern literature. Since my approach is rather historical than theoretical, I do not use Lacan's writings as a master text but as a heuristic tool-box to bring the alterity of premodern subjectivity to the fore. The question is, how can premodern subjectivity and Self in general and their gender implications be described, and how does this alien notion of subjectivity 'interact' with texts; to what degree did subjectivity shape literary texts and, conversely, how did texts shape subjectivity?

Since subjectivity is always mediated by discourses about the self, a study on subjectivity, sex and gender must address those premodern 'theories' of the self (soul and body)[43] which are predominantly manifest in theology, medicine and natural philosophy. This is also an implication of Lacanian thinking which had virtually no consequences in Lacan's writings. A case in point is Lacan's view of 'romantic love,' which he illustrates with a historical topic: 'medieval courtly love.' In his Seminar VII, where he discusses the "Ethics of Psychoanalysis," he postulates that courtly love exemplarily illustrates the psychic mechanism of the sublimation of libidinal drives, which found a "moral," an "ethic," and an "art" of love (178), by way of institutionalized deferral of pleasure and the transfer of cathexis upon the preliminaries of sexual intercourse (*Vorlust*). In Seminar XX, titled *Encore*, he suggests that courtly love is a smart ruse to supplement the absence of complementary genders, by way of pretending that the

---

[42] In his sketch of the counter-reformation "subject of control," Anthony J. Cascardi argues that the 'new subject' integrates "neo-Scholastic moral psychology" (243).

[43] See Veenstra (287).

obstacles to achieving fullness are man-made.[44] Yet Lacan's notion of love is suspiciously ahistoric: while he acknowledges the alterity of the art of love as a code of behavior, he does not account for family structures that are incompatible with our modern 'standard' model and hence imply a different configuration of the law-of-the-father, and he ignores the possibility that the premodern imaginary and symbolic orders provided, for instance, utterly different modes and images of 'identification,' gender roles or structures of 'symbolizing' and valorizing the biological facts of sexual intercourse. However, in spite of the totalizing thrust of Lacanian rhetoric and writing, which sweepingly colonizes the medieval past, Lacan's epistemology is based on the insight that symbolic and imaginary orders are culturally and historically specific and variable. In other words: the subject is produced by concrete socio-symbolic structures and an imaginary order represented for/by a concrete community.

My main methodological premise is to refine premodern faculty psychology – and its underlying epistemology – with psychoanalytic concepts. I emphasize the difference between premodern psychology as expressed in contemporary representations of subjectivity and our understanding of self and subjectivity. Naturally, difference is a relational term; that is, a 21st-century discussion of premodern subjectivity is necessarily also a discussion of still-hegemonic modernist subjectivity and its postmodernist rewriting. It is not my aim to posit faculty psychology as a determinative historical context that allows the recuperation of an authentic premodern subjectivity, but to use the conceptual apparatus of (post-)modern theories of subjectivity in order to trace (to make present the absence of) the non-articulated implications and over-determinations of premodern reflections of the self and its manifestations in literary texts – fully aware that these over-determinations are ultimately the result of a belated interpretation.

I will show how so-called faculty psychology provided both a model for the gradual build-up of structures of the self in the form of *hexis* or *habitus* through the 'deconstructive' assimilation of images, and a courtly mode of performative self-fashioning

---

[44] See Lacan (*Encore* 76). Central passages of *Encore* have also been translated and edited in Juliet Mitchell and Jacqueline Rose's anthology ("The Meaning of the Phallus"; "God and the Jouissance of Woman").

through amatory 'identification' with a mental image. I describe the premodern subject as a 'dispersed,' 'weak' subject constituted by a fold (in the Deleuzian sense) in the choric visual field. The courtly technology of the self, based on performance and the ostentation of passionate love (*amor hereos*) involves a gendered process which leads to the establishment of a masculine speaking 'I,' a caloric identity. Analyzing *Cárcel de amor*, with a particular focus on the initial wood-cut, I will contend that this identity is threatened by the internal logic of courtly subjectivity.

2.2. Faculty psychology and the fold of the Self

The *locus classicus* of the origin of modern 'individuality' in the Renaissance and the appraisal of the medieval sense of self is found in chapter two of Jacob Burckhardt's 1860 *The Civilization of the Renaissance in Italy* (*Die Kultur der Renaissance in Italien*):

> In the Middle Ages both sides of human consciousness – that which was turned within as that which was turned without – lay dreaming or half-awake beneath a common veil. The veil was woven of faith, illusion and childish prepossessions, through which the world and history were seen clad in strange hues. Man was conscious of himself only as a member of a race, people, party, family or corporation – only through some general category. In Italy this veil first melted into air; an *objective* treatment and consideration of the state and all things of this world became possible. The *subjective* side at the same time asserted with corresponding emphasis; man became a spiritual *individual,* and recognized himself as such. (98 [Burckhardt's emphases])

Since 1860, many of Burckhardt's own "prepossessions" have been dispelled by scholarship, showing the 'individuality' of medieval men, and the socio-cultural determination of the Renaissance individual.

It is, however, still worth musing over Burckhardt's metaphor of the veil which distorted the medievals' view of the 'reality' of the self, representing it in "strange hues." It is not without irony that we have reached, after half a millennium of psychological and a century of psychoanalytic inquiry, a point where the *méconaissance* of the subject is not seen as a vice of primitive cultures but as a constituent of the human condition. Some would argue that there is no self to be discovered behind the veil because the self is the veil. In Burckhardt's text, the veil metaphor is itself a veil. The woven fabric of the veil suggests a delicate texture, and, indeed, many premodern texts have come down to us which focus on the nature of man. Burckhardt implicitly acknowledges this fact, only to deprecate premodern reflections on the self as 'religious' (read 'dogmatic and static'), illusionary (read 'irrational'), and childish (read 'primitive, erratic'). The fact is, however, that the Middle Ages had a highly differentiated and rational psychology, which it bequeathed to Burckhardt's presumably self-aware Renaissance. I am referring to so-called faculty psychology.[45] This premodern psychology was a creative adaptation and transformation – often mediated by Arabian authors – of the heritage of Greco-Roman medicine and philosophy which was so dear to humanists from Petrarch's time to Burckhardt's.

Premodern theology, natural philosophy and medicine understood bodily and 'mental' functions as inextricably related.[46] Scholars developed a concept (primarily based on Galenic physiology and the Aristotelian works *De anima* and *Parva naturalia*) which ascribed distinct powers to particular organs. It was thought that there exists an intrinsic link between organs and functions, established by the workings of *pneuma* or *spiritus*.[47] Hence mental operations (perception, cognition, intellection), too, do not essentially differ from other bodily processes in that they are psychosomatic. In other words: "the human mind and soul (both designated by the term *anima*) are embodied" (Biernoff 83). Over a system of affinities, sympathies and correspondences, this psychosomatic body-soul compound was not

---

[45] The term 'psychologia' was coined in the Early Modern Period. Presumably, Johannes Thomas Freigius was the first erudite who used the concept, in 1575, in a sense akin to our modern understanding (Keßler and Park 455).

[46] See Bynum ("Female Body and Religious Practice" 228).

[47] As Agamben points out, *pneuma* is not just a medical notion (103-20): "si intrecciano [...] tutti gli aspetti della cultura medioevale, dalla medicina alla cosmologia, dalla psicologia alla retorica e alla soteriologia [...]" (106) ["all aspects of medieval culture, from medicine to cosmology, from psychology to rhetoric and soteriology are intertwined"].

marked off from its environment.⁴⁸ It was thought to be embedded in or even permeated by 'the world.' The "outside world, the linking senses, and the receiving subject were taken," as James F. Burke phrases it, "as part of an interlocking compendium in which none of these facets or functions of existence were conceived as freestanding" (*Vision, the Gaze, and the Function of the Senses* 19). Although the mental faculties are inextricably related, they are thought to possess a certain individual autonomy. This can be seen in the widespread medieval 'allegories' of psychagogic struggles in which the *singulare tantum* of the soul appears as a *plurale tantum* "of objective forces" (Jauß 245). Taylor calls it a "fragmented" self with a "multiplicity of 'mind' locations" struggling for the role of *hegemonikon* (118), where perceptions, thoughts and feelings occur.⁴⁹

In the Middle Ages and the Early Modern Period, two models of perception and cognition coexisted: extramission and intromission. The older one, based on Platonic ideas – which were primarily transmitted to the Middle Ages by Augustine – assumes that an interior 'fire' emits seeing rays through the eyes, which scan exterior objects. Seeing rays grasp the light or fire of the object, conveying sensorial data to the mind.⁵⁰ The concept of seeing rays never lost its influence on 'popular' imagination. It was also fundamental for the "magical world system" (Camille, "Before the gaze" 205) and bore on numerous literary texts.⁵¹ Beginning with the intense reception of Aristotelian thought in the twelfth century, the intromission model began to assert itself in

---

⁴⁸ See Vitz (85). In her recent *Sight and Embodiment in the Middle Ages*, Biernoff argues that the presumed soul-dichotomy should be analytically supplanted by a diagram of intellect/body-desire/flesh, implying that there are, in shifting constellations, female 'fleshly' parts of the soul and a male, rationally subjected body in each individual. The 'flesh' exceeds the boundaries of the body, 'intermingling' with the environment.

⁴⁹ The debate on the *hegemonikon* was also an age-old medical one; see Julius Rocca.

⁵⁰ See Michael Camille ("Before the gaze" 205).

⁵¹ Boccaccio's Fiammetta, for instance, falls victim to lovesickness due to pneumatic rays which are issued by Pamphilo's eyes and penetrate her soul (87); see Ioan P. Couliano (29-30). Also, popular phenomena like the Evil Eye ultimately assume the extramission of seeing rays; see James F. Burke (*Vision, the Gaze, and the Function of the Senses* 63-77). Toward the end of the 15th century, the extramission theory regained importance; see Couliano (28-52); see also Guillermo Serés's study of the Platonic motif of the "transformation of lovers".

the learned, natural philosophical milieu. Intromission theory assumes that objects emit 'forms' or *species* which travel through the environment (*species in medio*), usually the air. The exterior senses convey these *species* to the brain and the interior senses. Although intromission was all but universally accepted in the 14th century,[52] it is important to realize that intromission accommodated extramission, in order to avoid the problem of the precarious status of agency and free will in the intromission model: scholars like Roger Bacon argued that the *species* of the external world had to be 'ennobled' by *species* emitted by the eyes, which were nothing less than an extension of the viewer's sensitive soul beyond the visible limits of the body.[53]

The medieval understanding of the functioning of cerebral mental processes was firmly couched in terms of the "ventricular-pneumatic doctrine" (Manzoni 103).[54] Elaborating on the work of earlier scholars and opposing Aristotelian and Stoic teachings, the Greek philosopher and physician Galen (ca. 130-200 A.D.) declared that mental faculties can be located in different ventricles. According to Galen, the functioning of all mental activities and motor functions are executed through *pneuma* or *spiritus*, a substance generated, in a staged rarifying process (*concoctio*), from air and digested food. Via Byzantium, Galenic medicine was transmitted to the Arabs, who wedded Galen's pneumatology with Aristotelian natural philosophy and localized the mental and motor functions in the interior of the body.

In this form, faculty psychology was adapted and developed by Christian scholars, resulting in a universally accepted doctrine in many permutations. The medieval terminology and phenomenology varies from author to author, and even within the writings

---

[52] See Camille ("Before the gaze" 204), Bernhard Teuber ("*Per speculum in aenigmate*" 16-17), and Nelson (5). Franciscan scholars were of decisive importance for the conception of *species in medio* and its canonization; see Katherine Tachau and Biernoff (63-84). Despite their differences, both modes of vision have in common, as Nelson points out, that they are performative, connective and embodied, which distinguished them from the instrumental "modern eye" (4).

[53] See Biernoff (63-107). Bacon argues in his *Opus majus* (5.1.7.4) that the *species* emitted by objects are "*aided* and *excited* by the species of the eye" (quoted in Biernoff 87; Biernoff's emphasis).

[54] Regarding Galen's contribution to the physiology and anatomy of the brain see Rocca. In Galen's time (and well beyond) the question of whether the *hegemonikon* was the heart (as Aristotelians and Stoics had it) or the brain (as Galen and his Alexandrinian predecessors argued) was disputed.

of one author or a particular text we find inconsistencies.[55] For our purposes, it suffices to sketch a simplified model which illustrates the basic tenets of premodern psychology and epistemology.[56] In this basic model the mental faculties are located in three adjacent ventricles in which the *species* conveyed to the brain by the external senses are received, transformed and stored (caption 2).[57] The first ventricle is the location of imagination, the second of judgment (*vis aestimativa*), the third of memory (*memoria*). Imagination preserves the perceived *species*, de-composing it and associating it with relevant *imagines* stored in the chambers of memory. The *vis aestimativa*,[58] judgment, extracts so-called *intentiones*, which, according to Mary Carruthers, call forth "attitudes" or emotional "inclinations" and "intensities" toward the *imago* (*Craft of Thought* 124-26).[59] So the actual agency in judging things as harmful and repugnant or useful and attractive is not attributed to the perceiving, cognizing individual but to the objects.[60] Only in a secondary act, which may be described with the Aristotelian

---

[55] In the first chapter of *Images in Mind* I describe principal elements of faculty psychology, based on medical texts from medieval and Early Modern Iberia. Although Manzoni's sketch of the history of faculty psychology from a medieval point of view is teleologically skewed and marred by a serious lack of understanding of the cultural contexts (the author, for instance, does not distinguish between *anima sensitiva* and *anima rationalis*, and does not understand scholastic rationality), it provides much material and references to secondary literature. See the fundamental studies by Harry Austryn Wolfson, Murray Wright Bundy, E. Ruth Harvey, David Summers and Mary Carruthers (*The Book of Memory* 46-79). Michael Camille provides a concise overview ("Before the gaze").

[56] This basic model is not just an abstraction. Medieval authors like William of Conches (twelfth century), in his *Philosophia mundi*, associated each chamber with one faculty, in William's case *phantastica, logistikon, memorialis*; see Agamben (*Stanze* 93).

[57] It had been acknowledged since Galen's time that there were two anterior ventricles which were considered to be equivalent. The great majority of scholars who discuss faculty psychology, and most illustrations of the brain, assume a three-cell-model.

[58] 'Aestimativa' was probably introduced by the Arabic author Alfarabi (ca. 870-950) and subsequently adapted by important scholars such as Avicenna, Averroes, Albertus Magnus and Thomas Aquinas; see Manzoni (128-29). In other authors the estimative faculty is subsumed under the *vis cogitativa*; see below.

[59] Some scholastic philosophers use the term 'second intention' to refer to the relations established between sensual *species* and mental concepts; see Robert Myles (82-83).

[60] In 1551, the Spanish physician Bernardino Montaña de Monserrate uses the oppositive terms "prouechoso o dañoso" in his manual *Libro de la Anothomia del hombre* (fol. 124ᵛ). This work, which was addressed to non-experts in medical matters, provides an excellent summary of faculty psychology.

Caption 2: Gregor Reisch, *Margarita philosophica*. Freiburg im Breisgau: Schott, 1503. s.p.[61]

---

[61] The heading "anime vegetative" in this illustration is misleading and can be attributed to a printer's error. Manzoni's reproduction of the Basel 1517 edition clarifies that we see a representation of the faculties of the *anima sensitiva*, the animal soul: "De potentijs anime sensitiue" (Manzoni 130). In addition to the basic powers I describe, Reisch includes the "sensus communis" and the "fantasia," two forms of short-term memory also associated with judgment; see Summers (78-89). I will explain the term 'cogitativa' in the following section.

prohairesis ("moral choice"; Taylor 137), does the subject have the chance and duty to assert his or her self. The activity of the *aestimativa* causes orectic impulses (*appetitus*), which stimulate the heart, the seat of *spiritus* or *pneuma*. *Pneuma* is the vehicle of life-preserving vital heat and humidity. It is essential for all physiological processes and is, in highest sublimation, the medium of mental operations. Positive judgments of a *species* result in the desire to 'acquire' an object and to 'use' it (*appetitus concupiscibilis*); negative judgments have the opposite effect, that is, they cause a flight response or aggression (*appetitus irascibilis*). This psychosomatic complex is called 'passion' (*passio*). The resulting mental *imago*, which consists of *species* and 'judgment,' is finally permanently stored in the chambers of memory.

The operations I have just described were generally attributed to the *anima sensitiva*, the animal soul. However, from a theological perspective, man was distinguished by the rational soul (intellect, will, conceptual memory), an immortal substance which was not dependent on the body. According to Eckhart Keßler, the question of whether the *anima rationalis* was an immaterial stand-alone entity (and thus fell in the jurisdiction of metaphysics) or a 'form' which was tied to the body (and thus to be discussed in natural philosophy), was one of the crucial issues in premodern theology and philosophy.[62] The "Christian position regarding the ontological status of the soul," Keßler explains, "was firmly stated, i.e., that the human soul was a spiritual substance, self-subsistent, created in time by God, informing the human body and multiplied according to the multiplication of bodies" (513). Nevertheless, in the realm of Aristotelian natural philosophy there was a pronounced tendency to chain together mental operations and bodily processes.[63]

> [M]edieval theories of perception and knowledge often employed tripartite, not binary schemata; frequently making a sharper distinction between levels of soul than between soul and body. (Biernoff 25)

According to Aristotle, in all higher mental operations the rational soul depends on the *species* perceived and processed by the sen-

---

[62] See Keßler (487).
[63] See Keßler (533).

sitive soul. In *De memoria et reminiscentia*, Aristotle asserts that it is not possible to think without an image, and also that "memory, even the memory of objects of thought, is not without an image" (48-49; 449^b). This Aristotelian idea was adapted and elaborated by Thomas Aquinas in his comment to *De memoria et reminiscentia* (91-92; 311-15), where he repeats Aristotle's position. In a gloss to *De anima* (432a3-10) we read: "Sed cum speculetur, necesse simul phantasma aliquod speculari. Phantasmata enim sicut sensibilia sunt præterquam quod sunt sine materia" (lectio 13, col. 237).[64] He expresses the same idea in the *Summa*:

> Dicendum quod corpus requiritur ad actionem intellectus, non sicut organum quo talis actio exerceatur, sed ratione objecti; phantasma enim comparatur ad intellectum sicut color ad visum. (vol. 11, p. 12-13; 1a. 75,2)
> [The body is necessary for the activity of the intellect, not as the organ through which it acts, but in order to supply it with its object; for images stand in relation to the intellect as color in relation to the sight.]

The great issue for medieval thinkers was to come to terms with the issue of how the immaterial intellect gains access to and processes the 'material images' necessary for its functioning. Theologically, the immortal rational soul is the essence of man, but in its explanation of man's agency and interaction with the world, naturalist thinking tends to ignore the rational soul and attribute all higher mental functions to the *anima sensitiva*. Accordingly, the *vis aestimativa*, an instinct of sorts, was also called *cogitativa* when it operated 'rationally'.[65] This is manifest in Reisch's illustration in that the *cogitativa* is represented in the second ventricle as a 'superior' power of the *aestimativa* (caption 2). Faculty psychology, then, provided a model which was perfectly capable of accounting for and explaining the entire temporal existence of

---

[64] Robert Pasnau translates: "Instead, when one actually contemplates (*speculatur*) anything, one must at the same time form a phantasm for oneself. Phantasms are likenesses of sensible things, but they differ from them in that they exist outside of matter [...]" (391 [translator's emphasis eliminated]). It is important to notice, however, that the Latin text emphasizes the equivalence of *phantasmata* and *sensibilia*.

[65] See Camille ("Before the gaze" 212) and Keßler (487).

man. Notwithstanding most natural philosophers' affirmations that theology justly claims higher truths and the recognition of its importance for the salvation of the human soul, from their perspective, the *anima sensitiva* alone determined self and *Dasein*.[66]

The confrontation between theology and natural philosophy indicates that it is misleading to talk about *the* medieval or Early Modern subjectivity or *the* premodern self. A case in point is Ruth Mazo Karras's recent study *From Boys to Men: Formations of Masculinity in Late Medieval Europe*. Karras demonstrates that masculinity was construed differently in different socio-cultural milieus (the court, the university, the world of trade and crafts).[67] In the Middle Ages and in the Early Modern Period, competing and conflictive concepts and practices of the self co-existed: even if we bracket the fundamental gender aspect for the moment, it seems implausible that structurally equivalent subjects were constituted in the university, at court or in the rural peasant's world. It is imperative to differentiate between "procedures of confession and scientific discursivity" (Foucault, *The History of Sexuality: Introduction* 65), juridical-administrative mechanisms of subjectification,[68] and courtly-chivalric forms of *self-fashioning* and of the *fashioning of the self*, without losing sight of the intersections and interferences between them. The importance of faculty psychology resides in the fact that it established, in some measure, the epistemological parameters for different forms of premodern subjectification, fulfilling a more or less prominent function in all forms of the constitution of the self. It was particularly important, as I will explain in detail, in the case of the self-fashioning of the courtly elites, because the courtly discourse of nobilitation and self-aggrandizement through passionate love is incomprehensible without referring to faculty psychology.

As James F. Burke points out, from the perspective of faculty psychology, the *anima sensitiva* was an interface of sorts between man or woman and the world which allowed him or her

---

[66] Juan Huarte de San Juan is an excellent example; see chapter 2.4.3.

[67] David Warren Sabean's study of the subjectification which the authorities strategically implemented in Lutheran Germany and the tactical 'counter-subjectivities' of the common people is an example that demonstrates that it is necessary to differentiate even in presumably homogenous cultural spheres.

[68] See Foucault (*Die Wahrheit und die juristischen Formen*).

to "interact with the world around and process the data received through the senses" (*Vision, the Gaze, and the Function of the Senses* 15). It was, in other words, the material factor of the "potentiality for action" (Haidu 114). In his book *Vision, the Gaze, and the Function of the Senses in 'Celestina,'* Burke argues that the premodern subject can be construed in analogy to the Lacanian "scopic field":[69]

> [a] generalized, choric visual field that encodes within the precepts of the symbolic order. This gaze involves a vast number, an enormous array, of projecting, interwoven ocular planes that can be understood to proceed not only from the eyes of those who look but also from inanimate objects that in the ancient and medieval understanding were thought to emit species that in some fashion conveyed the imprint of their essence. (25)[70]

Lacan conceives of the generalized visual field as the aggregate of all individual gazes, imagined to emanate from people and 'objects': "things look at me, and yet I see them" (Lacan, *The Four Fundamental Principles of Psychoanalysis* 109). The subject is a function of the impersonal disembodied gaze: "That which makes us consciousness [sic] institutes us by the same token as *speculum mundi*" (75). In the same vein, the premodern subject can be understood as a *speculum mundi* constituted by a scopic field generated by extramission and intromission.

Premodern epistemology envisions a choric visual field which was affected by the *species* of inanimate objects (via intromission) and 'structured' by individuals' gazes (primarily via ex-

---

[69] Lacan's most concise and accessible text on the gaze and subjectification is the section titled "Of the Gaze as *Objet Petit a*" of his *The Four Fundamental Principles of Psychoanalysis* (65-119). Among the numerous introductions to Lacan's complex thinking and obscurantist idiom, Elisabeth Grosz's *Feminist Introduction* is particularly helpful because it focuses on the gender aspects. See also Roger Kennedy and Bice Benvenuto's introduction (with an emphasis on the clinical, psychoanalytical aspects) and the essays in the *Cambridge Companion to Jacques Lacan*, edited by Jean-Michel Rabaté.

[70] See also Madeline Caviness's notion of medieval "scopic economy," an attempt to "triangulate" medieval art, medieval texts and contexts and "modern and postmodern theories" in a feminist interpretation. Caviness does not pay sufficient attention to premodern "contexts," that is, the complex discourses on the workings of the mind and epistemology, and fails to historicize psychoanalytical premises sufficiently.

tramission).[71] Vitz argues that the benevolent or disapproving gazes of others bestow *value* upon the self, conveying or denying a fullness it cannot achieve by itself.[72] The tenet, rather alien to the modern mind, that personal gazes convey the qualities of the observer to the observed,[73] indicates that this bestowal of 'value' must not be seen as a merely psychological, that is, immaterial process. Biernoff makes the important observation that there is a fundamental difference between the modern notion of sight, as it underlies Freudian or Lacanian psychology, and the premodern one. Unlike in the modern understanding, vision is not an immaterial perception of a distanced object but a tactile, kinesthetic process.[74] Medieval scholars saw vision as a *passion*, that is, the actualization of a form or *species* emanating from an object, in the passive matter of the sense organs, the brain, and ultimately the 'embodied' mind. It is, as Biernoff explains, a sexualized operation in which the form 'conceives' an idea in the mind altering the matter of the recipient organism. *Species* are assimilated and, at the same time, assimilate: "intromission meant," in Biernoff's words, "that the passive matter of the eye (or the brain) was united as 'one flesh' to the formative essence of the visible world" (101-02). The interpenetration of self and world is even more blatant if we consider the effect of 'animate' gazes. Since seeing via intromission involves a prior 'ennoblement' of the object's *species* through an extension of the sensitive soul,[75] being exposed to the other's gaze means being penetrated and very materially 'influenced' by the other.[76] It is precisely in this

---

[71] According to Biernoff, the medieval gaze should not be confused with the necessarily phallic gaze of modern psychoanalysis (57-59). She differentiates between a male rational gaze as the medium of observation and a female fleshly gaze of desire. The viewer, male or female, assumes a gender-position according to the modus of gaze: "One might say that when a man looked with desire in the Middle Ages, he looked as a woman" (59).

[72] See Vitz (91-92). The 'popular' expression of the power of the gaze is the idea of the Evil Eye. As Burke points out (*Vision, the Gaze, and the Function of the Senses in* Celestina 22), the aggregate gaze of the crowd was thought to possess great visual power.

[73] For instance, William of Conches teaches this in the twelfth century; see Hahn (175).

[74] See Biernoff (97).

[75] See Biernoff (87-92).

[76] The importance of this concept is naturally even more patent in an extramissionist Platonist frame. Marsilio Ficino explains: "Quod autem radius emis-

sense that we have to understand Natalie Zemon Davis's claim that, as late as the 16th century,

> the line drawn around the self was not firmly closed. One could get inside other people and receive other people within oneself, and not just during sexual intercourse or when a child was in the womb. (56)

Of course, the effects of seeing and being seen were not just transitory; they were thought to be constitutive of Greenblatt's "sense of personal order" (*Renaissance Self-Fashioning* 1). James F. Burke explains that, in the perceptive-cognitive and intellective process, the sensorial input, that is, the incessantly shifting constellation of gazes and *species* emitted by objects, are checked against and fused with the contents of memory.[77] *Species* and gazes unremittingly penetrate the *anima sensitiva* and 'make up' the self. Not unlike the ancient Greek *cura sui* described by Foucault, it is a life-long 'working-in' of "vérités reçues par une appropriation de plus en plus poussée" ("L'herméneutique du sujet" 361) ["truths which are acquired through a more and more powerful appropriation"]. This mental discipline aims at the formation and confirmation of *hexis* or *habitus*.[78] It is, however, a process that cuts across the notions of 'activity' and 'passivity,' since this *cura sui* implied an interior management of external forces. In medieval understanding, the gradual build-up of mental structures ultimately consisted of, and, at the same time, resisted external 'influences,' thus constituting the individual 'potentiality for action.' The stark opposition of object world and subject is meaningless, and even the contours of the body fail to delineate a sharp distinction between individual and environment.

---

sus ab oculis vaporem secum spiritalem trahat et vapor iste sanguinem, ex eo perspicimus quod lippi et rubentes oculi spectantis proxime oculos radii sui emissione cogunt morbo simili laborare" (*oratio septima*, caput IV, p. 322) ["We can see that the ray which is emitted from the eyes carries with it *spiritus* and blood from the fact that those who look in the diseased and reddened eyes of others are infected by the rays coming from the others' eyes"].

[77] See James F. Burke ("The Insouciant Reader and the Failure of Memory in *Celestina*" 35).

[78] James F. Burke (*Vision, the Gaze, and the Function of the Senses* 30).

> [B]y virtue of the passage of species across and through it, the flesh of the skin and eyes constitutes a permeable membrane and not – or not only – the body's border. (Biernoff 90)

"Individuality" is, as Walter Haug points out (295), thinkable in this model, but it is understood as deficiency and failure. Ideally, James F. Burke explains, "the accumulation of many patterns in memory could be utilized by the highest faculties given to the human being, reason and intellect, to frame sets of rules and from them a perfected art of living" (*Vision, the Gaze, and the Function of the Senses* 30).[79] Hence Burke labels the self a "container" and its agency lies essentially in its capacity to choose what becomes part of it (*Desire and the Law* 19). The art of living entails a honing of the will, which Lee Patterson sees as the defining feature of the medieval subject.

> Medieval anthropology defined the subject as desire: as the Augustinian will, with its opposed movements of *caritas* and *cupiditas*; as the Boethian *intentio naturalis* that tends ineluctably toward the *summum bonum*; as the scholastic power of appetition, in which the intellectual appetite seeks to govern its *concupiscible* and *irascible* partners; or as *amor*, an inward sense of insufficiency that drives the Christian self forward on its journey through the historical world. (*Chaucer and the Subject of History* 8)

From the centrality of the orectic powers in medieval anthropology, Patterson derives the notion that medieval man was characterized by a "dialectic" between an alienated inward subject and a socially prescribed *persona*.[80] His argument rests on the premise that subjectivity equals an "inward sense of selfhood" (11). This premise, however, is neither backed by "me-

---

[79] A comparison between the *habitus* as a premodern model of the 'potentiality for action' and Pierre Bourdieu's notion of *habitus* is instructive. He describes a 'habitus' as a gradually acquired "system of dispositions" governing socially conditioned activities (78). He calls the embodied equivalent of the *habitus hexis* (87).

[80] Manfred Fuhrmann shows that in Roman culture *persona* referred not only to 'mask' but also to an individual's public 'image,' that is, not a subject in our modern understanding but a "perpetuated social role" (94). In other words, the *persona* that an individual constitutes in the course of his or her life is the result of self-fashioning.

dieval anthropology," which does not allow for an inward self opposed to the external world, nor by premodern literary texts in which, as Evelyn Birge Vitz has pointed out, the inside is not where 'I' is but the *telos* of desire.[81]

> [T]he inside does not correspond to 'I' or 'we' or 'here' – nor does outside refer to the contrary. The inside is not conceived egocentrically, nor even really as psychologically. The inside is here primarily a locus of affect or sensation or thought, not of personality, but of *value*. And the individual is not seen as an adequate source of value; he is not adequate to constitute an inside. (Vitz 91)

When the premodern self engages in introspection, like the presumed remote father of modern subjectivity, Saint Augustine, he or she finds, as Hans Robert Jauß attests, "impersonal forces" (244). Even those, like David Aers, who champion the Augustinian tradition as formative of medieval subjectivity's interiority, must acknowledge that the soul seeker turning inside does not find himself but God,[82] the ultimate expression of alterity. The interior of man is a heterotopical space in the Foucaultian sense, a juxtaposition of incompatible "emplacements" ("Des espaces autres" 758) which cancel out inwardness in the very process of introspection. Foucault justly cautions that even in the religious sphere, wherein subjectification was essentially based on "forms of attention, concern, decipherment, verbalization, confession, self-accusation, struggle against temptation, and so on" (*The Use of Pleasure* 63), the "restructuration" of the "'exteriority' of ancient morality" must not be confounded with a "gradual interiorization of rules, acts, and transgressions" (63). In the courtly culture of ostentation and display this is even more accurate: the inside is the outside. Although the "discursive field [...] *named* coherence and identity as proper while stigmatizing fragmentation and difference [...]" (Patterson, "Making Identities" 87; my emphasis), the premodern self was, on a fundamental level, neither autonomous nor 'decentered' (which would imply the possibility of a worldly center), but 'dispersed' with respect to the

---

[81] See Vitz (86).
[82] See Aers (183) and Bynum ("Did the Twelfth Century Discover the Individual?" 4).

worldly scopic regime.⁸³ Its struggle to gain 'self-control' (the control of the affects) and fullness through the forging of socially accepted and godly *habitus* cannot be achieved in this world.

According to Taylor, the Platonic outlook brought to the West the critical notion that truth, seeing and self are imbricated.

> [T]o be ruled by reason is to be ruled by the correct vision or understanding. The correct vision or understanding of ourselves is one which grasps the natural order, the analogue of health. (121)⁸⁴

Hence the premodern individual's equivalent to the Cartesian *cogito* is, as Burke observes, the "I see and am seen" (*Vision, the Gaze, and the Function of the Senses* 26-27).⁸⁵ We can infer that the subject is *what* it sees and *how* it is seen. The first aspect explains the loathing of the deformed or ugly and the appreciation of beauty. The latter translates into the importance given to public reputation or honor.⁸⁶ As Theo Kobusch points out, the *existimatio* of others, honor, reputation and prestige but also blemish or shame, constitute man as an *ens morale*, as the concrete being in its social context.⁸⁷ In the words of Petrus Aureoli "esse morale non constitit in re extra, sed in aestimatione hominum" (quoted in Kobusch 747) ["the moral being is not constituted by/in an external thing but in the esteem of the people"].

This is not to say that the self is determined by the others' gazes. Premodern practices of the self (writing and reading practices, religious and juridical ones, meditative practices) aimed

---

⁸³ While modern man is used to "draw an imaginary line around the perimeters of our bodies and define our subjectivity as the unique density of matter contained within that line" (Mansfield 82), the dispersed subject corresponds to a 'permeable' body which is, through correspondences, sympathies and, of course, gazes, part of the world; see also Porter (4).

⁸⁴ The Neoplatonic tradition emphasized the power passion-provoking images exerted on the subject; see Hahn (184) and Serés (*La transformación de los amantes* 49-63). Plotinus, for instance, wrote in the *Enneads* (4.3.8): "We are what we desire and what we look at" (quoted in Biernoff 85), and, in his *Epistolam Ioannis ad Parthos* (II,II, 14) St. Augustine states: "quia talis est quisque, qualis eius dilectio est" (quoted in Serés 49) ["because everybody is what he delights in"].

⁸⁵ See also Randolph Starn (209) and Richard D. Logan (with an overview of older scholarship that supports that position).

⁸⁶ See Fradenburg (171-85).

⁸⁷ See Kobusch (747).

precisely at taming the power of images and facilitating the shaping of socially sanctioned subjectivities. However, the matrix of these subjectivities was always a constitution of the self via 'image-like' sense impressions and gazes. In this model, the subject is neither opposed to a world of objects nor transcends it; it is in a relation of contiguity. The world is turned into self. Bernhard Teuber argues that Early Modern Spanish literature is informed by this notion of "weak subjectivity," which construes the self not in opposition to the *Umwelt*, but as a positioning of the self in which "Welterfahrung und Selbsterfahrung sind die beiden Seiten ein und derselben Medaille" (*"Vivir quiero conmigo"* 183) ["world experience and self experience are two sides of a single coin"]. According to Jörg Dünne, the self is based on repetition. While 'exterior' repetition, the Nietzschean "Ewige Wiederkehr," negates subjectivity, and 'interior' repetition creates the illusion of a self-grounding 'strong' subject (*Asketisches Schreiben* 59), 'weak' subjectivity is predicated on Deleuzian 'nude' repetition.[88] As Teuber and Dünne point out, in his interpretation of Foucault's theory of subjectivity, Gilles Deleuze provides a model for the premodern self. Deleuze argues that subjectivity can be described as a fold.[89] The subject's interior is "le dedans *du* dehors" (Deleuze, *Foucault* 134) ["the interior *of* the exterior"]. It is not a doubling of the exterior in an individual act of interiorization, but an effect of the episteme.

Referring to the courtly-aristocratic sphere, Olga Fradenburg describes this as

> [t]he perpetual need to assert honor as an interior essence [...]. [I]t is the knight's double imperative to confer interiority upon an exteriority – to make self out of the nonself – and to confer exteriority upon interiority; to make nonself out of the self. (207-08)

Fradenburg points out that this is a gradual and multiple process (fold on fold), implying that the fold is always 'visible' for the

---

[88] Dünne gives a graphic representation of these possibilities (*Asketisches Schreiben* 59). In his article, "Herborisieren und Selbstpraxis," he provides the gist of his argument.

[89] In *Le pli: Leibniz et le baroque*, Deleuze elaborates on the concept of the fold, arguing that it is the signature of 'baroque' subjectivity; see Dünne (*Asketisches Schreiben* 12-20).

exterior, the others. Medieval techniques of the self aim at avoiding opacity. Independent selfhood is not the goal of social life but a threat to it, a state of alienation that is to be avoided rather than sought out. And the isolated self does not precede confrontation with the world – is not the starting point for building an identity, but rather an effect, and a largely negative one, of the quest for renown.[90]

Hence, what we would call subjective interiority is a result of an illicit withdrawal from the choric visual field. Ideally, the self is a coordinate fixed by the others' gazes and by an environment that emits *species*. The basis of power in the 'feudal' world is, as Foucault observes, the fact that the individual belongs to a particular place.[91] This creates a particular kind of 'individuality' that requires that the subject perform his or her 'role' in a preordained place, according to shared expectations, gaining "esteem" (Crane 133) or garnering the benevolent gaze of the others.[92] This means the self is "vertically flexible," to use a category coined by Thomas Greene. There is an "upward and downward mobility of the human soul, which, in virtue and knowledge, is capable either of improvement or decline" (Veenstra 286); the individual's "horizontal flexibility," however, the "wealth and variety of human emotion and human ingenuity" and, therefore, the potential of self-fashioning, is limited.[93]

The workings of the scopic field in the subjectification of the individual accentuates the observation that, in the courtly milieu, subjectivity and masculinity must have been understood as performativity.[94] Through gestures, clothing, manners, behavior, acts, and words appropriate to his rank, the nobleman must

---

[90] See Crane (127).

[91] See Foucault (*Die Wahrheit und die juristischen Formen* 114).

[92] See Burke (*Vision, the Gaze, and the Function of the Senses* 22-23).

[93] See also Karlheinz Stierle, who argues that in the "Dante World" the difference between "objects" on one level is irrelevant, while in the "Petrarch World" the radical separation of human and divine planes bestows novel presence on the 'horizontal reality,' which Stierle sees as constitutive of the "discovery of the subject" (39-48).

[94] Regarding the court as a performance space see Filios (38-42). Filios studies one aspect of this self-fashioning in Medieval Spain, that is, medieval lyric poetry. In her view, transgressive erotic and scatological poetry and agonistic performances "provide a release valve for the tensions" (45) generated by courtly self-fashioning. Hence, although these performances often present the subject in abject *personae*, they ultimately confirm legitimate subject positions.

evoke the appearance which determines the essence: "Les valeurs de l'individu", in Paul Zumthor's words, "n'ont d'existence que reconnues et visiblement manifestées par la collectivité" (351) ["The values of an individual exist only inasmuch they are recognized and visibly made manifest by the collective"].[95] The nobleman's 'blank' genealogical identity is thus actualized through repetitive performance,[96] soliciting and attracting gazes which "project back to the subject the desired image of fullness and completion" (Fradenburg 210). The courtier-knight subjects himself to the scopic regime, gaining agency as the "impresario" (Starn 217) of his performance.

Fradenburg's study of late medieval Scotland shows that the tournament was one of the privileged scenarios for courtly spectacle. The tournament provided the knight with the opportunity to display his decorated body and his knightly prowess. According to Karras, knightly masculinity was defined as "the opposite of femininity, and dominance over other men [...] achieved through violence and through control of women" (11). The tournament was primarily a ritualized *mise en scène* of physical power and dexterity; the "control of women," the power to impress other men by proving one's attractiveness,[97] found its performative expression in the game of courtly love.

In the prologue to his famous song book known as the *Cancionero de Baena*, written toward the end of the reign of Juan II (d. 1454), the compiler Juan Alonso de Baena embarks on an apology for aristocratic 'sports' like jousting or hunting. Literature is the most profitable of noble diversions, he says. History books provide edifying and instructive *exempla* and invigorate the mental faculties. That is to say, proper readings, properly assimilated, fortify the noble *habitus*. Finally reaching the topic of lyric poetry

---

[95] According to Gert Althoff, publicly displayed emotions were used as "signs"; in other words, emotions were not the expression of 'authentic' affects but actualizations of an emotional *langue*; see also Joachim Bumke. Crane analyzes medieval maying rituals as performances of the self (39-72); see also James F. Burke (*Vision, the Gaze, and the Function of the Senses* 30). Norbert Elias's classic *Prozeß der Zivilisation* is, of course, a necessary point of reference. Regarding the socio-political basis of 15th-century Castilian nobility and their propagandistic self-representation, see María Concepción Quintiliana Raso.

[96] See Kimberlee A. Campbell, who studies the importance of repetitive patterns of self-performance in literary texts.

[97] See Karras (25).

in his exposition, he claims that also "el arte de la poetría e gaya ciencia" ["the art of poetry and 'gay science'"] endows its practitioners with "avisación e dotrina" (74) ["counsel and wisdom"]. This 'science' requires understanding, subtle *ingenium*, bookish erudition, personal experience and courtesy. Baena's description of the ideal poet culminates in the claim:

> otrosí que sea amador, e que siempre se precie e se finja de ser enamorado; porque es opinión de muchos sabios, que todo home que sea enamorado, conviene a saber, que ame a quien deve e como deve e donde deve, afirman e dizen qu'el tal de todas buenas doctrinas es doctado. (74)
> [he should also be a lover, and he should always pride himself and 'feign' being in love, because many wise men opine and confirm that the man who is enamoured – that is, if he loves whom he should and in the right way and where it is licit – that this man is an adept in all good knowledge.]

What is striking here is that Baena demands that the courtly poet should "feign" love, if he happens not to be in love.[98] As a matter of fact, in the 15th century, a host of Castilian noblemen authored or commissioned a plethora of love poems. This lyric avalanche was frequently censured for its conventionality and its supposed emotional insincerity.[99] However, as Jeanne Battesti Pelegrin remarks, the *poesía cancioneril* is predominantly, though strangely, 'autobiographic': "à travers le discours amoureux, elle est une discours sur soi, qui est un moyen de conaissance de soi" ("La poésie *cancioneril*" 97) ["through the amatory discourse, it is a discourse of the self which is a means of self-knowledge"].[100]

---

[98] Feign here should not to be understood in the modern sense, but as to 'fashion,' as in Pico della Mirandola's *Oratio de hominis dignitate*, where he says that the individual should fashion him or herself: "quasi arbitrarius honorariusque plastes et fictor, in quam / malueris tute formam effingas" ["so that you may, as the free and extraordinary shaper of yourself, fashion yourself in the form you will prefer"] (§5,22, fol. 132); see also Greene (242-43).

[99] Whinnom convincingly rehabilitated the aesthetic quality of the *poesía cancioneril* (*La poesía amatoria cancioneril*). There are patent parallels to Robert S. Sturge's interesting anlysis of the reception of Guillaume de Machaut's 'in-authentic' poetry and narratives (in particular, his *Voir-Dit*), in which he relates the appreciation of these texts to the prevalent concepts of subjectivity in criticism.

[100] This is also one of the underpinnings of Filios's study, although this author focuses on the unsettling of authoritative identity categories.

Hence Greenblatt's appraisal of Renaissance amatory poetry seems applicable: the conventionality of formulaic expressions is "the virtual assurance of their lived reality" (*Renaissance Self-Fashioning* 139). "[C]ourt poets," Greenblatt continues, "are as much written by their conventional lyrics as writers of them" (139).

The courtly poet of the fifteenth century, however, should be seen as a performer rather than a 'writer.' Lyric love poetry was, as a rule, composed for oral (possibly theatrical) presentation, mostly accompanied by music. "In its pragmatic contexts," Gumbrecht holds, "poetry at court was as tied to the body as in the 12th century or – presumably – in contemporary popular culture" (*'Eine' Geschichte der spanischen Literatur* 135; see also Battesti Pelegrin, "Le poésie *cancioneril*") ["In ihren Gebrauchszusammenhängen war Poesie bei Hof wohl so körpergebunden geblieben wie im XII. Jahrhundert oder wie – vermutlich – in der zeitgenössischen Volkskultur"].[101] Through his performance as a 'servant of love' the enamored knight staged himself before the eyes of an audience. As the courtly poet Suero de Ribera points out, the public praise of the female sex is a marker of nobility:

> A los de uil condición
> consiento que digan mal,
> seguiendo su natural
> syn freno de discreción;
> mas en los tales aferes,
> quando será menester,
> los fidalgos han de ser
> defensa de los mugeres. (658)[102]

[To those of base condition / I consent that they diffame, / following their nature,/ without restraint; / but in those affairs, / when it is necessary, / noblemen must be / women's defenders.]

---

[101] See also Filios. There are indications that Courts of Love, "tribunals consisting of groups of aristocratic ladies who would hear cases and make decisions on points of love" (Marino 47), existed in the Iberian Peninsula as late as the 16th century. Instructive in this respect is also Sylvia Huot's study on the 'material' transition from a culture of performance to a culture in which the book takes center stage in Late Medieval French literature.

[102] Ribera's poem is a reply to Pedro Torella's misogynist *Coplas de las calidades de las donas*. Both texts were included in the *Cancionero de Estúñiga* (ed. Salvador Miguel).

When the nobleman's love was reciprocated he could claim the "control of women" which assured him the esteem of his male peers. What is more important, however, is that even if rejected he could display his distinguishing and hence ennobling emotional sensitivity.[103] Although amatory courtly poetry was characterized by a certain solipsism in which the 'you' addressed to a beloved other was actually the "double inversé de lui-même" (Battesti Pelegrin, "La poésie *cancioneril*" 103) ["inverse double of oneself"], this self-affection necessarily unfolded in the midst of an expert public.

There was, as Gumbrecht observes, no split between staged role and 'real life': Subjectivity is performance.[104] Nevertheless, this does not exhaust the complex pragmatics of the frequently ephemeral love poetry. We have seen that the subjectification of the premodern individual was the effect of an interplay between being seen and seeing. In the game of courtly love, this latter aspect of subjectivity takes a peculiar twist, because the frame of reference of passionate love, as it is staged in courtly poetry, is a pathological malfunction of the mental faculties: *amor hereos*, lovesickness.

2.3. *AMOR HEREOS* AND THE CONSTITUTION OF THE SUBJECT

Lovesickness is a concept, at least in the English-speaking world, that still has meaning today: "So deeply affected by love as to be unable to act normally," or "Exhibiting a lover's yearning."[105] On Valentine's Day, it will make an occasional appear-

---

[103] Constantine the African translated the Arabic *ishk* (for lovesickness) as *eros*. In the work of his pupil, Johannes Afflacius, it has been transformed to *hereos*. Ultimately the form *hereos* prevailed, arguably because of its association with 'heroic' and its "peculiar medieval sense of 'belonging to a lord or nobleman'" (Wack 46).

[104] Although Filios acknowledges that in the courtly milieu "performance *is* normal behavior, and vice versa" (38), she argues that women's performance unsettled normative gender categories through "parodic mimicry" (3): Exaggerated performances in which the role and 'real' person overlap indicate the possibility that all identities are fake. I doubt that in an epistemic regime in which appearance and essence were inseparable and which knew of no 'private' self, the realization per se of the performative nature of subjectivity would produce anxiety.

[105] My source is http://dictionary.reference.com/ [8/16/2008], referring to the *American Heritage Dictionary of the English Language* (4th ed. 2006).

ance on news sites on the World Wide Web or spark a 'popular' publication on the topic.[106] Its premodern ancestor, *amor hereos*, is predominantly regarded, even among the scholarly community of medievalists and Renaissance specialists, as a historical curiosity or, at best, a marginal detail of cultural history.[107] In Early Modern Spain, however, particularly in the 15th century,[108] passionate love engaged courtly elites and fueled discussions among contemporary scholars. The topic had ramifications for questions of imagination in general and touched on central issues of the epoch, namely heresy and witchcraft.[109] We will see that the importance attributed to the topic is due to the fact that elite subjectivities and the gender order were at stake.

Much was written before the 18th century about lovesickness; eminent scholars from Constantine the African to Robert Burton inquired into its nature. It was perceived as a pressing, complex matter. Its reconstruction is thus equally complicated.[110] For our

---

[106] See, for instance, Frank Tallis's recent book with the telling title *Love Sick: Love as a Mental Illness*.

[107] Hjalmar Crohns, in his pioneering 1904 study on the history of "love as sickness," felt obliged to ask his learned reader's forgiveness for approaching this "ridiculous" topic (68).

[108] See Pedro M. Cátedra's fundamental *Amor y pedagogía en la Edad Media: estudio de doctrina amorosa y práctica literaria* and Antonio Cortijo Ocaña's additional "Notas sobre el Tostado *De amore*".

[109] See Folger ("Passion and Persuasion").

[110] Elsewhere, I discuss the topic and pertinent scholarship in detail (Folger, *Images in Mind*, 33-56). We must add to the studies I review in this book the recent publications by Marcelino V. Amasuno Sárraga on the *mal de amores* and *La Celestina*. Mary Frances Wack's edition of Constantine the African's *Viaticum* I.20, with its medieval glosses, is indispensable. See also Agamben (*Stanze* 130-45), and Donald A. Beecher and Massimo Ciavolella's instructive introduction to their edition and translation of Jacques Ferrand's 17th-century *Treatise on Lovesickness*. In the 15th century, passionate love became increasingly associated with witchcraft. In Heinrich Kramer's (Institoris) and Jacob Sprenger's *Malleus maleficarum*, it is discussed under the heading *philocaptio* (*quaestio* 7, part 1). However, the *Malleus* shows that *philocaptio* is a technical term for the *enamoramiento*, a mental process, which can also be triggered by magic: "Philocaptio igitur seu amor inordinatus vnius [sexus] ad alterum, triplici ex causa oriri potest. Aliquando ex sola incautela oculorum, aliquando ex tentatione Dæmonum solùm, aliquando ex maleficio Necromanticoru<m>, & Maleficarum simul & Dæmonum" (184) ["Philocaptio or inordinate love of one sex for the other can originate from three reasons. Sometimes from an imprudence of the eyes alone, sometimes from the Demons' temptation alone, sometimes simultaneously from the necromancers', witches' and the Demons' spell"]. I resolve abbreviations and superscripts according to the *Manual of Manuscript Transcription for the Dictionary of the Old Spanish Language* (ed. Harris).

purposes, it must suffice to sketch a model distilled from these texts. In the *philocaptio* a person of the opposite sex is perceived, that is, his or her *species* is received and processed in the first cerebral ventricle (*imaginatio*). In the next chamber, the seat of the *vis aestimativa*, utmost positive *intentiones* are attributed to it, based on physical attractiveness and the virtues ascribed to him or her.[111] In other words, on the basis of the *species*, this person is 'esteemed' as supremely 'useful' and hence desirable. Passionate love was seen, in Giorgio Agamben's words, as a " proceso essenzialmente fantasmatico, che coinvolge immaginazione e memoria in un assiduo rovello itorno a un'immagine dipinta o riflessa nel l'intimo dell'uomo" (*Stanze* 96) ["essentially phantasmatic process which draws imagination and memory into assiduously circling an image which is depicted or reflected in the interior of man"]. This means that the actual love object was not a person of flesh and blood but a mental image whose appraisal might or might not correspond to the person's actual qualities. The excessive character of lovesickness is, as pre-modern physicians emphasize, due to the fact that the new *enamorado* falls victim to misjudgment. The *intentiones* cause a*ppetitus concupiscibilis*, the urge to 'have' the person from whom the *species* emanates, accompanied by a boost of vital *spiritus* and the formation of a *species* with an overpowering emotional component. Due to this component, the mind creates an extremely effective mnemonic *imago*, and the lover cannot stop thinking of or remembering his beloved.

Love as passion ultimately results in a breakdown of the intricate interplay between the internal senses. The treasure-house of memory is obstructed and new sense-data cannot be processed properly anymore. The incessant gazing at the enticing mental *imago* prompts the heart to emit noxious quantities of hot *pneuma*. The heat of these emissions corrupts the natural humors (blood, bile, phlegm, melancholy), turning them into dangerous adust melancholy.[112] The multifarious psycho-somatic symptoms

---

[111] Regarding the impact of non-visual data in the *philocaptio* see Folger ("Passion and Persuasion").

[112] Below, I discuss adust melancholy in connection with Juan Huarte de San Juan's *Examen de ingenios* (2.3.4.). One of the essential functions of the brain, particularly the *pia mater*, was to "mitigate the warmth of the spirits emanating from the heart" (Avicenna, *Canon* 15, bk. III, ch. 2; translated and cited in Manzoni 118).

of lovesickness are well-known to the reader of premodern love literature: change in complexion, sleeplessness, fatigue, hollow eyes, tearfulness, and so on. Premodern physicians conceived of a broad range of cures because they considered *amor hereos* to be a fatal affliction.[113] In his *Commentarium in convivium Platonis, de amore*, the 15th-century Italian physician Marsilio Ficino provides a description of the effects of passionate love which requires no further explanation.

> Preterea, quocumque animi assidua fertur intentio, illuc et spiritus, qui animi sive currus sive instrumenta sunt, advolant. Spiritus in corde ex subtilissima sanguinis parte creantur. In amati imaginem phantastica infixam ipsumque amatum amantis animus rapitur. Eodem trahuntur et spiritus. Illuc evolantes assidue resolvuntur. Quapropter frequentissimo puri sanguinis fomite opus est ad consumptos spiritus recreandos, ubi subtiliores et lucidiores partes sanguinis quotidie in reficiendis spiritibus exanlantur. Propertea puro et claro sanguine resoluto, maculosus, crassus, aridus restat et ater. Hinc exsiccatur corpus et squalet, hinc et melancholici amantes evadunt. Ex sicco enim crasso atroque sanguine melancholica, id est, atra bilis efficitur, que suis caput vaporibus opplet cerebrum siccat, animam tetris horrendis imaginibus diu noctuque solicitare non cessat. (Oratio sexta, caput IX; p. 224-26)
>
> [Moreover, the *spiritus*, which are the vehicle and the instruments of the soul, fly to wherever the soul's *habitus* directs them. *Spiritus* are created in the heart from the most subtle part of the blood. In the lover, the lover's soul is raptured by the beloved's image inculcated in imagination. The *spiritus* are drawn there too, and flying there, they are incessantly consumed. Therefore, it is necessary that pure blood frequently provides the fuel to replenish the consumed *spiritus*, whence the subtle and lucid fraction of the blood is all exhaled in the restoration of *spiritus*. Hence the pure and clear blood is consumed, leaving polluted, thick, dry and black blood. This dries the body out and withers it and the lovers become melancholics because the dryness turns the thick and black blood into melancholy, that is, black bile which fills the head with its vapors and dries out the brain, unremittingly calling forth, day and night, horrible and gloomy images. (my translation)]

---

[113] I describe the most important cures of lovesickness and the underlying principle of 'distraction' and eidetic manipulation in *Images in Mind* (51-56).

Due to the continuous waste of *pneuma* and the patient's negligence of his bodily well-being, passionate love ultimately leads to a stage of anorectic exhaustion, a lethal amatory consumption. The patient 'burns out,'[114] losing humidity and heat.

In the courtly context, however, a re-semantization of the symptoms of *hereos* took place, as Couliano states:

> The phenomenon of courtly love results from a warped purpose that brought about a shift of emphasis concerning the concept of *health* as defined by medical science at the time. Through this *Umwertung*, the gloomy equilibrium of psychic forces recommended by learned treatises was transformed into a sickness of the intellect, whereas, on the contrary, the spiritual sickness induced by love ended by being extolled as the real health of body and soul. (21)

The rationale of this *Umwertung*, or "audace e radicale rovesciamento della teoria medica dell'amore eroico" ["audacious and radical inversion of the medical theory of *amor hereos*"] as Agamben puts it (*Stanze* 136), in the work of Dante and the *stilnovisti* was, according to the Italian philosopher, the Averroist notion of the *intellectus possibilis* and the mediating role of mental images: "[I]l fantasma (il pneuma fantastico), origine e oggetto d'amore, è appunto ciò in cui, come in uno specchio, si compie l'unione (*copulatio*) dell'individuo con l'intelletto unico e separato" (*Stanze* 126) ["The phantasm (the phantasmatic *pneuma*), the origin and the object of love, is precisely that in which, like in a mirror, the union (*copulatio*) between the individual and the only and separated intellect takes place"]. Love "inspires" because it is "essenzialmente e propriamente un 'moto spirituale'" (*Stanze* 146) ["essentially and properly a 'spiritual movement'"]. Agamben cautions against reductively viewing 'courtly love' as a "fenomeno sociale" (127).

One of its social aspects, which explains the re-semantization of lovesickness as an ennobling force, was, as I have explained, that it provided the possibility of displaying the symptoms of *amor hereos*, performing aristocratic subjectivity and masculinity

---

[114] See the ancient bronze statuette of the emaciated Perdica, one of the classic figures of lovesickness, reproduced in Wack's *Lovesickness in the Middle Ages* (4).

through a set of conventionalized behavior patterns and practices. Nevertheless, it is imperative to realize that the 'social' aspects must not be separated from epistemological ones: in the courtly milieu, lovesickness and amatory service was not just a role-play; the game of 'courtly love' painstakingly obeyed the laws of the premodern model of subjectification.[115] If we turn to Baena's prologue, we see that his apology of aristocratic life and courtly poetry is couched in naturalist terminology, interweaving the social and the psychological. It is instructive to take at face value his postulation that the courtly poet should be passionately in love or 'feign' passionate love.[116] In this context, to 'feign' means to 'imagine,' that is, to deliberately create the mental *imago* of a desirable woman on the basis of memories.[117] The effects of this imaginary work could be similar to the perception of a 'real' woman and the resulting passion.[118] Thus the *cortesano* who 'feigns' passionate love paradoxically demonstrates his superior rationality: persistently battling lower, bestial instincts (*appetitus*), he is a hero of self-mastery. The moderation of the passion he has to exert as a courtly lover requires a reflective stance,[119] a self-surveillance which would become a defining feature of modern subjectivity. It is, however, not necessary to invoke the workings of Foucaultian technologies of the self, nor to turn to Averroist philosophy in order to explain how *amor hereos* could be constitutive of the patient's self. The very phenomenol-

---

[115] Küpper holds that the *amour courtois* is primarily a "social ritual" ("code") which involves authentic feelings which are, however, not as "profound" as the passions caused by *hereos* ("(H)er(e)os: Petrarcas *Canzoniere* und der medizinische Diskurs seiner Zeit" 194-95). The problem with this view is that faculty psychology does not account for this distinction, based on the intensity of the affect. The power of courtly love as a vehicle of self-fashioning and communication is predicated on the 'reality' of *hereos* and the passionate nature of 'courtly love'.

[116] Glossing on this passage in Baena's prologue, Julian Weiss makes the observation that 'to feign' is derived from the Latin 'fingere,' which also means 'to create' (241).

[117] Greco-Roman Antiquity bequeathed upon the medievals not only faculty psychology but also a related "technique of the image, which can be organized for and against love" (Foucault, *The Care of the Self* 138-39).

[118] I describe this process in detail in my article "Passion and Persuasion." 'Feigned' lovesickness is also crucial in the psychological profile of Cervantes's Don Quijote; see Folger (*Images in Mind* 234-48).

[119] Roger Smith suggests that the discourse on passions was instrumental in the emergence of the modern 'I' in the 17th century (52).

ogy of passionate love shows that it was prone to be a *technê* of self-fashioning.

On one hand, the obsession (exogenous or feigned) with the *imago* halts the continuous folding of the outside to the inside and the formation of *habitus*, resulting in a disruption of the social competences expected from a nobleman.[120] In longer prose texts which deal with the topic of passionate love, the love-stricken knightly hero withdraws from the community, like Montalvo's Amadís, suffering the loss of his knightly prowess or sliding into an animal-like state. As I will presently show, the loss of humanity haunts San Pedro's *Cárcel de amor*. On the other hand, the fixation upon the *imago* – which is fantasized as an incessant gazing at a perfect body endowed with perfect virtues – has the effect of staving off potentially harmful visual sense impressions and memories. Since the subject is what he or she sees, the patient of *hereos* assimilates the beloved's qualities through obsessive contemplation. Aside from the performative potential of lovesickness, this is the reason for the *Umwertung* described by Couliano: "spiritual sickness induced by love ended by being extolled as the real health of body and soul" (21).

Although the subjectification through passionate love and the formation of 'orthodox' *habitus* have the same epistemic and medico-psychological bases, there is a fundamental difference. The normal process of the folding of the outside into the inside is effectively a deconstructive process: It involves the 'digestion' of visual perceptions by the mental faculties, fortifying mental structures which have been built up over a long period of time.[121] Naturally the *aemulatio* and *imitatio* of exemplary figures (saints and secular heroes) was a necessary part of this process.[122] It is no coincidence that representations of these figures appear conventional and 'flat' to the modern reader. Emulation of 'role models' was thought of in terms of typology and guided, particularly in

---

[120] The most caustic rebuttal of passionate love (as *amor desordenado*, or *loco amor*) in general and its courtly variant in particular is Alfonso Martínez de Toledo's *Corbacho*; see Gumbrecht (*'Eine' Geschichte der spanischen Literatur* 147).

[121] 'Digestion' was a common metaphor for the workings of memory, based on the processing of species (Carruthers, *The Book of Memory* 219-20).

[122] Bynum emphasizes that 'individuality' meant a choice between given roles ("Did the Twelfth Century Discover the Individual?").

the religious sphere, by the "Ideal der vollkommenen Selbstpreisgabe" (Moos, "Persönliche Identität und Identifikation vor der Moderne" 17) ["ideal of absolute self-renunciation"]. Premodern technologies of the self actually aimed at preventing the subject from being ensnared by images.[123] In the Middle Ages, it seems, the only legitimate identificatory processes were the *imitatio Christi* and "passion devotion."[124] Consequently, medieval literature did not provide the potential for identification, but for role play and masquerade: the pleasure of the recipients apparently grew, as Gumbrecht remarks,[125] with the distance between the role and the player's true identity. Burke gives this discrepancy a different twist, claiming that the official "law" and the "carnivalesque" desire are complementary in medieval thought: While the modern subject mimetically identifies, producing an "accurate copy of the essence of the object," in medieval subjectification a "negative outside was as likely as a positive one to flood in and constitute the 'self'" (*Desire and the Law* 19).

In passion devotion, however, medievals also strove to become an "accurate copy" of Christ. Biernoff points to the parallels between passion devotion and passionate earthly love: "No less than sexual lust, redemptive love is articulated through sight: it penetrates, inflames and transforms, leaving an indelible impression on the beholder's soul" (139). Both initiate a narcissistic process of identification, that is, in the Lacanian sense of incorporating an *other* or "assuming an image" (Smith, Paul Julian 96). In secular literature, it finds its most significant expression in the motif of the "transformación de los amantes" (*La transformación de los amantes* 15-53) ["transformation of lovers"], as Guillermo Serés calls it in his study of the origins of this notion and its repercussions in Spanish letters. The transformation of lovers has its roots in Platonism and mysticism (the lover as a mirror in which the lover recognizes himself), but it could also be accommodated to Aristotelian natural philosophy (55-86) and hence to

---

[123] As Fernando Gómez Redondo points out, Boccaccio's *Fiammetta* (which I will discuss in relation to Juan de Flores's *Grimalte y Gradissa*) is a detailed record of the noxious 'self-destructive' effects of an unbridled imagination and incautious reading.

[124] See Bynum ("The Female Body and Religious Practice"), Camille ("Mimetic Identification and Passion Devotion") and Biernoff.

[125] See Gumbrecht ("Lachen und Arbitrarität/Subjektivität und Ernst" 212).

medieval faculty psychology.[126] Glossing on Hugh of St. Victor, Serés explains that excessive passionate love

> comporta que el alma del amante, que recuerda la imagen, calca los contornos de la *species* permanentemente *impressa*, troquelada por los espíritus animales en el ventrículo cerebral y, por lo tanto, en el alma; comporta que el *phantasma* sea, en fin: la vestimenta, el hábito, del alma: 'Et siquidem ratio ipsa sola contemplatione eam susceperit, *quasi vestimentum*[,] ei est ipsa imaginatio extra eam, et circa eam quo facile exui et spoliari possit. Si vero etiam delectatione illi adhaeserit, *quasi pellis* ei fit ipsa imaginatio.' (75) [emphasis added by Serés][127]
> [has the effect that the lover's soul, which remembers the image, counterdraws the contours of the permanently impressed *species*, embossed by the animal spirits in the central ventricle, and therefore in the soul. This has the effect that the phantasma finally becomes the soul's vestiment and "habit": 'If reason apprehends it (the *species*), like a vestiment, through contemplation alone, it is outside and around of imagination itself so that it can easily be discarded and disappear. If, however, a pleasure adheres to it, imagination becomes like its second skin.]

Imagination, as the "vestimentum" or "pellis" (skin) of the soul, shapes it, eventually transforming the matter of the body. There is a significant semantic overlap between *vestimentum* and *habitus* as vestment and mental disposition:[128] the *habitus* is acquired by lifelong mental and bodily discipline, becoming, as Peter von

---

[126] The examples (mostly pieces of 15th-century *poesía cancioneril*) Serés adduces in order to illustrate the importance of the notion of "transformation of lovers" in the Middle Ages (87-136), show, in my opinion, that passionate love was conceived of as being firmly couched in naturalist discourse. As Serés notes, in Spain, the influence of Italian Platonists had repercussions in the 16th century.

[127] The quote is taken from Hugh's *De unione corporis et spiritus* (*Patrologia Latina*, vol. 177, col. 288). The sentence ends: "[...] ita ut non dolore exui possit, cui cum amore inhaesit" ["so it cannot leave without pain, that in which it is inhered with love"].

[128] It is worth noting that the connection between *habitus* as vestiment and mental and bodily disposition was, and is, obvious to Spanish speakers; the *Diccionario de Autoridades* lists the meanings of "El vestido ò trage que cada una trahe segun su estado, ministério ò Nación [...]", and "la facilidad que se tiene en qualquiera cosa que se hace ù dice, por repetirla muchas vezes" (t. 3, 106) ["The vestiment or garment everybody wears according to his state, office or nation [...] the capacity one has in anything made or said, by repeating it many times"].

Moos points out, a "second skin" ("Das mittelalterliche Kleid" 135).[129] "The radical stasis of the medieval personality," as Thomas Greene has called it (246), was radically undercut by passionate love. While the gradual and troublesome process ("difficile mobilis"; Greene 244) of the formation of *habitus* and *hexis* endlessly announced and deferred perfection and unity, amatory assimilation (of the beloved's *species* and by it) promised the near-instant transformation into an-other which was fantasized as perfect in body and soul.[130] It was the promise of wholeness and perfection in togetherness.

We have already seen that the ennobling subjectification through passion was a perilous process because the lover's performance in the courtly milieu ('being seen') and the contemplation of the perfect beloved ('seeing') was always already crossed out by the social debilitation due to blocked orthodox *habitus* ('being seen') and the obfuscation of the truth of faith ('seeing'). The implication and consequences of passionate love for the premodern understanding of sex and gender were even more momentous. An analysis of the Rosenbach illustration in *Cárcel de amor* will show that the courtly subjectification through love can be described as a masculine self-empowerment in Lacanian terms.

2.4. ONE SEX, MUCH (GENDER) TROUBLE

2.4.1. *Caloric identities*

According to Lacan, identity constitution is achieved through the appropriation of the phallus, the "authorizing signification of the Law," as Judith Butler calls it (56).[131] With 'phallus' Lacan

---

[129] According to von Moos ("Das mittelalterliche Kleid" 135), Erasmus calls the vestment "the body of the body".

[130] Leonardo da Vinci's plea for the excellence of the visual arts over poetry is based on the assumption that the beauty and harmony of images are instantaneously evident, shaping the painter himself in the creative process; see Summers (73-75).

[131] Lacan never clearly defines the term 'phallus,' providing instead a series of conceptual approximations on many occasions. However, he lays down fundamental aspects in a brief essay with the title "The Meaning of the Phallus." Regarding Lacan's key concept of the mirror stage, the primal *méconnaissance*

does not mean the bodily organ, the penis, but a symbol of the patriarchic power of negation and representation. The submission under the patriarchic law, *le nom du père* (the name/the 'no' of the father), is a positioning vis-à-vis the phallus, that is, a determination of gender roles. Woman 'is' the phallus because she is the signifier of the masculine desire for the other, and, at the same time, a signifier for its lack (through 'castration'). She 'appears' (in the mode of the masquerade) as the phallus,[132] reflecting its power. Only through the feminine other (and her desire) who 'is' the phallus, is the masculine subject capable of imagining that he 'has' the phallus (the object of the other's desire), thus establishing his masculine identity. According to Judith Butler, Lacan

> poses the relation between the sexes in terms that reveal the speaking 'I' as a masculinized effect of repression, one which postures as an autonomous and self-grounding subject, but whose very coherence is called into question by the sexual positions that it excludes in the process of identity formation. For Lacan, the subject comes into being – that is, begins to posture as a self-grounding signifier within language – only on the condition of a primary repression of the pre-individuated incestuous pleasures associated with the (now repressed) maternal body. [...] The dependency, although denied, is also pursued by the masculine subject, for the woman as reassuring sign is the displaced maternal body, the vain persistent promise of the recovery of pre-individuated *jouissance*. (58)

While Lacan's idea of oedipalization is tied to a specific socio-historical formation and therefore cannot be uncritically applied to the Middle Ages and the Early Modern Period, his concept of the 'transcendental signifier' as the structuring element of the patriarchal order and the positioning of the sexes is useful in reconstructing the premodern orders of sex and gender. At any rate, the analysis of the Rosenbach illustration of *Cárcel de amor*'s initial scene (caption 1) reveals perplexing parallels between Lacan's subject and the premodern subject.

---

which grounds all subsequent identifications, see his classic "Le stade du miroir comme formateur de la fonction du Je" and Elisabeth Roudinesco's study of Lacan's concept.

[132] See Lacan ("The Meaning of the Phallus" 84).

The initial encounter in the Sierra Morena is conspicuously understudied – in spite of the obvious importance the author gave to it.[133] San Pedro conceived of an "opening icon," a striking mnemonic image of the etiology of passionate love and its courtly implications which would guide a premodern reader's interpretation of the text.[134] Some attention has been paid to the figure of the "caballero salvaje,"[135] who can definitely be identified as a Wild Man. Alan Deyermond's interpretation that, in sentimental fiction, the Wild Man, a traditional figure in medieval literature and iconography,[136] represents the tension and violence which courtly love causes in the follower of its precepts ("El hombre salvaje en la novela sentimental" 108), is widely accepted. The thrust of Deyermond's argument is unquestionable, yet it fails to render the image's complexity. On one hand, it does not account for the essentially triangular constellation of passionate love (Leriano-*imagen*-Deseo), vis-à-vis El Auctor. On the other, it glosses over the figurine (*imagen*) carved into a crystalline stone which the Wild Man holds in his weapon-hand, a representation without precedent in iconography.[137]

The artist who executed the initial scene in Bernardí Vallmanya's Catalan translation presents the figurine as the focal point of the artistic arrangement, connecting the savage knight, Leriano and El Auctor. It shows the *imagen femenil* nude with a belt, an object in her hand, and flames radiating from her body. Harvey L. Sharrer demonstrates the debt of the wood-cut artist to medieval representations of Venus and the Virgin.[138] Elsewhere,

---

[133] See above note 10.

[134] See Folger (*Images in Mind* (201-14). The term "opening icons" was coined by V. A. Kolve in his analysis of Chaucer's *Knight's Tale* (91). In the 1493 original (ed. Mata, no pagination), the illustration is inserted between the prologue and the description of the encounter ("Comença la obra"), constituting a 'threshold' to the text.

[135] Remarkably, Grieve's study of the role of Girardian mimetic desire does not analyze the allegorical representation of Desire (*Death and Desire*).

[136] See my study of the role of the Wild Man in *Cárcel de amor* and his liminal status between the realms of humanity and animality (Folger, "Bestialische Leidenschaften"). About Wild Men see also Richard Bernheimer's classic *Wild Men in the Middle Ages*, Timothy Husband, and Dorothy Yamamoto's recent *The Boundaries of the Human in Medieval English Literature* (144-196). Oleh Mazur and Fausta Antonucci focus on the figure of the *salvaje* in Golden Age Spain, providing overviews of medieval antecedents.

[137] See Fraxanet Sala (436).

[138] See also Husband (65-67).

however, I show that the *imagen* must be related, in spite of its iconographic filiations, to the phenomenology of *amor hereos*.[139]

On the primary diegetic level, San Pedro's *imagen femenil* literally represents a mental *imago* of Princess Laureola, the object of the fantasies of the lovesick hero Leriano. Agamben has interpreted the love-inflicting *phantasma* as a 'lost object,' describing it in terms of the Freudian notion of fetish. Defying the metaphysical dichotomy of absence and presence, the fetishistic phantasm makes present the unattainable presence of the love object: in a situation in which 'real' possession is impossible, the *phantasm*/fetish is a means of 'appropriating' the desired object by making it 'appear' lost.[140] Although Agamben's account is congruent with Lacan's notion of the woman *as* the phallus, it fails to acknowledge the gendered nature of the narcissistic introjection in premodern passionate love. This gender aspect is perfectly illustrated by the opening scene of *Cárcel* and the supplementary Rosenbach wood-cut. Deseo holds the *phantasma* in his right hand while he has a defensive weapon, the iron shield, in his left hand. Since it is the *imagen* the knight uses to subdue another knight ("con la hermosura desta imagen causo las aficiones y con ellas quemo las vidas [...]"; San Pedro 5-6 ["with the beauty of that image I cause passions; and with those I burn lives"])[141] it can be inferred that the *imagen femenil* in his right hand, the weapon's hand, substitutes for a weapon. In the knightly world, a weapon, however, is much more than a technical artifact or a simple tool. Armature must be seen as a "'self-extension'" of the knightly subject (Fradenburg 185),[142] and the nature of this "self-extension"

---

[139] Following a hint by Erich von Richthofen, I base the identification of the sculpture as mental *imago* on striking parallels between *Cárcel* and Dante's *Vita Nuova* (Folger, *Images in Mind* 201-14); see also Folger ("*Cárceles de amor*"). To the evidence I present in these earlier works, it is worth adding a poem by the Comendador Escrivá which nicely illustrates my argument: "En aquel punto que os vi, / imagen en mí esculpida, / con mis ojos imprimida / dentro de mi alma os metí" (*Cancionero general* 1514, quoted in Serés 143) ["When I saw you / image sculpted in me, / impressed by my eyes / I inserted you in my soul"].

[140] See Agamben (45).

[141] My translation. Whinnom translates "aficiones" with "passion" (5). The plural here is necessary to convey the congruence with faculty psychology. The term might also be translated here as *intentiones*.

[142] Regarding the role of clothes as identificatory markers and identity-shaping "second" skin in general see von Moos ("Das mittelalterliche Kleid") and Groebner (54-67).

Caption 3: Wild Man, Cathedral of Ávila (16th century)

can be easily determined if we follow the chain of metaphorical substitutions. The figurine occupies the position which the literary and iconographic tradition of the Wild Man reserves for the maze (caption 3).[143] The maze, particularly in vertical orientation, is an unambiguous symbol of the penis.[144] Since, as Thomas Laqueur amply demonstrates, the penis per se was not the marker of sexual difference, it may seem counter-intuitive to understand it also as a representation of the phallus in the Lacanian sense. It must not be forgotten, however, that "the chain of signifiers in which the phallus finds its context varies historically" (Grosz 121).[145] The 'originary' marker of sexual difference is, as I will show in due time, vital bodily heat. Vital heat is what women lack and what they desire in sexual intercourse. The erect male penis is a marker of vital heat: it distinguishes man from woman, who has a penis which is internal, due precisely to this lack of vital heat. The weapon equally indexes prowess, physical strength owing to vital heat. Hence if we acknowledge this "chain of signifiers" and substitutions (vital heat-weapon-erect penis-woman-*imagen femenil*), it becomes plain that, in the premodern world, woman as a phantasm of male imagination 'is' the phallus.[146]

The 'owner' of the phallus, however, is not the submissive lover Leriano, but his jailer: Deseo, the Wild Man. This Wild Man is an oxymoronic figure,[147] as we can see in his characterization of himself:

---

[143] See Bernheimer (1) and Husband (2). In his discussion of weapons used by Wild Men, Oleh Mazur holds that "Spanish prose offers a much greater variety of weapons than any other European country" (108). He leaves, however, no doubt that the typical weapon is the maze.

[144] Antonucci speaks of a "símbolo de virilidad" (21) ["symbol of virility"].

[145] According to Grosz (121), Lacan argues that in ancient Greece the phallus did not represent an organ but was an insignia, a marker of class differentiation. The weapon, or sword, had an equal function and is, perhaps, a more adequate signifier for the phallus than the penis. Cynthia Hahn (175) suggests seeing the representation of the Cross as a/the 'transcendental signifier' of the Middle Ages.

[146] In his "God and the Jouissance of Woman", Lacan emphasizes that the woman as love object is necessarily a fantasy.

[147] While the Wild Man is typically, as Deyermond holds, the "término opuesto a los valores cortesanos de la sociedad medieval" (18) ["the opposite term to the courtly values of the Middle Ages"], the *salvajes* in Spanish sentimental romance "se identifican con los amantes cortesanos y el amor ideal" (21) ["identify with the courtly lovers and ideal love"]. See also Hayden White and Yamamoto (144-196), who see the Wild Man as the Other that enables 'negative' self-definition. The 'hybridity' of Deseo points to improper sexual conduct, since monstrosity

siempre me crié entre los onbres de buena criança, usaré contigo de la gentileza que aprendí y no de la braveza de mi natural. Tú sabrás, pues lo quieres saber, yo soy principal oficial de la casa de Amor; llámanme por nonbre Deseo. (San Pedro 5)
[Since I was ever nurtured among men of good breeding, I shall use you with the gentle courtesy that I have learned and not with the ferocity which comes naturally to me. Know, then, since you wish to know, that I am chief officer in the household of Love; men know me by the name of Desire. (5)]

The courtly idiom he uses is a token of his *gentileza*, and his 'possession' of the phallus. While the Wild Man is incapable of speech, producing instead unintelligible sounds, in *Cárcel de amor* the courtly lover Leriano groans ("con lastimado gemido" ["with a piteous moan" (4)]), repeating a confused statement: "En mi fe se sufre todo" (4) ["in my faith everything is suffered/can be sustained"].[148] Therefore, Timothy Husband's contention that, in *Cárcel de amor*, "the wild man is elevated from a symbol of mere sexuality to a rare, allegorical one of unfullfilled sensual desire" (65) must be qualified. The emphasis in the Wild Man's self-characterization is not on longing but on self-control. In spite of his natural ferocity, Deseo, the personification of Desire, is distinguished by a courtly ethos and control of affects ("gentileza") which he describes as the result of a subjectification ("me crié") in a courtly milieu ("entre onbres de buena criança"). Similarly, Leriano the courtly knight is plagued by a ferocious desire, without succumbing to his beastly impulses. While the Wild Man was traditionally seen, as Husband remarks (65), as the "natural opponent of the knight," Leriano and Deseo, who are literally tied together in the otherworldly landscape of the dark valley, resemble each other and yet embody complementary aspects of the courtly lover's "characterology" (Rogers 1-17): We witness an obvious doubling of the knightly protagonist Leriano, into the sentimental lover enslaved by passion and his "shadow 'other'" (Yamamoto, 187), the Wild Man. In the image, this doubling is signified by a

---

was often related to "unnatural coitus between different species, or [...] unnatural type of copulation" (Jacquart and Thomasset 162); see also Camille ("Hybridity, Monstrosity, and Bestiality in the *Roman de Fauvel*" 164-65).

[148] Whinnom rather freely translates: "In the constancy of my love, all suffering can be borne" (4).

parallelization of the postures of Leriano and Deseo (caption 4), and, in the text, it is manifest through the rays of fire which bind Deseo and his captive.[149] The Rosenbach woodcut is emblematic of Lacan's dictum that "[i]f the phallus is a signifier then it is in the place of the Other that the subject gains access to it" ("The Meaning of the Phallus" 83), because Leriano 'has' the phallus only in the field of the Other – through his double.[150]

Gilles Deleuze describes the logic of the double:

> [L]e double n'est jamais une projection de l'intérieur, c'est au contraire une intériorisation du dehors. Ce n'est pas du dédoublement de l'UN, c'est un redoublement de l'Autre. Ce n'est pas une reproduction du Même, c'est une répétition du Différent. Ce n'est pas l'émanation d'un JE, c'est la mise en immanence d'un toujours autre ou d'un Non-moi. Ce n'est jamais l'autre qui est un double, dans le redoublement, c'est moi qui me vis comme le double de l'autre: je ne me rencontre pas à l'extérieur, je trouve l'autre en moi [...]. (105)
> [The double is never a projection of the interior. It is, on the contrary, an interiorization of the exterior. It is never a de-doubling of the One, but a re-doubling of the Other. It is not a reproduction of the Same, but the repetition of the Different. It is not an emanation of an 'I' but the becoming immanent of an other or a Non-Me. In the doubling, it is never the other who is the double; it is me who sees himself as the other's double: I do not meet myself in the exterior but find the other in me.][151]

Deseo is not a projection of Leriano, a reflection of the inner tensions which courtly love causes, as Deyermond has it.[152] In the

---

[149] According to Biernoff (139), in images of St. Francis's stigmatization, divine love is frequently depicted as rays of light emanating from the wounds of a Seraph to pierce Francis's own body. Possibly, San Pedro was inspired by this tradition. San Pedro alludes here to the "seeing rays" of the extromission model, suggesting that Leriano was "infected" and captured by the gaze of his beloved.

[150] According to George Herbert Mead, the conception of the "double" is related to the "beginning of the self as an object" (140), which is a defining feature of modern subjectivity.

[151] See also Foucault's reflections on the relation between the double and "the thinking of the outside" ("Das Denken des Draußen"). He argues that there is the subject *of* enunciation: the subject leaves behind a "grammatical fold," a speaking (153).

[152] Rohland de Langbehn notes that his "buena crianza" restrains him from pursuing his passion ferociously (*Zur Interpretation der Romane des Diego de San Pedro* 148).

paradoxical way Deleuze describes, Deseo is what Leriano is not, and what he finds in himself. In the wood-cut, the parallelization between Leriano and Deseo indicates that we are not confronted with a specular reflection, but with a *fold* (caption 4). The axis of the fold separates the plane of Leriano's imaginary assimilation from a phenomenal sphere in which we see, beside the observer El Auctor, Leriano's masculine body in courtly attire. The choric visual field that constitutes Leriano's self is represented, *en miniature*, by the *gazes* of a 'real' public (El Auctor) and the specular gazes of the phantasmatic image of a desirable woman and his alter ego (Deseo), the Wild Man (caption 5).

The female figurine signifies Laureola, who figures in the text as a female *other*. Leriano's attempt to conquer her and El Auctor's struggle to decipher her emotions and thoughts by interpreting her bodily reactions are frustrated.[153] The *imagen femenil* is alien, and the Wild Man too, is an image of otherness. Compared to the size of Leriano, which is presented by the confrontation with the same-size El Auctor as normal, the alter ego is the *Other*. In the imaginary order, defined by the axis of the fold, Leriano, in his figuration as a courtly Wild Man, 'has' the phallus in the shape of the *imagen femenil*. Leriano's alter ego is, on one hand, a hyper-masculine figure.[154] His hirsuteness was, for contemporary medicine and natural philosophy, a clear indication of the excess of vital heat, and therefore virility.[155] His obvious physical power, the possession of

---

[153] The rationale of Nicolás Núñez's continuation is precisely to eliminate the threatening indeterminacy of her 'body language.' In a dream vision, Laureola appears with epigrams attached to her garments, spelling out her thoughts and feelings (Folger, "*Cárceles de amor*").

[154] Regarding the Wild Man as a "lecherous creature" see Mazur (136-37) and also Yamamoto (163). Glossing on Vincent of Beauvais, Camille points out that "monsters" were often seen as "engendered [...] by means of an unnatural type of copulation" ("Hybridity, Monstrosity, and Bestiality in the *Roman de Fauvel*" 164). The monstrous Wild Man, then, also symbolizes sexual "perversion".

[155] See, for instance, the Aristotelian *Problemata*: "¿Por qué tanto las aves como los hombres peludos son lascivos? [...] [P]orque son capaces de cocer una gran cantidad de humedad a causa de su calor? Los pelos y las plumas son la prueba" (V, 31; p. 115-16) ["Why are birds and hirsute men lascivious? (...) Because they are capable of cooking a great quantity of humidity due to their heat? The hair and the feathers are the proof"]. Juan Huarte de San Juan, whose *Examen* I will discuss in due course, argues that the fact that woman does not have a beard demonstrates that she is not "templada ni caliente" (612) ["balanced nor hot"]; regarding the role of (female) hirsuteness in Huarte's notions of sex and gender, see Susanne Thiemann. Regarding medieval and early modern views of

Caption 4: Leriano/Deseo, two aspects of the courtly lover

Caption 5: Fold Leriano/(Laureola)Deseo

weapons and the dominance he, Deseo, exerts over another male are further factors of the courtly subject's masculinity.[156]

The viewer is offered a spectacle in which the masculinity of the Wild Man, the control he exercises over female bodies, shines through Leriano, the courtly *persona* – his submissive, socialized body, his courtly *criança*. The courtier/knight's self appears as a screen, "stain" or "spot," in Lacanian diction (*The Four Fundamental Principles of Psychoanalysis* 97), between the geometric point (El Auctor as the 'I' of enunciation) and the Other (Deseo cum female phantasm). Thus the opening icon of *Cárcel de amor* manifests the paradox of courtly love, that is, the co-presence and interdependence of abjection and self-empowerment:[157] A properly gendered courtly *persona* as the slave of his beloved is the double of a tamed yet sexualized Wild Man, who 'possesses' a female body. This body is instrumental in the constitution and stabilization of the masculine subject.

Disrupting the laborious sedimentation of *species* into *habitus*, the woman's *imago* can *appear* as the 'transcendental signifier' which promises to halt temporarily the "mouvements péristaltiques" (Deleuze, *Foucault* 104) ["peristaltic movements"] of the folds and the Lacanian *glissement* of the signifiers over the signifieds.[158] Hence San Pedro and his congenial illustrator created not only an emblem of the differentiation of sexes and genders through passionate love and love service, but also the primal scene of the masculine speaking 'I''s genesis (Butler 58). The silent spectacle of the exchange of gazes is only disrupted by Leriano's occasional lament: "'En mi fe, se sufre todo'" (San Pedro 4). These words are oddly displaced in the mouth of the captive, but they aptly characterize Deseo and Laureola('s *imago*). Somebody else speaks through Leriano. His discourse is in the field of the Other.[159] He becomes the masculine subject of enunciation through the phantasmatic 'appropriation' of the phallus (by his double).

---

the topic in general see also Cadden (181-83) and Will Fisher. One characteristic of the Wild Man is his aggressive sexuality; see, for instance, Antonucci (21-30) and Mazur, who holds that the Wild Man "embodies *amor ferino*" (136-37).

[156] See Karras (12).

[157] El Saffar speaks of a "dynamics of fear and dependency that suggest a period prior to the Renaissance in which resistance to, but captivity still within, the figure of the Mother is the dominant collective experience" ("The 'I' of the Beholder" 183).

[158] See Lacan ("The Instance of the Letter in the Unconscious" 419).

[159] See Lacan ("The Meaning of the Phallus" 78).

On one hand, the subjectification through love is complementary to the performance of the dispersed subject. On the other, it lays the foundations of a subject that is not grounded in the Other of the choric visual field, but in a totalizing, instantaneous transformation through assimilation – of and by the beloved.[160] Nonetheless, the image of empowering, masculine subjectivity in *Cárcel* manifests, at the same time, the precarious nature of courtly self-fashioning. The Wild Man is not only a cipher for masculinity, but also for the loss of humanity, the sliding into the realm of the beastly, and, therefore, for the loss of rationality.[161] Loss of rationality and the association with "nature" implies effemination, as Sherry B. Ortner argued in her classic "Is Female to Male as Nature Is to Culture?". This effemination of the Wild Man is reflected in his double, Leriano. Although the *Umwertung* of this loss is part and parcel of the establishment of Leriano as a masculine subject, there are clear indications that this very masculinity is threatened. We must not forget that *Cárcel*'s initial abduction scene certainly rang a bell for contemporary readers. Iconographic and literary representation abound in which a Wild Man kidnaps a maiden, threatening her with rape.[162] Leriano, the passionate lover, stands in for the maiden, being the potential object of sexual debasement and radical loss of self-determination.[163] As we will see in due course, Juan de Flores, in his *Grisel y Mirabella*, fleshes out these somber implications.

San Pedro, on the other hand, provides the prisoner of love with the opportunity to perform his role as perfect courtly lover and brave knight. Once Leriano has returned to Macedonia we see him fully incorporated in the community, blamelessly performing his role as a courtly lover. He shows his individual prowess as a fighter when he defeats the traitor Persio, and, after Laureola's incarceration, he shows that he is a superior strate-

---

[160] Burke points out the crucial importance of *assimilatio* for medieval thinking (*Desire and the Law* 15-16). However, it must be emphasized that the immediately transformative assimilation I am describing here belongs to the genealogy of modern identification.

[161] See Gilian Clark ("The Fathers and the Animals"). Elsewhere, I analyze the blending of femininity and animality in *Cárcel de amor* (Folger, "Bestialische Leidenschaft").

[162] See Antonucci (38-41).

[163] Note that Leriano is the object of gazes of the bystanders (caption 5), implying, as Caviness points out (22), effemination.

gist.[164] Leaving the court as wished by Laureola, he exerts the self-control expected from the perfect courtly lover, eventually becoming a 'martyr of love.' There is reason, then, to see in Leriano, as most critics do, a model knight and ideal courtly lover. San Pedro clearly indicates in the prologue that this was precisely his intention.[165] But upon careful reading, his work presents a bleak picture of courtly love and courtly self-fashioning through performance.

Although in *Cárcel* San Pedro staged, as it were, the entire program of traditional aristocratic subject constitution, El Auctor expresses a certain annoyance with the "endlessness of the aristocrat's need to prove his unalterable possession of honor" (Fradenburg 171) in public displays of his domination of other males by means of physical superiority. Describing the duel between Leriano and his rival, he states that "la fuerça de los golpes mostraron la virtud de los ánimos" (San Pedro 34) ["the power of their blows showed the virtue of their souls"],[166] but he has no intention of indulging in the popular display of feats of arms: "por no detenerme en esto que parece cuento de historias viejas, Leriano le cortó la mano derecha [...]" (34) ["so as not to dwell on what must seem a tale from old stories, Leriano struck off Persio's right hand"].[167] Obviously, San Pedro gave greater importance to Leriano's conduct as a courtly lover as a proof of his "virtud de ánimo" and his masculinity.

---

[164] See Rohland de Langbehn (*Zur Interpretation der Romane des Diego de San Pedro* 67-68).

[165] The author proposes to improve upon a criticized work of his, imitating an "oración" he wrote earlier (San Pedro 3). The chastised text is most certainly his *Tractado de amores de Arnalte y Lucenda*; the model of the *imitatio* can be identified as his *Sermón*, because Arnalte is presented as a protagonist far from exemplary and the *Sermón* provides an *ars amandi* for the perfect lover; see Folger (*Images in Mind* 199-200).

[166] My translation. Whinnom's translation "the fury of their blows displayed the temper of their spirits" (33) emphasizes their state of mind without paying attention to the display of masculinity which is clearly the theme of the scene.

[167] Whinnom translates "from some antique chronicle" (34); he explains that he "removed an ambiguity in the Spanish" (103, note 21). Although Whinnom is right in pointing out that formal juridical duels before the king are documented in many chronicles and manuals of chivalry, it stands to reason that San Pedro refers here to romances. Needless to say, the chivalric "tales" despised by San Pedro were by no means literarily obsolete, but held great appeal for San Pedro's contemporaries.

Yet the denouement, that is, Leriano's gloomy death, conceived of in order to demonstrate that Leriano is a hero of self-control and thus a superior male, is disconcerting. There is the fundamental fact that Leriano has failed to prove his attractiveness to Laureola, his power to exert "control of women" (Karras 11). Leriano tries to convince his audience that his death is a virtuous and manly act of martyrdom, but he "convinces no one, within the text or outside of it, for he is clearly dying of rejection [...]" (Sears, "Prisoners of Love" 275). Ingesting Laureola's letters – which are not a token of a past glory of reciprocated love, but documents of Laureola's refusal to mirror his desire – he makes a desperate attempt to recuperate or achieve his fullness through a metonymic incorporation of his beloved, but the literal dissolution of meaning is emblematic "of a 'dead-end' speech situation" (Brownlee, *The Severed Word* 171) and thus the fading of the masculine speaking 'I.'

It is misleading to interpret Leriano's death as a suicide and, therefore, a radical act of self-determination.[168] He is in the grip of his passion and ultimately surrenders to a force he is incapable of mastering. There can be no doubt that, at the end of San Pedro's *Cárcel*, Laureola – who is impervious to passion and resists the power of courtly persuasion – is endowed with agency.[169] The fact that San Pedro created, possibly unwittingly, a weak hero and a strong heroine, probably accounts for the fact that *Cárcel* was avidly read by a female public – as far as we can judge from the fact that all of the French translations were commissioned by women.[170] This subversion of the gender hierarchy

---

[168] Regarding the diverging opinions on the reason and rationale of Leriano's death, see Folger (*Images in Mind* 219-21).

[169] In her study of troubadour poetry, Kay suggests that the *domna* is a third, "mixed" gender (86). The internal logic of premodern caloric gender economy, however, has the advantage of avoiding essentialized notions of gender, proffering instead a scale model. In misogynist discourse, as in the works of Pedro Torellas, female self-determination is typically devalued as ingratitude and unreasonable arbitrariness: "Non quieren por ser queridas / nin galardonan seruicios, / mas, todas desconocidas, / por sola tema regidas, / reparten sus beneficios" (648, l. 5-9) ["They won't love for being loved / nor do they reward services, / rather they are all ungrateful, / ruled by arbitrariness / they give (their) rewards (benefits)"].

[170] See Orth. In the light of San Pedro's prologue, Orth's contention that Leriano's praise of women "emphasizes the intended appeal to a distinctly virtuous feminine audience" (211) is highly dubitable. According to Parrilla ("La ficción sentimental y sus lectores" 22), the inventories of 16th-century libraries provide

in San Pedro's work was also what incited Nicolás Núñez to write a 'continuation' in which he strips Laureola of her superiority and resurrects Leriano as an active, 'manly' subject.[171]

At any rate, Leriano's mother clearly perceives her son's death as a defeat:

> ni te valió la fuerça del cuerpo, ni la virtud del coraçón, ni el esfuerço del ánimo; todas las cosas de que te podías valer te fallecieron. (San Pedro 78)
> [the strengths of your body could not assist you, nor the goodness of your heart, nor the valour of your spirit. All the things to which you might have had recourse failed you. (80)]

She laments the insufficiency of Leriano's physical, moral, and mental virility, and she is not the only one.

> [T]urbada la lengua y la vista casi perdida: ya los suyos, no podiéndose contener, davan bozes; ya sus amigos començavan a llorar; ya sus vasallos y vasallas gritavan por las calles [...]. (76-77)
> [his tongue was already faltering, and he could scarcely see. It was then that his servants, unable to contain themselves, began to wail, that his friends started to weep, that his vassals, men and women, cried aloud in the streets [...]. (78)]

The view of his emaciated body and failing mental faculties causes the distress of family, friends and vassals, male and female. In a cruel *contrafactum* of the medieval *ars moriendi*,[172] Leriano so-

---

no evidence for a predominantly female readership of *Cárcel*. It is significant that the French translations were related to a media change, that is, the production of lavishly illuminated manuscripts, indicating a mode of perception typical for earlier sentimental fiction: "el debate crítico, la especulación sobre casos amorosos" (Parrilla, "La ficción sentimental y. sus lectores" 24) ["critical debate, the deliberation of love cases"]. The feminist thrust of *Cárcel* was particularly emphasized by Joseph F. Chorpenning. The rationale of the late-medieval Iberian *Querelle des femmes* was, for both misogynists and 'pro-feminists,' the assertion of male superiority (Folger, "Liebeskrankheit").

[171] Elsewhere, I suggest that Núñez's interstitial rewriting of the last paragraph of *Cárcel*, which was published along with all but a few Spanish editions of the texts, made the text palatable to a male public, contributing to its editorial success ("*Cárceles de amor*").

[172] The relation to the *ars moriendi* has been pointed out by E. Michael Gerli, though without elaborating on the disturbing subversion of the idea of 'good dying' amidst "family and loved ones" (Gerli, "Leriano's Libation" 416). Regarding scholarship on Leriano's death, see Folger (*Images in Mind* 218-25).

licits the approving and benevolent gazes of the public but presents a spectacle of dissolution and effemination.

The ambiguity of *Cárcel*'s explicitly apologetic stance toward amatory subjectification and disclosure of its antinomies can by no means be attributed to the author's lack of sophistication. There is an intrinsic reason for the fact that, in *Cárcel de amor*, like in other sentimental romances, "[...] the woman paradoxically embodies redemptive and destructive qualities" (Grieve, "Mothers and Daughters in Fifteenth-Century Spanish Sentimental Romance" 346). This is perfectly illustrated by the *imagen femenil*, that is, the *imago* of a female body enwombed in the subjectifying fold Leriano-Deseo. Following the logic of the fold, the Other, the feminine and the bestial which constitutes, by way of 'exclusion,' the masculine self, is also 'inside.' It is an integral element of this self.[173] Since self and Other are ontologically continuous, this fold is an 'open fold,' exposed to the gazes of a courtly public. Like El Auctor, who is the witness to Leriano's subjection and his loss of agency and senses the animality lurking behind the mask,[174] the courtly community sees how the patient of *amor hereos* fails to comply with the social expectations of a courtly subject,[175] knowing that his fantasies cannot be separated from sexual appetites, always in danger of getting out of control. In short, sex and gender are unsettled in passionate love, because this love is predicated – in spite of the solipsistic dimension of lovesickness – on the ostentation of the affliction, that is, on a face-to-face situation. This means that the lover who tries to assert his subjectivity is always subjected to the probing, evaluating gazes of the others.

While gender and subjectivity were alien categories to premodern men, they could draw on natural philosophy to explain Leriano's 'unmanly' end. There was, as it were, a medical diagnosis for the effemination of the passionate lover and the ensuing crisis of masculine identity formation. In light of the tremendous progress science has made in the exploration of the human body and mind since the 15th century, it is necessary to caution against

---

[173] See Teuber "'Vivir quiero conmigo'" (184-86).
[174] See note 26, chap 3.
[175] According to Rohland de Langbehn (*Zur Interpretation der Romane des Diego de San Pedro* 159), *Cárcel* presents love as a force which alienates the individual from society ("gesellschaftsentfremdende Macht").

deprecating premodern images of the body, banishing them from the realm of 'historical reality' as mere curiosities or aberrations. However, the significance of "imaginary anatomy varies," as Lacan emphasizes, "with the ideas (clear or confused) about bodily functions which are prevalent in a given culture" ("Some Reflections on the Ego" 13). Elisabeth Grosz explains that the

> lived anatomy of the body [...] is organized not by the laws of biology but along the lines of parental or familial significations and fantasies about the body – fantasies (both private and collective) of the body's organization. [...] The body is lived in accordance with an individual's and a culture's *concepts* of biology. (44)

As I have already mentioned, in the Middle Ages and the Early Modern Period, it is essential to understand these concepts of biology not as merely physiological but as psychosomatic. Although the masculinized 'I' emerges from a fantasizing of the desired female body, the 'imaginary anatomy' implies that the bodily reality of the amorous suffering effects an eventual loss of masculinity. I am not only talking about the medical risks of *hereos* in the narrower sense, as they were discussed by contemporary physicians and natural philosophers,[176] but also about an essential instability revealed by *amor hereos*, an instability which has, in turn, repercussions on the culturally sanctioned gender hierarchy.

Premodern science knew that man and woman are essentially identical in terms of physiology, but differ accidentally. Their bodies differ in complexion, shape, texture, physical strength, etc., but they have the same sexual organs. The 16th-century Spanish physician Juan Huarte de San Juan, about whose famous *Examen de ingenios* we will hear more presently, formulates this doctrine as follows:

> Y es que el hombre, aunque nos parece en la compostura que vemos, no difiere de la mujer, según dice Galeno, más que en tener los miembros genitales afuera del cuerpo. Porque si hacemos anatomía de una doncella hallaremos que tiene den-

---

[176] See Folger (*Images in Mind* 33-56).

tro de sí dos testículos, dos vasos seminarios, y el útero con la mesma compostura que el miembro viril sin faltarle ninguna deligneación.

Y de tal manera es esto verdad, que si acabando Naturaleza de fabricar un hombre perfecto, le quisiese convertir en mujer, no tenía otro trabajo más que tornarle adentro los instrumentos de la generación; y si hecha mujer, quisiese volverla en varón, con arrojarle el útero y los testículos afuera, no había más que hacer. (608)

[And it is a fact that man, although he appears in the shape we see him, only differs from woman, as Galen says, in that his genitals are outside of the body. Because if we anatomize a girl we see that she has two testicles inside, two spermic ducts, and the uterus in the same shape as the male member, in all details.

And so it is true that if Nature has produced a perfect man, if she wanted to transform him into a woman she only would have to retract into the body his organs of reproduction, and in the case of a woman, if she wanted to turn her into a man, all she [Nature] would have to do is push her uterus and testicles out.]

Thomas Laqueur has studied this "one-sex model" in his influential study *Making Sex: Body and Gender from the Greeks to Freud*.[177] According to Laqueur, in

> the old model [...] men and women are arrayed according to their degree of metaphysical perfection, their vital heat, along an axis whose telos was male[. It] gave way by the late eighteenth century to a new model of radical dimorphism, of biological divergence. (5-6)

In other words, observable somatic differentiations between men and women are secondary and causally related to a single sex-determining factor: vital heat. Women are women because they are cooler then men.[178] Some scholars, like Huarte de San Juan,

---

[177] Although Joan Cadden has filled many of the lacunae in Laqueur's sketchy picture of notions of sex in the Middle Ages and claims to have discovered "evidence of other models not reducible to Laqueur's" (3), her own study provides, in my opinion, ample proof that the thrust of Laqueur's thesis is indisputable.

[178] Pedro Torella's famous *Coplas de las calidades de las donas* illustrate the

asserted that the coldest man was still warmer than any woman: "[Se] infiere claramente que no hay hombre que se pueda llamar frío respecto de la mujer, ni mujer caliente respecto del hombre" (610) ["It can be clearly inferred that no man can be called cold in relation to woman, nor any woman hot in relation to man"].[179] This does not mean, however, that there is a categorical divide of the sexes, but a continuum.[180] The "caloric model of sexuality," as Greenblatt calls it ("Fiction and Friction" 45), is not based on an essentialized binary opposition of the sexes, but on a caloric scale which sexes the body.[181]

The sudden sex change, manifest in a popping out of the sexual organs, was not a theoretical musing but an experienced historical reality, as indicated by cases reported, for example, by Michel Montaigne and the 16th-century surgeon Ambroise Paré.[182] While it is more common that woman turns into man, there are also cases of the opposite occurring. In a 16th-century case of lesbianism, the culprit claimed that the "terror of imprisonment had caused his penis to retract" (Greenblatt, "Fiction and Friction" 31). It is possible to dismiss this case as mere lie born out of the desire to outsmart the prosecutors; it is necessary, however, to realize that this ruse only made sense if it could be made plausible. A physician would explain that the fear of the prisoner caused *appetitus irascibilis*, a reduction of vital heat, which eventually led to a retraction of the sexual organs.

This volatility of sex, indexed by the genitals as secondary sexual markers, is at odds with Laqueur's claim that, before the 16th century,[183] "sex, or the body, must be understood as the

---

popularity of this tenet and its misogynist thrust (here referring to the lack of heat in procreation): "Mvger es un animal / que dize hombre ynperfecto, / procreado en el defecto / del buen calor natural / aquí se incluyen sus males / e la falta del bien suyo [...]" (p. 654; v. 91-96) ["Woman is an animal / that is called imperfect man / procreated by defect / of vital heat / here (in this text) are contained her vices / and her lack of virtue (...)"].

[179] See also Cadden (171).
[180] See Bynum ("Female Body and Religious Practice" 221).
[181] The tradition goes back to Antiquity, with Pliny as the most important *auctor* (Laqueur 128). Even seasonal change threatens the sexual identity: Constantine the African recommends in his book *De Coitu* that intercourse occur in Spring "when warmth and moisture are well-mixed. Warmth increases desire and masculinity, whereas cold reduces desire and renders effeminate" (Delany 57).
[182] See Laqueur (7 and 126-42).
[183] Laqueur acknowledges that the one-sex model was the cause of gender anxiety, increasingly during the 16th and 17th centuries (114-92).

epiphenomenon, while *gender*, what we would take to be a cultural category, was primary or 'real'" (8). In other words: gender made sex. Focusing on human anatomy, however, he concentrates on an 'epiphenomenon' in sexing, losing sight of vital heat as the primary factor. If we radically historicize the empirical data that matters or does not matter in medieval and early modern sex and gender constitution, it is obvious that the internal logic of the one-sex model poses a lingering threat to the stability of the presumably fixed categories of gender in the Early Modern Period. That is, even if bodily features like genitals, which are unambiguous sex markers to us, did not matter, the no less 'real' economy of vital heat did – emerging as a matrix of sexual differentiation and gender constitution.

Glossing on Jerome, Susan A. Crane points out that the woman who wishes to renounce earthly pleasure and serve God will be called man. "Jerome neatly formulates both the dichotomous difference of the sexes and the fluidity of sexuality along the axis of virtue" (97). This "axis of virtue" is not unconnected to the sexing axis of caloric heat. It actually doubles it. Virtue and virility are causally and reciprocally related, as are vice and femininity. A 'cold body' is imagined to be of female sex and gender. A change in one of the terms of the equation will effect a shift on the axes: an increase in vital heat will produce a more masculine body and a more virtuous subject; heightened virtue will necessarily push the body closer to the male *telos*. Thus "soul and body were [not] 'gendered' in any essential or even consistent sense; rather, their hierarchical organisation in a specific context determines the attribution of gender" (Biernoff 33).

Caroline Walker Bynum's work cautions against the undifferentiated assumption that the Middle Ages equated the female with abjection.[184] In the realm of spirituality, male visionaries would often describe and picture themselves as female. In the chivalric sphere, however, effemination through mundane passion threatened public *existimatio* and bodily integrity, haunting the imagination of courtly writers. Spanish sentimental fiction indicates that the one-sex model generated gender anxiety, even

---

[184] According to Bynum ("The Female Body and Religious Practice in the Later Middle Ages"), the body-soul dichotomy was more pronounced in Patristic and Early Modern thinkers than in their medieval counterparts.

before anatomical advances in the 16th and 17th centuries began to undermine it.[185]

2.4.2. Juan de Flores and gender anxiety

Juan de Flores, a contemporary of Diego de San Pedro and, as rector of the university of Salamanca and chronicler of the Catholic Kings, a man with close ties to the court,[186] authored some of the most remarkable Early Modern Spanish texts. In *Triunfo de Amor*, an allegorical courtly amusement related to sentimental fiction, and his so-called *Crónica incompleta*, he reflects upon the bewilderment caused by social upheaval and Isabel's ascent to power, uncovering, as Gerli points out, "the performative nature of courtly society and the central place of gender in it" ("Gender Trouble" 173).[187] In his best-known works, *Grimalte y Gradissa* and *Grisel y Mirabella*, he makes even more disturbing inquiries into the volatile nature of gender and sex.

Grimalte y Gradissa, composed most likely between 1480 and 1485 and probably first printed in 1495 in Lérida by Heinrich Botel,[188] is a 'sequel' to Giovanni Boccaccio's open-ended sentimental fiction *Elegia di Madonna Fiammetta*. In the prologue,

---

[185] See Laqueur (114-92). In her recent book *Isabel Rules: Constructing Queenship, Wielding Power*, Weissberger analyzes the gender implications in Castilian texts from the second half of the 15th century, related to the rule of Queen Isabel.

[186] Regarding the identity of Juan de Flores see Carmen Parrilla García ("Introducción," ed. *Grimalte* 3-24; "Un cronista olvidado") and Joseph J. Gwara ("The Identity of Juan de Flores"). I discuss scholarship, textual tradition and the intertextual relation between *Fiammetta* and *Grimalte y Gradissa* in *Images in Mind* (171-94). See also Whinnom's checklist (*The Spanish Sentimental Romance* 56-62). Weissberger ("Authors, Characters and Readers in *Grimalte y Gradissa*"), Brownlee (The Severed Word, "The Counterfeit Muse"), Haywood, and Grieve (*Desire and Death in Spanish Sentimental Romance*) address, more or less explicitly, issues of gender and subjectivity. Recently, Fernando Gómez Redondo has read Boccaccio's *Fiammetta* as a pioneering introspective account, that is, an *exemplum ex negativo*, of a 'personality change' due to harmful literary imaginations, and Flores's *Grimalte y Gradissa* as a literarization of a 'successful' reading.

[187] See also Weissberger (*Isabel Rules*, "Isabel's 'Nuevas leyes,'" and "'¡A tierra, puto!'").

[188] See Barbara Matulka (458) and Pamela Waley ("Introduction" 11-12). Regarding Flores's possible source see Folger (*Images in Mind* 171-74) and Mita Valvassori.

Flores, who, "por la siguiente obra mudo su nombre en Grimalte" (3) ["for the present work changed his name into Grimalte"],[189] tells his readers that his beloved Gradissa, upon reading Boccaccio's work, demands that her hapless suitor reconcile the abandoned, lovesick Fiometa (as she is called in the Castilian text) and her fickle lover Pamphilo. Grimalte fails, Fiometa dies of amatory consumption, and Pamphilo, grief-stricken, flees into the wilderness. Gradissa positively resolves not to take the risk of accepting Grimalte's advances, but Grimalte does not give up. It takes him twenty-seven years and the help of hunting dogs to locate Pamphilo in a deserted place in Asia.[190] Withdrawn from the subjectifying gazes of a civilized community and immerged in a visual field emanating from 'wild objects,' Pamphilo is not his former self.

> De tan desfigurado facion stava que si no lo hoviera visto denante, ningun humano iuyzio lo podria a ninguna difformidad comparar. Porque todos los senyales de persona racional tenia perdidos por muchas razones. [...] Y esta cosa lo havia mudado en salvaje pareçer, porque no solamente los cabellos y barvas tenia mucho mas que su statura crecidas, mas assi mismo era muy vieio por la continuacion de andar desnudo, y los cabellos de la cabeça y barva le davan cauteloso vestir. Y su andar era tal que soplian las rodillas a los pies, los quales pareçian en ell scusados miembros. Pues ell, por su andar y pareçer diverso, en todos sus senyales a hun fiero animal pareçia. (67)
> [His appearance was so disfigured that, if I had not seen him before me, no human understanding could have compared him to any deformity because he had lost all signs of a rational person, for many reasons. (...) And this thing had given him the appearance of a wild man, since not only his hair and beard had grown longer than his height but he was also aged because of the constant walking around naked, and the hair

---

[189] According to Lillian von der Walde Moheno, Grimalte is the "personaje eje" ("La experimentación literaria del siglo xv" 81) who establishes narrative coherence yet is "independent" (79) from the historical author. This view does not account for the crucial importance of self-fashioning and projection of *other* selves in *Grimalte y Gradissa* and sentimental romance in general.

[190] According to Walthaus, Flores uses the spatial setting of the novel ("semantización del espacio" 16) to supplant allegory as a means of exteriorizing emotions.

of the head and the beard provided him with scanty vestiment. And he walked in way that his knees substituted for the feet, which looked like needless members. So he resembled, because of his strange walk and appearance, a wild animal, in every aspect.]

The once handsome nobleman Pamphilo has become a Wild Man.[191]

Oleh Mazur classifies Pamphilo as the "wordly 'anchorite'" (15) type of the Wild Man, but there can be no doubt that the former courtly lover is the victim of a mental derangement, another subcategory of Mazur's rather arbitrary taxonomy. He suffers from a melancholic state which robbed him of this humanity. It is, in all likelihood, not a result of passionate love, but a consequence of the excessive pain or remorse he felt at Fiometa's death.[192] At any rate, Flores is playing a cruel trick on his character, because Pamphilo, who rejected Fiometa's love, possibly feigned passionate love, or simply satisfied his lust, is suffering from the same symptoms as the patient of lovesickness.

This becomes clear when Grimalte is finally able to break Pamphilo's vow not to talk by imitating his bestial behavior: "las manos puestas por el suelo en la manera que aquell andava, siguiendo sus pizadas, tomandolo por maestro de mi nuevo officio" (69) ["the hands on the ground like the other one, following his steps and accepting him as the master in my new vocation"]. Uprightness is the sign of "human 'godlike nature and essence'" (Summers 86). It is, as David Summers points out, necessary for the mental operations which distinguish man from animal.[193] Imitating Pamphilo's animal *habitus*, Grimalte forsakes part of his rationality and humanity. He becomes a double of Pamphilo, losing part of his *dignitas*, and restoring part of Pamphilo's humanity (as a speaking subject) by losing part of his. Like San Pedro in *Cárcel de amor*, Flores thus stages a doubling of courtly *persona* (Leriano/Grimalte) and animal-like Wild Man (Deseo/Pamphilo); not

---

[191] As John Block Friedman points out (180), the famous 14th-century jurisprudents Baldo and Bartolo agreed that a loss of human appearance equals a loss of human soul.

[192] See Folger (*Images in Mind* 177-94). Mazur also discusses the "Love madness type" (18-19).

[193] Summers (86) refers to Aristotle's *De partibus animalium* (686a32).

with an empowering effect, however, but accompanied by emasculation and animalization. And, like in *Cárcel*, the doubling of the courtly lover is predicated on a female *phantasma*.

At night the 'twins' witness the "spantables visiones" ["distressing visions"] which have been haunting Pamphilo. They watch Fiometa being tortured by devils, "gentes abominables" ["hideous people"] (71).

> La pusieron encima de un carro que levavan dos cavallos y los apareios que yo vi alli tormentar a la mas que tormentada Fiometa, por ser increibles de creher las callo. Y despues que ela alli puesta, desnuda de sus vestidos, mostravan a Pamphilo quanto la havia mudado su desconocimiento de aquello que ser solia. [...] De tal manera que quanto su graciosidat en el mundo me era alegre, tanto que mas me dava pena el agora remirarla. Y no se que diga della para que en mi vida bastasse a cuentar lo que de su figura me parecio. (71-72)
> [They put her on a coach, which was pulled by two horses, and the artifices I saw which they used to torture the more than tormented Fiometa – I do not want to talk about them, because they were incredible to believe. And after she was there displayed, stripped of her clothes, they showed Pamphilo how much his disregard had changed her. (...) Hence, as much as her grace was a pleasure to me in the world, so much did it hurt me to see her now. And I do not want to say more about her because my life would not be enough to tell everything I saw of her figure.]

The irony is that Pamphilo, who renounced the admiration of her image in his mind when she was still famous for her awful beauty,[194] is now confronted with this horrible vision. Grimalte's encounter with the Wild Man in the otherworldly Asian wilderness is a veritable *contrafactum* or un-making of the opening icon of *Cárcel*: Whereas in *Cárcel* the third term of the constitution of the male subject is the *imagen* of the enticing Laureola, in *Grimalte y Gradissa*, the "spantables visiones" (71)[195] centered in the *imago* of

---

[194] It is worth noting that Flores has a nude female body displayed, keeping in line with his *contrafactum* of erotic phantasies. While the artist of the *Cárcel* woodcuts used nudity to emphasize the sexual attraction of Laureola, in Flores's text nudity marks abjection, both of Fiometa and her 'admirers'.

[195] San Pedro's El Auctor refers to the initial encounter with the unfortunate prisoner of love as an "estraña visión" (5) ["strange vision" (4)].

Fiometa's mutilated, appalling body un-make the courtier. "The desirable woman of the romances has," as Dorothy Yamamoto observes,

> a white, soft body, its smooth, caressable surface a metaphor for its uncontested appropriation by the hero. When that surface is broken, the result is not wildness, or the irruption of animal features, but a loss of specularity – the woman no longer reflects back those qualities which both sign her femaleness and substantiate male identity. (199-200)

While the female image in *Cárcel* works as a Lacanian "reassuring sign" (Butler 58) of male identity and humanity, this mutilated female body is instrumental in the abjection of the courtier and knight (and his double).

Grimalte is apparently capable of extracting himself from this phantasmatic hell, yet when he appears in a courtly environment before his Gradissa, it becomes clear that the *persona* side of the double has not escaped unscathed. Gradissa will remorselessly reject the final passionate plea of the elderly man,[196] ultimately thwarting Grimalte's attempts to reestablish his masculinity by proving his attractiveness and soliciting affectionate female gazes. Whereas San Pedro tries to resignify Leriano's bodily decay, loss of virility and speech, and the radical restriction of the potentiality for action as an act of heroism, Flores lays bare the disastrous long-term effects of courtly self-fashioning through passionate love, both the solipsistic interior contemplation of a mental image and the public courtly service.

In *Grimalte y Gradissa* the fantasy of the bodily disintegration of the courtly lover is figured by the lover's loss of humanity and the mutilation of the beloved object; in his earlier sentimental fiction, *Grisel y Mirabella*,[197] the fantasy or "'image of the body in bits and pieces' (*imago du corps morcelé*)" (Lacan,

---

[196] Gómez Redondo has emphasized that Gradissa's rejection is due to her careful reading of Boccaccio's novel as a negative example, suggesting that she represents a female reader capable of *identifying* with the heroine. Like most critics of *Grimalte y Gradissa*, Gómez Redondo does not concede much importance to the portion of Flores's work which narrates the events after Fiometa's death.

[197] According to Walde Moheno (*Amor e ilegalidad* 15), Flores composed *Grisel y Mirabella* around 1475.

"Some Reflections on the Ego" 13) as a result of passion is bleakly literalized.[198]

Grisel y Mirabella, published in 1495 (Lérida: Henrique Botel), and subsequently translated in various languages, is set in Scotland. The beauty and graces of the King's only daughter cause mayhem among the "flor de caballería de casa del Rey" (55) ["the flower of the King's knighthood"], many of them dying of lovesickness ("preso de su amor"; 54) ["captured by her love"], some of them slain by their rivals; for instance, an unnamed knight by his friend Grisel. Although the King decides to imprison his daughter in a tower and remove her from the gazes of his knights, the passion of one of them, Grisel, is not only requited but also consummated. This brings the couple into conflict with the *Ley de Escocia* [Law of Scotland], which severely punishes extra-marital relationships:[199] The lover who is responsible for the affair is put to death: "el quien mas causa o principio fuese al otro de haber amado, mereciese muerte [...]" (62) ["the one who is reason and instigator of having loved deserves death"].

When the love between Grisel and Mirabella is revealed to the King, both lovers claim to be guilty. Their struggle for responsibility is commonly labeled a *debate de generosidad* [debate of generosity],[200] but it should not be forgotten that it is also about agency:[201] Should Grisel be found 'innocent,' his prowess as a courtly lover would be challenged. Even under torture both lovers are steadfast. The king decides to hold a public debate with the aim of determining the greater guilt of men or women in

---

[198] Regarding scholarship on *Grisel y Mirabella*, see the bibliographical references in Walde Moheno's *Amor e ilegalidad*, Mercedes Roffé's *La cuestión del género en 'Grisel y Mirabella'*, and the essays edited by Joseph J. Gwara in *Juan de Flores*. While critics like Grieve (*Desire and Death in Spanish Sentimental Romance* 55-73), Jorge Checa, Lillian von der Walde Moheno ("El episodio final de *Grisel y Mirabella*"), Marina Brownlee (*The Severed Word* 162-75), and Roffé (*La cuestión del género en 'Grisel y Mirabella'*) have emphasized that Flores's work is symptomatic of a general crisis in legal, social and cultural ('courtly love') authority, Weissberger (*Isabel Rules*) engages in the discussion of the crisis of gender relations in Flores's works.

[199] See Pablo Alcázar López and José A. González Núñez (35-36).

[200] Regarding *Grisel y Mirabella*'s debt to the tradition of 'literary debates,' see Roffé ("*Grisel y Mirabella*: a la luz del debate medieval").

[201] Grieve thinks that Mirabella is found guilty because of her enticing appearance (*Desire and Death in Spanish Sentimental Romance* 70), but there are clear indications that she has the more active part in the relationship, initiating sexual intercourse.

general. Each sex has a champion: Brazaida (Briseida/Cressida), an emblematic figure of womanhood,[202] smart and experienced in matters of love, and Pedro Torrellas (Pere Toroella), the Catalan poet who, due to his infamous "Maldezir de las mugeres" (also: "Coplas de las calidades de las donas") ["Vituperation of women"; "Verses about the qualities of women"] was the Spanish epitome of misogyny.[203] For no apparent reason, the judges condemn Mirabella to be burnt at the stake. Throwing himself into the flames, Grisel averts her execution, yet he fails to save her life:

> [F]uese en camisa a una ventana que miraba sobre un corral donde el Rey tenía unos leones, y entre ellos se dejó caer. Los cuales no usaron con de aquella obediencia que a la sangre real debían [...] mas antes miraron a su hambre que a la realeza de Mirabella, a quien ninguna mesura cataron: y muy presto fue dellos despedazada, y de las delicadas carnes cada uno contentó el apetito. (86)
> [Wearing only a shirt, she went to the window which overlooked a courtyard where the King had some lions and threw herself among them. Those (the lions) did not show the respect they owed to royal blood (...) and cared more for their hunger than for Mirabella's royalty, to whom they showed no temperance: And very soon she was lacerated, and each of them satisfied his hunger with her delicate flesh.]

A number of critics have drawn connections between the King's 'incestuous' desire for his daughter and the devouring lions.[204] Although this connection is plausible, it is essential not to reductively interpret the lion as a mere metaphor for royalty, ferocity, and wantonness.[205]

---

[202] Regarding the literary origins of this character see Alcázar López and González Núñez (41), Walde Moheno (*Amor e ilegalidad* 125), and Weissberger ("Authority Figures in *Siervo libre de amor* and *Grisel y Mirabella*" 259). Flores was probably inspired by the Briseyda character in Rodríguez del Padrón's *Bursario*; see Folger (*Images in Mind* 84-95).

[203] Regarding this poet, see Peter Cocozzella.

[204] See, for instance, Grieve (*Desire and Death in Spanish Sentimental Romance* 59-64), Brownlee (*The Severed Word* 191-210), and Weissberger ("Role-Reversal and Festivity in the Romances of Juan de Flores" 328).

[205] Regarding the symbolic and metaphoric meanings of the lion, see Walde Moheno (*Amor e ilegalidad* 209-10). According to Brownlee, Mirabella "is destroyed by her father's identity" (*The Severed Word* 206).

THE PREMODERN SELF 99

According to Giorgio Agamben, the premodern "anthropological machine" ("anthropologische Maschine"; *Das Offene* 47), which defines humanity, operates by inclusion of an exterior non-human into the human realm. This can be the Wild Man, or an animal assigned human characteristics,[206] like the lion associated with the King of Scotland. While in *Cárcel de amor* the subjectifying constellation man-woman-animal (corresponding to Leriano-Laureola-Deseo) eventually leads to the death of the male protagonist but temporarily generates a properly gendered male protagonist, Flores unleashes the destructive potential inherent in male desire in his modeling of the triangle (Grisel-Mirabella-Lion). Although Lillian von der Walde Moheno sees in Grisel's suicide a "triumph" of the individual over the codified and unwritten laws of society and an assertion of the individual,[207] there can be no doubt that passionate love is a somber, destructive force in Flores's romance, and that Grisel, the male subject, is annihilated, consumed by flames (and passion).

The further plot development leaves no doubt that his last desperate action to (re)gain agency was futile. The desirable and desired female body, robbed of its royal aura which should, according to the bestiary tradition, earn the respect of the king of animals, is dismembered and devoured. The lion in *Grisel y Mirabella* is not 'tamed' like the *salvaje* in *Cárcel*.[208] Bestial violence destroys the female body, and the sexual overtones and allusion to rape in this scene – the "delicadas carnes" which satisfy bestial 'appetites' – suggest that the lion represents a double of the courtly lover, and an equivalent of the Wild Man.

The gory end of the love affair is not the end of the novel, however, only the prehistory of a crescendo of passionate violence. Torrellas has fallen in love with Brazaida. Driven by desire, he approaches her with a letter, written with "loca confianza" (86) ["foolish confidence"]. Brazaida informs the Queen, who wants to avenge the death of her daughter. A rendezvous is set up

---

[206] See Agamben (*Das Offene* 47).
[207] See Walde Moheno (*Amor e ilegalidad* 206).
[208] In his study of the motive of the "heredero anhelado, condenado y perdonado," Deyermond ventures that Flores's refusal to "forgive" Mirabella might have been related (subconsciously) to the fact that the heiress to the throne had lost her virginity (114).

which turns into a horrible surprise for Torrellas.[209] The Queen and her female entourage have set up a trap.

> Atáronle de pies y de manos, que ninguna defensa de valerse tuvo. Y fue luego despojado de sus vestidos y atapáronle la boca porque quejar no se pudiese: y, desnudo, fue a un pilar bien atado; y allí cada una traía nueva invención para le dar tormentos; y tales hobo que, con tenazas ardiendo y otras con uñas y dientes, rabiosamente le despedazaron. [...] después que fueron alzadas las mensas, fueron a dar amarga cena a Torellas [...]. Y después que no dejaron ninguna carne en los huesos, fueron quemados; de su ceniza, guardando cada cual una bujeta por reliquias de su enemigo [...]. (93)
> [They tied his feet and hands, so that he was defenseless. And then he was stripped and gagged so that he could not complain. And, naked, he was tied well to a pillar, and then each of them came up with a new invention to torture him. And there was such that some mauled him with red-hot pincers and others with fingernails and teeth. (...) After the tables were set they made for Torrellas a bitter dinner. (...) And after they had left no flesh on the bones, those were incinerated; each of them kept a little box with the ashes as a relic of their enemy (...).]

This denouement is a 'condensed' and, at the same time, 'explicated' mirror image of the disastrous outcome of the passionate love between Grisel and Mirabella. Torrellas's body is lacerated like Mirabella's, and the remnants are cremated like Grisel's.[210] While Mirabella faced an animal with human characteristics (the lion), Torrellas falls victim to animalized women.

With the killing of Torrellas, Flores apparently pays his dues to poetic justice, whence the commonly accepted view of Flores as a 'feminist' writer.[211] The misogynist Catalan poet is the epitome

---

[209] Once again, Flores employs the strategy of literalizing courtly metaphors: In his misogynist *Coplas de las calidades de las donas* Torellas had likened women to animals (649 and 654); now he falls victim to the women who turn into animals – ironically pushed over the verge by misogynist discourse. See also Nicasio Salvador Miguel's study of the "tradición animalística" in Torrellas's work.

[210] Deyermond speaks of a "combination" of the deaths of Grisel and Mirabella ("El heredero anhelado, condenado y perdonado" 117).

[211] See, for instance, Gwara's recent "'La muger en la sardina, de rostros en la ceniza'".

of a poisoner of the choric 'phantasmatic' field (composed of *species* and *intentiones* of images and sounds), and his death seems to indicate a cleansing of this field and a stabilization of order. However, as a courtly poet, Torrellas is also a proponent and protagonist of the traditional economy of *existimatio*, and his death indicates a crisis of an entire episteme. The death of the sole heiress to throne, Mirabella, means not only a political catastrophe, as Deyermond remarks, and, in Brownlee's pointed diction, a breakdown of Scottish society,[212] but also the very collapse of the patriarchal order.[213] The full implications of this collapse become apparent in the gruesome final scene of violence, torture, mutilation, murder and, apparently, anthropophagy. Here the man-woman-animal subjectifying fold finds its most unsettling inflection: "la escena transparenta," according to Walde Moheno (*Amor e ilegalidad* 243), "la angustia inconsciente del hombre a ser dominado – e incluso devorado, castrado, absorbido – por ese otro sexo al que se tiende, pero no se alcanza a comprender" ["the scene reveals man's unconscious yearning to be dominated – even devoured, castrated, absorbed – by the other sex, which is desired but cannot be comprehended"]. Torrellas is gradually stripped of his supposed male superiority in a process that amounts to nothing less than the systematic annihilation of the male subject. Fetters and gag deny him agency and the ability to speak. His nude body, divested of its courtly attire, an element of his performative self,[214] is exposed to scornful female gazes. The scene suggests sexual debasement and rape: the courtly lover's haunting fantasy of being a mere victim of sexual violence, suggested by *Cárcel de amor*'s image of Leriano being taken prisoner by the Wild Man, a potential rapist, comes true. The ultimate consequence is castration and the 'loss' of the phallus. The once-powerful speaking subject, the orator, author and poet, is reduced to anguished screams, to raw, bleeding flesh, to bones, to ashes. Like the lions who consume

---

[212] See Deyermond ("El heredero anhelado, condenado y perdonado" 114) and Brownlee (*The Severed Word* 206).

[213] Regarding the prominence of legal terminology in *Grisel y Mirabella* and the intersection of legal and literary discourses, see Helen Cathleen Tarp; see also Walde Moheno (*Amor e ilegalidad*).

[214] See Fradenburg (185).

Mirabella,[215] the courtly ladies shred Torrellas's body into pieces, shattering the Law of the Father.

The connection between Freudian melancholy, in which the 'I' introjects, or devours, a desired object, and anthropophagy has been traced by Agamben.[216] The finale of *Grisel y Mirabella*, then, is a cruel literalization of Torrellas's desire to be a 'love object' and a usurpation (destruction *and* appropriation) of male subjectivity by the ladies of the court. While Grieve sees, in the *mise en scène* of the courtly topos of 'wanting to die for love,' not a triumph of femininity but a radical breakdown of the social order,[217] Weissberger interprets this breakdown as "a carnivalesque reversal in which unruly women seize control and wreak havoc on the misogynistic society that has victimized one of them" ("Role-Reversal and Festivity in the Romances of Juan de Flores" 204). At the end of *Grisel y Mirabella*, Flores presents us with the vision of a 'courtly' society from which the courtly lover has been excised and in which "unruly women" have appropriated the Phallus. This appropriation is figured by the fetishistic "relics" of Torrellas's body. Torrellas's quest, for a position of 'having' the phallus through the desire of the other, is thwarted by desire and passion, which convert him into an object of passion – the parallels with the scene in the lion court suggest, once again, rape – leading to a loss of masculinity, an effemination, and ultimately annihilation.

In both *Grimalte y Gradissa* and *Grisel y Mirabella* the *phantasma* of the desired and enticing female body returns as a specter:[218] in Pamphilo's "strange vision" as a mutilated, tortured body that degrades the male subject to the state of an animal, and the animalized women of the court who have been associated by Deyermond with the "fantasmas femeninos" of the Wild Hunt

---

[215] Again, Flores literalizes "courtly" *topoi*: in his *Maldezir*, he likens women to animals (648-49, l. 19-27); see Nicasio Salvador Miguel.

[216] See Agamben (*Stanze* 27).

[217] See Grieve (*Desire and Death in Spanish Sentimental Romance* 57).

[218] Manuel da Costa Fontes argues that the final palinode of Martínez de Toledo's misogynist *Arcipreste de Talavera* can be read as a "nightmare." *Triunfo de amor* is another text in which Flores has a vision of the *mundo al revés* ["world upside-down"] in terms of social order and gender: "the inversion of traditional gender roles [...] expands into a fully imagined topsy-turvy world" (Weissberger, "Isabel's 'Nuevas leyes': Monarchic Law and Justice in *Triunfo de amor*" 103); see also Gerli ("Gender Trouble").

("El hombre salvaje en la ficción sentimental" 30).[219] This vision of a loss of humanity and of devouring bestial femininity as a result of failed courtly subjectification was certainly one manifestation of the nightmare that haunted premodern patriarchal regimes.[220] I think that a similar nightmare is the rationale behind San Pedro's *Cárcel de amor*. Yet while Flores mercilessly lays bare the fault-lines of the mode of subjectification based, on one hand, on the repression and incorporation of the female body, which is fantasized as desirable and desiring, and, on the other, on a doubling into courtly *persona* and animal, San Pedro reacted in a diametrically opposed manner. The author of *Cárcel* fathoms in his text the antinomies and dangers of courtly self-constitution, striving, however, to shape his hero Leriano into a perfect, that is, masculine courtly lover.[221]

Before I turn back to *Cárcel* I will examine Juan Huarte de San Juan's *Examen de ingenios*, a text which is driven by the same preocupations, although it belongs to an entirely different discourse and was written nearly a century after *Cárcel*. I have been arguing that San Pedro's failure is ultimately related to the medical reality of the one-sex-model and the inherent danger of effemination through amatory 'consumption'. Saying that danger was inherent is not the same as saying that it was inevitable. Medical 'solutions' were sought – without abandoning the one-sex-model or the caloric identities this model instituted, yet probing the possibilities it provided for anatomizing sex, and consequently, naturalizing gender.[222]

---

[219] See also Walde Moheno (*Amor e ilegalidad* 237-39), who associates this scene with witchcraft.

[220] Weissberger sees in the ending of Flores's romances a "carnivalization of the sentimental genre, a process which may reflect and reinforce a subversive resistance to the male authority that modern scholars have assumed is upheld in these texts" ("Role-Reversal and Festivity in the Romances of Juan de Flores" 200).

[221] The majority of critics see in Leriano the perfect knight and courtly lover. Grieve, on the other hand, thinks that San Pedro "deliberately" (*Death and Desire* 30) exposed the antinomies of courtly love and their incompatibility with everyday life. Although I agree with her appraisal of Leriano and courtly love in general, I think that San Pedro failed in his attempt to *save* the courtly lover (Folger, *Images in Mind* 215-27).

[222] The change in the early modern economy of gender is, of course, a complex with a plethora of aspects; as Dangler points out in relation to Spain (83-109), educational politics, for example, were crucial in changing women's gender status.

2.4.3. *Juan Huarte de San Juan's* Examen de ingenios para las ciencias: *a naturalist approach to the problem of gender*

My starting point was a 'medical problem,' as a metonymy of an epistemological issue, and its impact on subjectification and the hegemonic economy of gender and sex. The literary texts I have discussed so far, Juan de Flores's sentimental fictions, are essentially diagnostic and heuristic with respect to the troubles inherent in the model of caloric identities. If we look for remedies for the crisis I have described, it makes sense to first examine contemporary medical discourse and the solutions it offered. Some readers will object to my choice of text, Huarte's *Examen*, written a century after *Cárcel de amor*. This choice is justified by the fact that no essential changes in medicine and 'psychology' occurred in this century; the *Examen* is, in my opinion, a text firmly couched in the terms of traditional natural philosophy, and, at the same time, it explores the resources this medical discourse uses to counteract the inherent gender trouble – to the point of questioning its own premises. On one hand, the *Examen*'s difficulties in grappling with the issue of sex and gender, a century after they were laid bare by authors of the Isabeline epoch, indicates that the patriarchal order relied on other discourses and practices for self-preservation, not least on literature, as I will show shortly in my analysis of *Cárcel*. On the other, the partial success of the *Examen* highlights the supplementary nature of literature in a complex process of cultural change in the Early Modern Period.

According to Laqueur, the one-sex model did not lose its sway until the end of the 17th century,[223] when changes in medical premises also affected the gender issues related to the older model. The change was mainly effected by medical innovation and anatomical discoveries like blood circulation, which would eventually discredit age-old Galenic humorology. It was, however, also possible to approach the problem of gender instability medically, without postulating two anatomically distinct sexes;

---

[223] Bienvenido Morros Mestres's recent *Otra lectura del Quijote* provides ample evidence of the preponderance of faculty psychology and the all-but universally accepted reality of lovesickness in Golden Age Spain.

that is, within the confines of faculty psychology and natural philosophy.

Juan Huarte de San Juan's *Examen de ingenios para las ciencias* (*The Examination of Men's Wits*)[224] is known to scholars of Spanish letters because it has been postulated as an important influence on Cervantes,[225] a kind of blueprint for the psychological make-up of the ingenious *hidalgo* Don Quijote de la Mancha.[226] Accordingly, modern historians of medicine celebrated Huarte's work as an important vestige of the beginnings of modern "differential psychology,"[227] suggesting that his work was influential because of its 'innovative' psychology. This view must be qualified. While it is a fact that the *Examen de ingenios* was a remarkable international success, as attested by the numerous editions and translations,[228] its reception in Spain was less favorable. The first edition, published in 1578, fell into the wheels of inquisitorial censorship. The author had to rewrite his text, which was finally published in 1594. The reason for the Inquisition's intervention was by no means that Huarte's psychology was 'revolutionary' but the author's persistent "mezcla" ["mixing"], as Domingo Ynduráin calls it, of "ontología y dialéctica, religión y ciencias naturales" ("En torno al *Examen de ingenios* de Huarte de San Juan" 48) ["ontology and dialectics, religion and natural sciences"]. Huarte was obviously well acquainted with the most progressive trends in European philosophy: his stern naturalism and deterministic concept of human nature were in conflict with the Catholic doctrine of free will. The reason that the *Examen de ingenios* did not fall victim to an interdiction is that Huarte's "differ-

---

[224] In 1594, Richard Carew translated the text, based on Camillo Camili's Italian version, into English. Here, all English translations from Huarte are mine.

[225] Arguably, outside the realm of Spanish letters and history of science, Huarte is best-known through Noam Chomsky's reference to him as a key thinker in the development of *Cartesian Linguistics* (78-80).

[226] Seminal in this respect was Rafael Salillas's 1905 study with the telling title *Un gran inspirador de Cervantes: El doctor Juan Huarte y su 'Examen de ingenios.'* See also M. de Iriarte and Otis H. Green's influential article. Green's generalizations have been qualified by more nuanced analyses by, among others, Harald Weinrich, Malcolm Read, Chester S. Halka, Luis S. Granjel, Juan Bautista Avalle-Arce (99-100) and Teresa Scott Soufas (1-35, particularly p. 18, note 57). See Serés's excellent introduction, which also provides a selected bibliography.

[227] See Iriarte and Halka (13).

[228] See Serés ("Introducción" 114, 119-22).

ential psychology" (Iriarte) was firmly couched in traditional Hippocratic medicine and Galenic humorology.[229] In spite of Huarte's polemic stance against some authorities of traditional natural philosophy, primarily the (pseudo)-Aristotelian *Problemata*,[230] his approach is not empiricist.[231] He wanted to methodically 'rationalize' the old system.

It was Huarte's principal objective to show "for what profession each one is apt," as Richard Carew put it in the subtitle of his 1594 English translation. Huarte was interested in the individual's intellectual abilities, determining in which function he or she was most useful to society.

> En una palabra, el *Examen* es la obra de un arbitrista desaforado que, en lugar de resolver un problema concreto, soluciona la totalidad de la organización social, la material y la espiritual..., porque en ningún momento pretende alterar el orden establecido (como sí hacen los utopistas), sino garantizar el cumplimiento de un orden definido ya por los teólogos..., y por la realidad. (Ynduráin, "En torno al *Examen de ingenios* de Huarte de San Juan" 17)
> [In a word, the Examen is the work of a grandiose *arbitrista* (sc. a self-declared state counselor) who, instead of resolving a concrete problem, works out a solution for the totality of social organization, both material and spiritual..., because he never pretends to alter the established order (like utopians do) but to guarantee the order defined by theologians..., and by reality.]

The paradoxically conservative utopian thrust of Huarte's work, his preoccupation with the "totality of social organization" necessarily implied a 'reform' of the volatile orders of sex and gender, which San Pedro, Flores, and other authors of the Isabeline court articulated in their works.

The key term of Huarte's *Examen* is *ingenio* (*ingenium*), a term for which he provides a definition:

---

[229] See Ynduráin ("En torno al *Examen de ingenios* de Huarte de San Juan" 8). See also Dangler's discussion of Huarte, in which she sees a "more intensified preoccupation about the social order" (102), within a largely conventional naturalist-scientific framework.

[230] See Ynduráin ("En torno al *Examen de ingenios* de Huarte de San Juan" 8).

[231] See Ynduráin ("En torno al *Examen de ingenios* de Huarte de San Juan" 37).

[E]n cuanto al nombre ingenio, el cual desciende de este verbo ingenero, que quiere decir engendrar dentro de sí una figura entera y verdadera que represente al vivo la naturaleza del sujeto cuya es la ciencia que se aprende. (193-94)
[Regarding the name *ingenio*, which is derived from the word *ingenero*, which means engender in oneself an entire and true figure which realistically represents the nature of the subject of the studied science.]

Ingenium is the result of the interplay of all mental faculties, which is, according to Huarte, strictly determined by an individual's economy of bodily humors. Huarte presumes three basic faculties which are assisted or hampered by the humors: *imaginatio*, *entendimiento* and *memoria*. He is an emphatic partisan of the *entendimiento*, vehemently arguing that its advancement is necessary for the common welfare. Terminological inconsistencies, typical of all but a few medical authors of the time, have misled modern students of Huarte's work. Although Huarte ascribes the mental activities he analyzes to the workings of the *ánima racional* (303), that is the rational soul, there can be no doubt that he actually describes the perceptive and cognitive activities of the animal soul, the *anima sensitiva*. "Con esta mesma virtud animal entendemos, imaginamos y nos acordamos" (321) ["With the same animal faculty we understand, imagine and remember"]. Accordingly, Serés's assertion that he eliminates the *vis aestimativa* from his model of the human soul is misleading.[232] Huarte discusses the *vis aestimativa* as an aspect of rational judgment, using the term *entendimiento*, equivalent of the *vis cogitativa*, as we have seen in connection with Gregor Reisch's description of the sensitive soul.

Like many of his learned peers in Europe, Huarte affirms the higher dignity of theology and his incompetence in questions of metaphysics.

El error de Galeno está en querer averiguar por principios de filosofía natural si el ánima racional, faltando del cuerpo, muere luego o no, siendo cuestión que pertenece a otra ciencia superior y de más ciertos principios. (382)
[Galen's error lies in wanting to ascertain the principles of natural philosophy, namely, if the rational soul, without body,

---

[232] See Serés ("Introduction" 63).

dies or not, which is an issue that belongs to a higher science with more secure principles.]

Huarte clearly does not explicitly deny the existence of an immortal, individual soul, but *de facto* he attributes all mental operations to somatic factors, ignoring faculties which are independent of the body, that is, Intellect and Will. This position has affinities with nominalistic and Averroist trends and the ideas supported in the circle of Protestant scholar Philipp Melanchthon.[233] His naturalist determinism got him in trouble in Spain and assured his positive reception in Protestant countries.

As a utopian *arbitrista*, Huarte was naturally concerned with the order of the sexes. We have already seen that the Spanish natural philosopher, in spite of a penchant for polemics and his philosophically progressive outlook, did by no means question the bases of Galenic medicine and naturalist psychology. The existence of one sex with two accidental manifestations is an indisputable fact for him. For Huarte too, vital heat is a fundamental factor not only in sexing but also in the shaping of the individual potentiality for action, because it is essential for the workings of imagination: "de la frialdad nace la mayor diferencia de ingenio que hay en el hombre" (328) ["from coldness comes the greatest difference in *ingenium* in man"]. Since judgment (*entendimiento*) requires dryness, the ideal complexion of a genius is, according to Huarte, an adust-melancholic temperament. Everything burnt has "vario temperamento" ["varied temperament"]:

> De aquí se infiere que los melancólicos por adustión juntan grande entendimiento con mucha imaginativa: pero todos son faltos de memoria por la mucha sequedad y dureza que hizo en el celebro la adustión. (458)
> [From this it can be inferred that melancholics, through combustion, unite great understanding and much imagination, but all of them lack memory because of the dryness and the hardness caused in the brain by combustion.]

The dryness of this humor guarantees a superior faculty of discernment, and its hot-cold nature the workings of imagination.

---

[233] See Park (478-81) and Keßler (518).

The lack of memory (and the ineptitude in learning Latin) typical of Spaniards,[234] according to Huarte, is the price for mental *agudeza* [acuity].

Huarte is convinced that women, due to their humoral disposition, naturally lack mental acuity.[235]

> Porque pensar que la mujer puede ser caliente y seca ni tener el ingenio y habilidad que sigue a estas dos calidades, es muy grande error; porque si la simiente de que se formó fuera caliente y seca a predominio, saliera varón y no hembra; y por ser fría y húmida, nació hembra y no varón. (614)
> [Because it is a great error to believe that woman can be warm and dry or have the ingenium and abilities implied by these qualities, because if the seed from which she was formed had been predominantly warm and dry, she would have turned out to be a man and not a woman, and because (the seed) was cold and humid she was born as a woman and not a man.]

Sex is determined by the temperaments of the male and female 'seeds.' The individual sexed as female is necessarily phlegmatic and should she cease being phlegmatic – a possibility Huarte categorically discards – she would cease to be woman.

In Huarte's work we can perceive a shift in the medical foundations of the fixity of gender difference and the correspondence of sex and gender. Vital heat is a volatile factor, easily altered, for instance, by pathological conditions like passionate love. Humidity, on the other hand, is a natural condition of those individuals born as female, thus being 'naturally' excluded from the ranks of social elites which Huarte envisions, and tied to the behavioral patterns he associates with the unalterable female humoral economy. With his dyadic model, Huarte manages to assuage the gen-

---

[234] "Y esto es verdad, forzosamente han de tener [sc. los españoles] ruin memoria y grande entendimiento; y los alemanes, grande memoria y poco entendimiento. Y, así, los unos no pueden saber latín, y los otros lo aprenden con facilidad" (Huarte de San Juan 415) ["And truly, (Spaniards) have necessarily miserable memory and great understanding, and Germans great memory and little understanding. And so, the latter are incapable of learning Latin, and the former learn it easily"].

[235] There is, to my knowledge, no satisfying systematic study of the gender implication of Huarte's *Examen*; Gabriel-André Pérouse's essay on Huarte and women is conspicuously apologetic of the author and utterly insensitive to gender issues.

der anxieties related to 'sex change': the individual, born female, turned into a male by excessive vital heat which turns her/his sexual organs inside out will not meet the conditions (*entendimiento*) Huarte postulates as necessary for the social elites. A sex change would not essentially affect gender.

Generally Huarte is interested in women only in connection with his eugenic agenda: he tries to determine which female bodies with which humoral dispositions are best suited to deliver 'geniuses,' naturally males.[236] Finally, in the context of this discussion, Huarte explains why the possibility can be excluded that at least the brains of the humid and cold female bodies could have a disposition favorable for the workings of the mental faculties. It is true, he concedes, that the *ingenium* is determined by the head's temperament

> pero es tanta fuerza y vigor el útero y sus testículos para alterar todo el cuerpo, que si estos son calientes y secos, o fríos y húmidos, o de otra cualquier temperatura, las demás partes dice Galeno que llevan el mismo tenor. Pero el miembro que más asido está de las alteraciones del útero, dicen todos los médicos que es el celebro [...]. (613)
> [but the uterus's and the testicles' strength and power are so great as to alter the whole body, and if those are warm and dry, or cold and humid, or whatever temperament, the other parts of the body have, Galen says, the same characteristics. But all physicians say that the member that is most affected by the changes of the uterus is the brain.]

The male and female 'testicles' are so powerful that their temperament (hot and dry in a man's case; humid and cold in a woman's case) determines the entire body's complexion, particularly the brain, and, consequently, the mental abilities. Although men and women have anatomically the same sexual organs, the specific humoral differences of these sexual organs determine "ingenio y habilidad" (614) ["ingenium and talent"] and their place in society, that is, their gender. In sum, Huarte de San Juan adheres to the one-sex model, but in his *Examen de ingenios* an

---

[236] Huarte dedicates a whole chapter to the question "[*w*]*hat diligence ought to be used, that children male, and not female may be borne*" (*Examination of Men's Wits* 286).

anatomization of gender differentiation is in the offing, interlinking sex and gender in ways that would be typical for the later epoch.

However, it is important to realize that Huarte fails to resolve one essential problem of the one-sex model: even though woman is barred from improving her status, man's status is still physiologically precarious. There is a whole range of complexions which can characterize male individuals, Huarte writes, "[p]ero frío y húmido, y frío y seco, no se puede admitir (estando el hombre sano y sin ninguna lesión)" (618) [but cold and humid, and cold and dry, cannot be admitted (if the man is healthy and uninjured)"]. With this disclaimer to Huarte's doctrine of man's natural superiority, we return to the topic of subjectification through passionate love: *amor hereos* is precisely one of these pathological conditions that eventually leads to cold and dry complexion, which makes him, in Huarte's view, 'unmanly.'

Huarte de San Juan's *Examen de ingenios* shows that, a century after San Pedro and Flores articulated the gender trouble inherent in the one-sex model, this trouble had not yet been resolved 'scientifically.' Although remarkable 'progress' in terms of medicine, psychology and natural philosophy was made in Early Modern Spain, other discourses and dispositives were at work in the fixing of sexual identities, stable gender roles and subjectivities. In *Cárcel de amor*, San Pedro staged the problem dramatically and the unknown illustrator visualized it emblematically. In one and the same text the author defines the problem and crosses it out – by means of *literature*.

CHAPTER 3

CÁRCEL DE AMOR: L'ÉCRITURE DE SOI

"L E clerc écrit au XVIᵉ siècle et le chevalier aime" (107) ["In the 14th century, the 'clerk' writes and the knight loves"], says Jacqueline Cerquiglini in her study of Guillaume de Machaut's *Voir Dit*, a work that foreshadows many of the characteristics of Spanish sentimental fiction. Cerquiglini sees the *Voir Dit* as "radically transgressive" ("de transgression maximale"; 121):

> [I]l propose, à travers son propre personnage d'amant, la figure d'un clerc-chevalier, c'est-à-dire d'un clerc (quelqu'un n'appartenant pas à la classe aristocratique) qui se rêve chevalier. (121)
> [Through his own *persona* as a lover, he proposes the figure of the clerk-knight, that is, a clerk (somebody who does not belong to the aristocratic class) who dreams himself a knight.]

In San Pedro's *Cárcel de amor*, more than a century later, the *letrado*, El Auctor, writes, and the knight, Leriano, loves. Nonetheless, his text is not looking back to the medieval past; his 'dream' of 'being a knight' is no less transgressive.

3.1. From performance to identification

San Pedro's *Cárcel de amor* and the initial illustration of the Rosenbach edition display the phenomenology of courtly male self-fashioning through passion and the performance of amatory service, laying bare the inherent gender problem: "*Cárcel de amor*," in the words of Ruth El Saffar, "presents an image of the masculine ego fragmented and caught in an idealization of the Mother imago" ("The 'I' of the Beholder" 184). This fragmentation and the entrapment by an overpowering (ultimately devouring) female *imago* is predicated on the face-to-face situation in courtly self-fashioning. The 'mental presence' of the *imago*, upon which the subject's gaze is fixed, effects a physiological effemination. Conversely, the gazes of the others compromise the suffering subject's gender status. The protagonist Leriano and his woes, then, are emblematic of an 'old' mode of courtly subjectivity. San Pedro's narrativization of passionate amorous relationships encapsulated in *cancionero* poetry leads,[1] probably unintentionally, to a radical and pessimistic questioning of this mode.

Like in other texts labeled as sentimental fiction, in *Cárcel de amor* we see, as Gumbrecht points out, a clash between the logic of the courtly game and the logic of "everyday verisimilitude" (*'Eine' Geschichte der spanischen Literatur* 164). Focusing on Leriano as the representative of the courtly-chivalric logic, Marina Brownlee shows how "Leriano's eating of the words serves as an emblem of a 'dead-end' speech situation. Words are presented as sterile objects rather than communication" (*The Severed Word* 171). E. Michael Gerli's Lacanian reading points to the protagonist's struggle and failure to assert himself as a (masculine) speaking subject.

---

[1] Elsewhere, I argue that the idealization of passionate love in lyric poetry must give way to critique and/or irony in longer narratives (Folger, *Images in Mind* 21); see also Rüdiger Schnell (128-29). Brownlee speaks of a "bankruptcy of discursive generic traditions" (*The Severed Word* 172). In relation to the reception of John Gower's *Confessio Amantis*, Cortijo Ocaña discusses the trend toward prosifications and narrativization in 15th-century Spain (*La evolución genérica* 71-74). For French literature, Huot has studied the 'material' aspects (editing, compiling etc.) of the displacement of the performer by 'the book.' We owe a theoretical reflection on the complex emergence of prosimetric 'pseudo-autobiographies' in Guillaume de Machaut's *Voir Dit* to Jacqueline Cerquiglini. The author argues that the "pièces lyriques sont source du sens, fondatrices du texte. La narration est 'montée' à partir d'elles" (32) ["the lyric pieces are the source of sense, foundations of the text. The narration is 'mounted' as a departure from them"]. I think that her concept of *montage* can be used to explain how sentimental fiction, analogous to the *Voir Dit*, uses amatory poetry to 'mount' a text consisting of lyric poetry, prose narration and authenticating letters. I am not referring here to the actual genesis and elaboration of individual texts. With an established tradition of sentimental fictions, Flores was able to commission Alonso de Córdoba to write lyric poetry to insert into his *Grimalte y Gradissa*.

> Leriano is in this way motivated by the unconscious desire to conquer the power of language – to grasp the symbolic phallic signifying authority of language – and to guarantee a space for himself in the world as a whole human subject. As he reaches out for Laureola, he desperately seeks mastery over language and a reassurance in its ability to communicate and satisfy his emotional hunger through dialogue and conversation. ("Leriano and Lacan" 121)

In another important recent article, Gerhard Penzkofer has tackled the issue of subjectivity in *Cárcel de amor*, shifting attention from Leriano to the narrator, El Auctor. According to Penzkofer, San Pedro's experimentation with narrative tradition (particularly the intradiegetic first-person narrator) and his probing of innovative representations of consciousness and modeling of self-experience amount to nothing less than the invention of a "Poetik der Introspektion" (245) ["poetics of introspection"]. Penzkofer claims that in *Cárcel* introspection supplants the allegorical representations of affects and passion, making it possible for the passionate subject to internalize his emotions as an integral part of the self.[2]

Although the thrust of his argument clearly points in the direction of my interpretation of the text, it is necessary to avoid the pitfall of blurring introspection and inwardness or interiority. The fact that, in the description of the Prison of Love, Leriano's mental faculties are building blocks of an 'interior' space, in which we find Leriano chained to his fiery chair, does not amount to proof that subjectivity is imagined as interiority. If Leriano, his chivalric courtly *persona* as a prisoner of his passion, is *surrounded* by supposedly inner qualities, this spatial arrangement suggests that the subject's affects are located outside and that agency is wrested from the 'I' by external forces.[3] This is the traditional medieval outlook in which the 'I' wishing "to define or analyze the nature of his experience, [...] must present it in transindividual and external terms, and not as 'his'" (Vitz 85). The Prison of Love illustrates how the 'I' is constituted in a fold by an

---

[2] See Penzkofer (254).
[3] Glossing on Arnaut, Kay points out that "subjective allegory erodes the distinction between inside and outside, self and other, and thus problematizes the notion of 'self'" (55).

exterior which is, as Deleuze argues,[4] the outside *of* the inside. The subject's self-exploration is a movement going inside but looking at the outside, it is, in Penzkofer's words, an introspection without "*introspectum*" (245). The probing of the self has no object; the hero is both object and subject of his passions.

In *Cárcel de amor*, the interior void of the subject is filled, Penzkofer continues, by means of a doubling of hero and author which prefigures a Lacanian identification with an idealized other and a narcissistic sublimation of the self,[5] that is, in Lacan's words,

> la transformation produite chez le sujet, quand il assume une image, – dont la prédestination à cet effet de phase est suffisament indiquée par l'usage, dans la théorie, du terme antique d'*imago*. ("Le stade du miroir" 94)[6]
> [the transformation that takes place in the subject when he assumes (...) an image – an image that is seemingly predestined to have an effect at this phase, as witnessed by the use in analytic theory of the term 'imago.' ("The Mirror Stage" 76)]

Penzkofer's emphasis on the role of narcissistic identification in *Cárcel* is an important observation. I will show, however, that a shift of focus to El Auctor makes it necessary to postulate that San Pedro explores two different forms of subjectivity in his text: the 'traditional' courtly subjectivity embodied by Leriano, and an 'innovative' self-fashioning performed by the writerly subject, El Auctor. In spite of its chivalric hero's disastrous end and the disturbing gender implications of its denouement, *Cárcel de amor* is ultimately a success story about the constitution of a masculine speaking 'I' or, to be precise, a writing 'I' which, as I will show, is 'properly' gendered.

If San Pedro, instigated by male courtiers ("cavalleros cortesanos"; 3 ["courtly knights"]), wanted to provide an example of the courtly lover,[7] what function did the character of El Auctor

---

[4] See Deleuze (*Foucault* 134).
[5] See Penzkofer (257-58).
[6] See also Lacan ("Some reflections on the Ego" 12).
[7] The widely accepted notion that Leriano is an exemplary lover is not unquestioned. Theresa Ann Sears, for example, judges Leriano's death as a "martyr of love" as "unconvincing" ("Prisoners of Love" 275), Anthony van Beysterfeld sees in *Cárcel* "una nueva teoría del amor" ["a new theory of love"] which

have in this plan? In an insightful recent article, Sol Miguel-Prendes has associated San Pedro's *Cárcel* with premodern "'prayer-book mentality'" ("Reimagining Diego de San Pedro's Readers" 12). She argues that the work is "a vision of meditation on the sufferings of the protagonist, the noble Leriano, madly in love with Princess Laureola" (12),[8] modeled on the *imitatio Christi*. "Cárcel's reading," Miguel-Prendes adds, "requires another act of contemplation [...]: the private, silent reading of a text that leads to a visual re-enactment of Christ's torments with the help of a *retablo*" (13).[9] Hence the obvious fact that San Pedro modeled the death of his hero Leriano on the passion of Christ – from the initial image of Leriano as a man of sorrows in the Prison, to his 'salvation' of and 'sacrifice' for Laureola, to the libation on his deathbed and his final words[10] – is not sufficiently explained as a calque on the popular 'sacro-profane' hyperbole in *cancionero* poetry; it fulfills the important function of triggering emotional identification trained in passion devotion.

This observation is important because it sheds new light on the fascination sentimental fiction exerted on 15th-century read-

---

debunks the precepts of courtly love and foreshadows Golden Age love concepts. Marina Brownlee holds that San Pedro, in an "exemplary meta-linguistic act" ("Imprisoned Discourse in the *Cárcel de amor*" 189), strikingly departs from the "cooperative principle" (190) of speech acts, failing to "effect an amorous liaison between the two protagonists" (200). In *Images in Mind*, I argue that it was most likely San Pedro's intention to save the traditional courtly lover, but that the author ultimately failed, due to the internal logic of *amor hereos* (200). Elsewhere, I show that the rationale of Nicolás Núñez's continuation was to patch or gloss over the subversive potential of San Pedro's *Cárcel* ("*Cárceles de amor*"); see also Brownlee ("Imprisoned Discourse in the *Cárcel de amor*" 200).

[8] See also Severin's study on *Religious Parody and the Spanish Sentimental Romance*.

[9] Emphasizing the importance of interior spirituality and *imitatio Christi* in 15th-century Spain, Dolz i Ferrer claims that the 'prototype' of sentimental fiction, *Siervo libre de amor*, was also destined for private, silent reading ("El vocabulario del alma en el *Siervo libre de amor*" 85-88). In his reading of the text, *Siervo* is essentially a religious meditation, which unduly ignores the courtly dimension of the text and its contemporary reception.

[10] The parallels to Jesus Christ's passion and the Eucharist have been pointed out early by Anna Krause (269-70) and by Bruce W. Wardropper, who sees in Leriano's 'perfect' love a reflection of Christ's perfect love ("El mundo sentimental de la *Cárcel de amor*" 176). See also Whinnom (*Diego de San Pedro* 101, 109). Despite acknowledging the Christian subtext ("Cardona, the Crucifixion and Leriano's Last Drink"), Whinnom rejects the idea that Leriano is a figure of Christ ("Introduction" 16). See Miri Rubin regarding "The Eucharist and the Construction of Medieval Identities".

ers: while medieval techniques of the self were intended to facilitate the gradual build-up of *habitus* and prevent mimetic entrapment by earthly images – and what Petrarch called the "varietas mortifera" ["mortifying variety"] –[11] passion devotion required a totalizing, ravishing gaze (*autopsia*) that transformed and individuated the self through an "emotional and cathartic identification of one's physical existence with the identity of the man of sorrows" (Sawday 32).[12] Naturalizing the mental habits of passion devotion in secular literature, the authors of sentimental fiction enabled their readers to identify with the protagonists and re-enact their suffering.[13]

The particularity of San Pedro's *Cárcel* is that it provides a sophisticated protocol of this identificatory process, literally accompanied by a *retablo*: the first image in the series of the Rosenbach illustrations. Michael Camille has studied the imbrication between 15th-century passion devotion and the visual arts. In his brilliant analysis of an "Angel Pietà" by Meister Francke, Camille explains that figures depicted as gazing at Christ's suffering define an "emotional locus of identification for the viewer within the image [...]" ("Mimetic Identification and Passion Devotion" 192). Indeed, San Pedro's El Auctor models and provides "a stage of identification" (192) too. In the initial scene compassion wins over El Auctor's fear and he follows the suffering Leriano and his alter ego Deseo: "no hazer el ruego de aquel que assí padecía figurávase inhumanidad [...]" (San Pedro 5) ["not to respond to the plea of one who suffered so appeared to be inhuman cruelty" (4-5)]. He is the only witness to Leriano's torments in the Prison of Love, that is, he becomes involved in the unfolding of the fold of Leriano's subjectivity, an image of the agonizing 'dispersed self.' El Auctor becomes Leriano's messenger, 'teacher' and confidant,[14] who shares his hope and despair. El Auctor's desperation upon receiving Laureola's final rejection causes, as Rogelio Miñana observes,[15] a "voluntad pseudo-suicida" ["pseudo-suicidal volition"]:

---

[11] See Greene (246).
[12] Sawday's description refers to 17th-century Protestant religious practices.
[13] I am excluding, of course, Juan de Flores's caustic reworkings of earlier "serious" works (*Siervo libre de amor*; *Sátira*).
[14] See Rohland de Langbehn (*Zur Interpretation der Romane des Diego de San Pedro* 146).
[15] See Rogelio Miñana (143).

> [P]ues vista su determinada voluntad, paraciéndome que de mi trabajo sacava pena para mí y no remedio para Leriano, despedíme della con más lágrimas que palabras, y después de besalle las manos salíme de palacio con un nudo en la garganta, que pensé ahogarme por encobrir la pasión que sacava; y salido de la cibdad, como me vi solo, tan fuertemente comencé a llorar que de dar bozes no me podía contener: por cierto yo tuviera por mejor quedar muerto en Macedonia que venir bivo a Castilla [...]. (San Pedro 63)
> [When I saw that her will was resolute, because it seemed to me that my efforts could bring only punishment for me and no help for Leriano, I took my leave of her with more tears than words, and, after kissing her hands, left the palace with such a lump in my throat that I feared I should strangle in the effort to conceal the grief with which I departed. And as soon as I was outside the city and found myself alone, I began to weep so violently that I could not help crying aloud. Assuredly I felt that it would have been better for me to die in Macedonia than return to Castile (...). (65)]

He does not succumb to his suicidal impulses, but "transfers" (Miñana 143) them to Leriano: "quando llegué a Leriano dile la carta, y como acabó de leerla díxele que ni se esforçase, ni se alegrase, ni recibiese consuelo, pues tanta razón avía para que deviese morir" (San Pedro 63) ["when I reached Leriano, I gave him the letter, and when he had finished reading it, I told him that he should not attempt to resist further, nor dream of being happy, nor listen to the words of comfort, for there were too many good reasons why he should die" (65)]. El Auctor, who had freed Leriano from the dungeon of his solipsistic love, now orchestrates his death, projecting his own death wish onto his double. Accordingly, Leriano stages his own death, dying, as a figure of Christ, for El Auctor's 'sins.'[16] The protagonist executes the suicide the 'I' cannot narrate, while the first person narrator models the identification with suicidal passion for his readers. In the final scene, the dying Leriano mutters his last words, his eyes fixed on El Auctor's ("puestos en mí los ojos"; 79) ["he fixed his

---

[16] El Auctor is 'guilty' of having repeatedly misjudged Laureola's intentions and feelings, falsely advising Leriano (Folger, *Images in Mind* 215-17).

eyes upon me" (82)]. The scene mirrors the initial encounter which El Auctor observes, "puestos los ojos en la estraña visión" (5) ["my eyes fixed on this strange vision" (4)]. Leriano's death deeply affects El Auctor: "con sospiros caminé; con lágrimas partí; con gemidos hablé" (79) ["With sighs I set out on my journey; with tears I departed; with moans I spoke" (82)].

Hence we see a progression from initial pity to sharing experiences and intimate feelings. This is why Bruce W. Wardropper suggests that "Leriano and El Autor embody two sides of San Pedro's character, the sentimental and the rational [...]" ("Allegory and the role of *El Autor*" 39). "[P]sicológicamente ambos personajes han vivido emociones, si no idénticas [...] sí al menos análogas" ["psychologically, both characters have lived through emotions which were at least analogous if not identical"], Belmar Marchante observes, which leads her to postulate a split into "un 'yo' externo (autor-actor) con un 'yo' interno (Leriano)" (320) ["an external 'I' (author-actor) with an internal 'I' (Leriano)"]. Battesti Pelegrin identifies El Auctor as the "double de héros" ("'Je' lyrique, 'je' narratif dans la *Cárcel de amor*" 13) ["hero's double"],[17] painstakingly listing the instances in which El Auctor speaks and acts *in the place of* Leriano. The most important is undoubtedly the initial encounter.

> '[E]l auctor' se substitue à Leriano, et enrichit, pour le lecteur, le portrait psychologique de ce dernier. C'est lui par exemple au début du récit qui nous dit la beauté de Laureola (coup de foudre fatal au héros), image féminine sculptée dans la pierre: "*la cual era de tan estrema hermosura que me turbava la vista.*" (14 [Battesti Pelegrin's emphasis])[18]
> [El Auctor replaces Leriano and enriches for the reader the psychological portrait of the latter. It is he, for instance, who, at the beginning of the narration, tells us about Laureola's beauty (the reason for the hero's fatal falling in love), an image sculpted in stone: "*which was of such extreme beauty that it dazzled my eyes.*"][19]

---

[17] See also Sylvia Roubaud.
[18] It must be added that both characters suffer from passions (love and pity) that hamper their rational judgment; see Folger (*Images in Mind* 216).
[19] The translation of the quote from *Cárcel* is Whinnom's (4).

The bond between the *doppelgänger* is, as Penzkofer observes, of a narcissistic nature:[20] the novel's plot is set in motion by El Auctor's compassion for Leriano ("no hazer el ruego de aquel que assí padecía parecíame inhumanidad" San Pedro 5 ["not to respond to the pleas of the one who suffered so appeared to be inhuman cruelty" (4-5)]); his love for Leriano transforms him into a go-between ("tanta afición te tengo, [...] y tanto me ha obligado amarte tu nobleza [...]" 12 ["I have such great affection for you, and your nobility so much obliges me to love you" (12)]), and when he describes Leriano's death El Auctor thinks that his feelings are obvious to his audience: "Lo que yo sentí y hize, ligero está de juzgar" (79) ["What I felt and what I did can easily be imagined" (82)]. San Pedro's El Auctor is – becomes – another double of Leriano, modeling narcissistic identification with Leriano and enabling the reader to empathize,[21] 're-enacting' the hero's love woes and – like in a passion devotion – his death throes.[22] We have seen that El Auctor's death wish is projected onto Leriano, who dies 'in the place' of El Auctor, who survives as a locus of readerly identification.

Two factors are instrumental in this identificatory process, one narrative, the other 'visual.' Elaborating on Gerli's insight that the metafictional aspects of sentimental romance, in particular the

---

[20] See Penzkofer (257-58). Robert Rogers shows that a narcissistic relation is characteristic of the double as "mirror image" (18-39). Rogers's study of the double in literature addresses the "decomposition" of the ego, from an orthodox Freudian perspective, as a reflection of the psychological state of the author, without taking into account the performative effect of writing and reading in subjectification.

[21] There are clearly parallels between the works of San Pedro and Flores. According to Waley ("*Cárcel de amor* and *Grisel y Mirabella*"), Flores honed his writer's skill as a reader of *Cárcel*. Weissberger speaks of Gradissa as an "exceedingly empathetic reader of sentimental fiction" ("Authors, Characters and Readers" 68), identifying her as a "fictionalization" of the reader (72). The fact that a male writer provides a female "emotional locus of identification" (Camille, "Mimetic Identification and Passion Devotion" 192) with a female heroine (Fiometa) has intriguing implications for premodern female subjectivity and related gender aspects, which exceed the scope of this study.

[22] According to Rey, San Pedro's intention to narrate the death of a perfect courtly lover is the rationale behind the narrative structure of *Cárcel* (98); see also Parrilla (61-64), who rejects all attempts to "identify" El Auctor and Leriano, arguing that the narrative economy of *Cárcel* requires two different characters (a protagonist and his chronicler). Of course, doubling, as Grieve observes, is not equivalent to duplication (*Death and Desire* 38; see also Rogers 1-17). Moreover, psychological identification is predicated on two subjects.

frame story structure, this ingenious redoubling interplay of a text within a text typical of many of the Spanish sentimental romances asks us to alter our perception of writing fiction and assent imaginatively to the idea that we are witnessing actual events ("Metafiction in Spanish Sentimental Romances" 57).

Miñana argues that through the 'intrusion' of the frame (through El Auctor), the "acercamiento de los planos de la ficción y la realidad" (137-38) ["converging of the spheres of fiction and reality"], the reader is 'pulled' from an 'authorized' frame (San Pedro's real world) into the fiction. In other words, Gerli and Miñana suggest that the narrative structure of *Cárcel de amor* makes it possible to imaginatively experience the story *as if* it were real and not as part of the reader's social reality. This particular structure is, according to Gumbrecht,[23] a defining generic feature of sentimental fiction; it marks the frontier between everyday roles and roles which become accessible only via identification based on 'literary reading.' While in medieval performances of literary texts the performative space was contiguous with 'reality,' the narrative structure establishes a fictional space – or theatrical space, as Gumbrecht and Egginton put it – leading the reader from his everyday world (Peñafiel) to the fictional World (the valley in the Sierra Morena, Macedonia), and back to 'reality' (Peñafiel). The ability to perceive fiction as being indexed as 'as if' is the structure of literature and hence the precondition of identification.[24]

The second decisive device for facilitating identification is 'visual,' that is, a channeling of the gaze through images. The opening scene of *Cárcel* is an instance of *enargeia*, an attempt to "place things before the eyes" by means of description. *Enargeia*, in the words of Paul Julian Smith, "aims to create a credible image which will take the audience into the presence of the object itself," a "linguistic gesture [which] will provoke emotions appropriate to this graphic persuasiveness" (45). Thus the wood-cut in the Rosenbach edition is a supplementary tool which functions like the *retablos* mentioned by Miguel-Prendes:[25] It evokes an im-

---

[23] See Gumbrecht (*'Eine' Geschichte der spanischen Literatur* 193).

[24] Glossing on Jenaro Talens, Miñana points out that the frame story structure inscribes literature as a social practice (136), and that this practice is, in *Cárcel*, private, silent reading (145).

[25] See Miguel-Prendes ("Reimagining Diego de San Pedro's Readers at Work" 13).

age (Leriano) to identify with, and with El Auctor it provides the "emotional locus of identification" (Camille, "Mimetic Identification and Passion Devotion" 192), the perspective point from which the viewer/reader gazes at Leriano.

Conversely, assuming this mediating position means being the object of the others' gazes (caption 6). In the illustration, Leriano, the Female Image, and Deseo (and Leriano's horse),[26] figments of the author's imagination, look back, gaze, at El Auctor, in lieu of the viewer or reader. The characters of *Cárcel de amor*, the text, establish a choric visual field which constitutes El Auctor's subjectivity; El Auctor, in turn, functions as a relay of identification with the protagonist.

In the Rosenbach wood-cut, the artist represents El Auctor and Leriano as mirror images. As I have argued earlier, Leriano's own subjectivity can be described as a fold which includes the courtly *persona*, its double, the wild man, and a phantasmatic representation of a female body. Although the abject other (the female, the animal) is 'involved' in El Auctor's (and the reader's) identification with the mirror image of a male gendered and sexed courtly *persona*, *Cárcel* stages an "Abspaltung des Fremden und die narzißtische Verdoppelung des Eigenen" (Penzkofer 258) ["de-merging of the alien and a narcissistic doubling of the self"]. The Rosenbach image illustrates that this *other* is deferred or barred: El Auctor is depicted at a distance from the Wild Man, Deseo, separated from him by Leriano. His immediate object of identification is not a female *other* but a male knight. The savage yet bridled passion incarnated in Deseo is 'repressed,' turning Leriano into a 'metaphor,' a signifier for a signified which is "retained as a latent signifier" (Coward/Ellis 106).[27]

---

[26] The gazing horse further complicates the illustration: It shows that 'things' also look back, and it is a further refraction of the knightly identity 'on' the fold. Elsewhere I interpret the mirroring between knightly subject (Leriano) and writerly subject (El Auctor) with reference to Agamben's "anthropological machine" (Folger, "Bestialische Leidenschaften").

[27] Pertinent in this context is also Agamben's "anthropological machine," which can produce the human (Agamben's study is completely oblivious of gender) either by the exclusion of something recognized as internally human (the 'humanoid' animal, the racially other), or by the inclusion of an exterior non-human (the Wild Man, the slave, the foreigner, "figures of the animal in human shape") (*Das Offene* 47). Both modes, ascribed by Agamben to the 'moderns' and the 'old' respectively, coexist and are imbricated in *Cárcel de amor*.

CÁRCEL DE AMOR: L'ÉCRITURE DE SOI

Caption 6: El Auctor as an identificatory stage and subject, constituted through 'imaginary gazes'; fold El Auctor/Leriano(/(Laureola)Deseo)

Indeed, Leriano's status as subject is 'reminiscent' of the Lacanian shorthand for the relation between signifier and subject:[28] Leriano stands in as a subject for El Auctor, who is the signifier of another subject, 'San Pedro.' In *Cárcel*, we witness an epistemological transformation analogous to the shift from performance and spectacle to representation, which William Egginton has detected in Golden Age theater. Egginton argues that the separation between actor and spectator transformed the stage and the represented characters into a

> screen as a mirror, as a space where a subject's reality is projected in a more or less distorted form, and in which space the subject recognizes him or her self. But in order for this recognition to take place, the spectator has to identify with a perspective, a point of view from which the image makes sense; this point is termed the gaze. [...] [W]ithin the epistemology of the stage the spectator becomes convinced that what he or she sees are merely appearances and that there exists beyond the screen of appearances an essence that is somehow more real. Spectorial subjects, therefore, are not transfixed by what they see on the stage, but rather by what they fail to see, but desire anyway. (*How the World Became a Stage* 403-04)

The parallels with *Cárcel* are apparent: Leriano is at the level of the screen, he is the object of El Auctor's projection and identification. El Auctor, the "spectorial subject," is affected, yet unlike the bound Leriano, he is not transfixed. Behind the appearance of the subjects lurks Desire. El Auctor provides the relay, the point of view which enables the reader to "assume the gaze" and internalize the Other's gaze, represented in the *Cárcel* wood-cut by the looks of Deseo, the Image and El Auctor (caption 5).

Egginton relates the "epistemology of the stage" to changes in theater practice – in the first instance, the establishment of steady theaters, the *corrales* – and discerns the rationale of this institution in the accommodation of subject and ideology. In *Cárcel* the shift is related to the media change from manuscript to print and new reading habits, and the rationale of the 'new subject' is to overcome the gender trouble inherent in traditional courtly

---

[28] See Egginton (*How the World Became a Stage* 397).

modes of subjectification. We must turn to the gender aspect in order to approach the issue of the role of literature in the epistemological transformation and explore the potential which writing practices provide for (authorial) self-fashioning.

The shift from the *imagen femenil* to the metaphor of the courtly knight foreshadows the shift from mother to father *imagines* which El Saffar detects in the Spanish Golden Age.[29] In epistemological terms the deferral of an alienating Other translates into a dissolution of the face-to-face situation. This dissolution in the amatory relationship characterizes, to a certain degree, Leriano's love for Laureola: the communication between the two is primarily effected through letters.[30] Although epistolary discourse implies a separation of the partners, the opening scene, in which Leriano is physically bound by the presence of the *imagen*, suggests that the letters he sends to his beloved are conceived as presence in potentiality.[31] *Cárcel* goes one decisive step further, enabling an identification with a male body and courtly *persona* which does not involve obsessive gazing at a female body and performance of masculinity before the eyes of a courtly public, but an "act of contemplation," a "silent reading of a text that leads to a visual re-enactment" (Miguel-Prendes, "Reimagining Diego de San Pedro's Readers at Work" 13).

The invention of the printing press was only one factor in the development of silent reading, but it was a decisive one. Gumbrecht argues that it meant that the "body had been screened out of the consciousness of communication" (Gumbrecht, "The Body vs. the Printing Press" 187). The fixity of the text, the proscription of "any modification by way of the lecture, copying, printing, or reception" (187), had the effect that the receiver suddenly perceived the "'intentional meaning' of an author, who disqualified as inadequate any modification by way of the lecture, copying, printing, or reception" (187). The bracketing of the physical presence, however, also implied a greater freedom for the reader regarding the choice of texts and a potential liberation from the

---

[29] See El Saffar ("The 'I' of the Beholder" 182). Grieve traces the origins of this shift in the second half of the 15th century ("Mothers and Daughters in Fifteenth-Century Spanish Sentimental Romance").

[30] Regarding the importance of epistolary discourse as a means of psychological exploration and 'sentimental education' see Canet Vallés (232).

[31] See Gumbrecht (*'Eine' Geschichte der spanischen Literatur* 180).

coercive aspects of a collective reception/performance. As a solitary reader of sentimental fiction, the recipient was shielded from the communal gaze, free to imaginatively identify with the abject lover, without running the risk of being feminized.

A silent solitary *reader* identifies, via El Auctor, with the lovesick (male) knight. This reader is, like El Auctor, a parasite with regard to courtly self-fashioning: he is 'nurtured' by the courtly subject without running the risk of effemination and abjection. This parasitic structure of communication is constitutive of modern forms of literature.[32] Unlike self-fashioning processes which emulated actual historical beings or publicly 'personified' socially prescribed *personae*, the imaginary worlds of literature made "playful identification," based on the subject's 'distance' and self-affirmation, possible.[33] Instead of corporally and visibly participating in the performance of a fictional text and being immerged into the choric visual field, the disembodied reader is transported into a fictional realm of his own where he finds the means to fashion his self. And it is a new form of subjectivity that *Cárcel de amor* foreshadows.

El Auctor's identification with Leriano effects a fold within the fold. In Leriano's subjectification, an exteriority becomes an interiority *of* the exteriority; the subsequent folding establishes an interiority of an interiority. As Gerhard Poppenberg holds, the interior of the Golden Age subject is the stage of a psychomachia whence this subject appears, from our perspective, as "profoundly schizoid and agonal" (152) ["zutiefst schizoid und agonal"]. Nevertheless, the interior is imagined as an interior.[34] The resulting subject is no longer 'horizontally' structured by the accumulation of folds. He is 'vertical' in relation to the choric visual (and aural) field, and hence not dispersed (as the aggregate of multiple folds in the constitution of *hexis*) but, as a *mise en abîme* of

---

[32] Michel Serres has studied the role of the parasite in communication. For Gumbrecht, the works of the Marqués de Santillana mark the beginning of modern forms of literature (*'Eine' Geschichte der spanischen Literatur* 158).

[33] See Wolfgang Matzat ("Frühneuzeitliche Subjektivität und das literarische Imaginäre" 357).

[34] Poppenberg studies Golden Age "spirituality." Although it is likely that there was more than one configuration of subjectivity in the Early Modern Period, the 'spiritual subject' he describes is certainly a descendant of the subject constituted by passion devotion and similar technologies of the self.

folds, manifold and punctual.³⁵ This subject transcends the choric field, forming a fold that is invisible for an outside and thus establishes a 'real' interiority. While the disperse subject is fixed by its immediate embedding into the visual field, the manifold subject is horizontally mobile.

New reading *habitus* were instrumental in the emergence of new forms of subjectivity and the stabilization of the order of sexes as well as gender roles. The development of solitary and silent reading was a slow process that spanned centuries.³⁶ Although there was more involved than the displacement of manuscripts as the primary medium of written communication ("in the state of potentiality"; Gumbrecht, *'Eine' Geschichte der spanischen Literatur* 180) by the printing press, the change in media had a profound impact. This impact can be traced in *Cárcel de amor*, addressing the question of the text's rationale.

I have described the self-fashioning modeled in *Cárcel* as parasitic, meaning that literature makes it possible to fashion the self through imaginatively modeling it on 'actual' courtly subjects. But who were the beneficiaries of this parasitic-literary self-fashioning? The *incipit* of the text explains that Diego de San Pedro composed *Cárcel de amor* at the request of "Diego Hernandes, alcaide de los donzeles, y de otros cavalleros cortesanos" (3) ["Don Diego Fernández, Master of the Light Cavalry, and other courtly knights" (3)].³⁷ Colbert I. Nepaulsingh has ventured reservations regarding the authenticity of the paratexts: he argues that the *incipit* which assures us that the title of the work is *Cárcel de amor*, and the epigraphs which identify the narrator as El Auctor are editorial additions which may not necessarily conform to the *voluntas auctoris*.³⁸ However, this does not devalue the readings of earlier editors. Moreover, San Pedro's 'authentic' introduction is addressed to a "muy virtuoso señor" (3) ["most noble lord" (3)],

---

³⁵ Taylor describes the modern subject in its extreme expression in Hume's work as the "punctual self" (159-76). Elsewhere I describe the pluralization of the subject in greater detail (Folger, "Geschlechterentwürfe und die (Ent-)pluralisierung des Subjekts").

³⁶ See Paul Saenger's fundamental *Space Between the Words*.

³⁷ In a note, Whinnom explains: "Diego de Fernández de Córdoba, seventh *Alcaide de los Donceles*, was related by marriage to Don Juan Téllez-Girón, in whose service San Pedro spent much of his life. The *Donceles* were the young palace noblemen who formed a privileged troop of light cavalry" (101, note 2).

³⁸ See Nepaulsingh (174-75).

and both *incipit* and salutation indicate that the addressee is a (young) male knight with relations to the court, a man of arms with a taste for courtly love. El Auctor, now turned San Pedro, evokes this pragmatic context in the final line when he kisses the hands of "vuestra merced" (79) ["your lordship" (82)].[39] If the text as a vehicle for identificatory self-fashioning is addressed to a courtier, then the 'new' courtly subject is a parasite of its own past. However, it is important to realize, as Ulrich Winter does, that this pragmatic framing of *Cárcel* has extradiegetic rather than paratextual status. In other words, "das präsentische, inszeniert als mündliche Erzählen" (Winter 330) ["the presentist, staged as oral narration"] is part of the fiction and does not tell us about the actual pragmatics.

Although Stephen Gilman argued in his classic *The Spain of Fernando de Rojas* that *Cárcel* was nothing less than "the first novel written for the printing press" (327-28), the intended and actual audience and media status of sentimental fiction is still uncertain. Carmen Parrilla García argues that the first generation of sentimental romances, which were or posed as handwritten letters written by a first-person narrator to a confidant, sought to encourage "el debate crítico, la especulación sobre casos amorosos" (24) ["critical debate and speculation about cases of love"].[40] The novels of Diego de San Pedro and Juan de Flores were written when the media parameters had changed. Flores's *Grimalte y Gradissa* textualizes and models silent reading and emotional identification with the characters, indicating, as Weissberger argues,[41] that it was written for the printing press. Since the publication of Weissberger's article, Saenger's studies have shown that silent reading had a long evolution before the advent of the printing press, and Dorothy S. Severin's more recent study on the audience of *Grimalte y Gradissa* qualifies and supplements Weissberger's thesis.[42] Severin argues that Flores, most likely a di-

---

[39] Regarding the problem with Whinnom's translation of this passage see note 20.

[40] In *Images in Mind* (84-95) I argue, based on an analysis of Rodríguez del Padrón's seminal *Bursario*, that the hermeneutics of love was at the heart of 15th-century sentimental fiction.

[41] See Weissberger ("Authors, Characters and Readers in *Grimalte y Gradissa*").

[42] See Severin ("Audience and Interpretation").

rector of the University of Salamanca and chronicler of the Catholic Kings, wrote his works "originally [...] within an entirely male milieu," and that they "were probably first performed in for [sic] an all-male and highly-educated audience at the University of Salamanca [...]" ("Audience and Interpretation" 69).[43] Later, poetry by Alonso de Córdoba was added to *Grimalte y Gradissa*, probably intended for musical performance. In this form the text could appeal to a courtly audience and, after it was disseminated by the printing press, to "bourgeois" readers ("Audience and Interpretation" 69).

Although scholarship lumps *Grimalte y Gradissa* and *Cárcel de amor* together under the generic label of sentimental fiction, and there is the possibility that *Cárcel* was one of the structural models of Flores's second sentimental fiction,[44] we can infer from Severin's study that the receptive parameters of *Cárcel* were rather different. It is likely that San Pedro was university-trained like Flores, but he envisioned (extradiegetically), as we have seen, a courtly audience, or an audience that had an interest in emulating courtly performativity. There are several reasons why the possibility of a performance can be discarded and why *Cárcel* was most likely a text tailored to the exigencies of the printing press.[45] Unlike earlier specimens of sentimental fiction, *Cárcel* does not contain lyric portions which would have made it attractive for a courtly performance and collective reception, and the author dispensed with the acoustic conceits and rhymed prose[46] typical of oral recitation. Unlike *Grimalte y Gradissa*, which could be performed by a cast of four performers (Grimalte and Gradissa, Fiometa and Pamphilo), a staging of *Cárcel* would

---

[43] Regarding the changes Flores made for the printing press see also Severin (*Del manuscrito a la imprenta en la época de Isabel la Católica* 11-22). Gumbrecht, too, thinks that sentimental fiction initially targeted a small, educated audience (*'Eine' Geschichte der spanischen Literatur* 178). Regarding the relation of sentimental romance to the university milieu and the academic 'genre' of *repetitiones* see Pedro M. Cátedra's *Amor y pedagogía en la Edad Media*.

[44] See Waley ("*Cárcel de amor* and *Grisel y Mirabella*").

[45] Severin dedicates a few pages of her *Del manuscrito a la imprenta en la época de Isabel la Católica* to San Pedro (5-9). She speculates that the author reacted to the editorial success of his *Arnalte y Lucenda* with the composition and preparation of *Cárcel* for the letter press (7). See also Severin's "Diego de San Pedro from Manuscript to Print".

[46] See Weissberger ("Authors, Characters and Readers" 63).

have required a virtually unmanageable cast of *dramatis personae*, mass scenes (the battle between the king's armies and the troops of the insurgent Leriano), fantastic sceneries (the allegorical Prison of Love) and details (fire rays emanating from the *imagen*).[47] Most importantly, *Cárcel* was conceived, as Miguel-Prendes has demonstrated,[48] for contemplative, silent reading. Since the text was perfectly suited for private reading it was, independent of the authorial intention, prone to mechanical reproduction and divulgation. This was certainly one of the reasons for its great editorial success in the 15th and 16th centuries.[49]

Cárcel, the printed text, addressed a "pubblico eterogeno" ["heterogeneous audience"], according to Vicenzo Minervini (12-13); noblemen and bourgeois circles who saw in it a "perfect codex" for "imitating" the traditional elites. Although it is unlikely that Leriano was a model for actual 'imitation,' it is important to realize that *Cárcel* modeled techniques of identification with 'noble subjects' and made them available to traditional elites (the nobility),[50] new elites (the rising bourgeoisie, *letrado* functionaries) and possibly also to readers belonging to the lower echelons of society.[51] We also must not forget, as Severin reminds us, that "men wrote these works [sc. of sentimental fiction] with one intention, but the message was probably received rather differently by the accidental audience of women" ("Audience and Interpretation" 70). As a matter of fact, Myra Dickman Orth's study of the

---

[47] It should be mentioned, however, that late medieval Castilian court spectacles known as *momos* could be rather complex, occasionally involving the whole court; see Miguel Ángel Pérez Priego (149-55).

[48] See Miguel-Prendes ("Reimagining Diego de San Pedro's Readers").

[49] Regarding the editions of *Cárcel* see Corfis. The fact that no manuscript has come down to us suggests that the text did not circulate in manuscript form before the printing. In this sense, the reception in France was, as it were, a courtly reappropriation; see below.

[50] Compare my analysis of Fernán Pérez de Guzmán's *Generaciones y semblanzas*, completed before 1460, and Hernando del Pulgar's 1480 *Libro de los claros varones de Castilla* [Toledo: Juan Vasques], as tools for the interpellation of 'noble subjects' (Folger, "Noble subjects").

[51] Although the literacy rate in Golden Age Spain was probably less than twenty percent (see Beverley 219), it cannot be inferred that powerless individuals could not acquire more or less basic writing and reading skills. Men like the hapless *conquistador* Alfonso Borregán (see Folger, "Alonso Borregán writes himself") are proof to the contrary, and the literary figure of the *pícaro*, if we choose not to discard him or her as a violation of the principle of verisimilitude, indicates that the literate 'subaltern' was at least part of the cultural imagination.

manuscript adaptations of the printed text in 16th-century France shows that all of the translations, commissioned with lavish illustrations, were dedicated to women of high birth. Orth's claim, that the reason for their interest was the praise of women which the moribund Leriano utters, is certainly not the whole truth.[52]

Cárcel, as Gerli phrases it, "probably satisfied the psychological and emotional needs of a new type of reading public not circumscribed by gender and hungry to participate imaginatively in the lives, feelings, and experiences of others" ("Toward a Poetics of Spanish Sentimental Romance" 481, note 4). Though this audience was not "circumscribed by gender" it is, nevertheless, imperative to take gender into account. While San Pedro may have envisioned *Cárcel* as a tool which enabled the male reader to identify with a male courtly subject – without running the risk of effemination – female readers may have identified with the female, yet masculinely-gendered, "victorious heroine"[53] Laureola, or even with the feminized image of the love-stricken Leriano, asserting both a female identity and the position of a male 'speaking' subject. The intervention of a male reader, Nicolás Núñez, who 'fixed' the 'gender trouble' in his *cumplimiento* of *Cárcel*, shows that some male readers found the possibility of cross-gendering disturbing.[54]

At any rate, subjectification through literature – particularly when disseminated by the printing press – had far-reaching consequences for the Early Modern gender order. According to Ruth El Saffar, the Renaissance was, from a psychological perspective, a prolonged "emancipatory" process "by which men escaped the bondage of servitude to woman, to nature, to the land, to home" ("The 'I' of the Beholder" 178). "The forces at work during the Renaissance," El Saffar holds,

> had the effect of deepening the split within the masculine subject, and, as an effect of that split, of making that masculine

---

[52] See Orth (211). Orth's article seems to indicate that the seven manuscripts under study do not contain Núñez's *cumplimiento*, which made the text amenable to a 'male reading' (Folger, "*Cárceles de amor*").

[53] See Weissberger ("Role-Reversal and Festivity in the Romances of Juan de Flores" 208).

[54] See Folger ("*Cárceles de amor*"). Some later editions titled Núñez's continuation "cumplimiento" [supplement/completion/repairing] (Corfis 21-39).

subject capable of relating to the feminized other only through a pattern of dominance and control. (179)[55]

Moreover, she specifies the historical factors of the Early Modern subject:

> That divided subject, perforce alienated from body, passion, and all else associated with maternal care, is above all the product of specialized schooling and the introduction of the arts of reading and writing into the lives of young men aspiring to power in the new nation states that were developing in Western Europe. (180)

Since El Saffar associates the emergence of the split subject with the rise of bureaucracy and reading and writing practices, it is worth dwelling a little longer on the figure of El Auctor.

3.2. El Auctor and his forebears in *Sátira de infelice e felice vida* and *Siervo libre de amor*

El Auctor is, as we have seen, an entrance point of sorts that facilitates the identification with a 'noble subject.' The artist who illustrated the Rosenbach edition represented him in figure, posture and through spatial arrangement as a specular image of Leriano. However, in contrast with Leriano's courtly attire he wears a cloak: the illustrator imagined him not as a member of the traditional elites, but as a *letrado*, a man belonging to the class of university-trained functionaries who played such a crucial role in the genesis of the Spanish nation state from the time of the Catholic Monarchs.[56]

---

[55] In an earlier essay ("The Evolution of Psyche under Empire"), El Saffar traces this process of the increasing "oedipalization" of the novelistic hero in Early Modern Spain, analyzing *La Celestina*, *Lazarillo* and *Don Quijote*. Since the transition from the phantasmatic desiring and suffering to the realm of the symbolization counteracts lethal symbiotic identifications (see Küchenhoff 188), sentimental fiction as a writing practice is part and parcel of this emancipatory process of man and the abjection of the feminine.

[56] See José Antonio Maravall and William D. Phillips. Regarding the "power of writing and the writing of power" in 15th-century Castile in general, see the overview by Elisa Ruiz García.

According to El Saffar, *letrados* were not only instrumental in the rise of "Empire," but also paradigmatic for a new form of subjectivity, because they embodied a new individualist "mentality," a sense of self based not on genealogy ("earlier notions of regional or tribal loyalty") but on "ideological linkage" ("The 'I' of the Beholder" 165-166).[57] Although little is known about the historical Diego de San Pedro, it is reasonable to conjecture that the author of *Cárcel de amor* belonged to this class of *letrados*. He did not belong to the higher echelons of nobility, was possibly of *converso* descent, and, as he indicated in his last known work, the *Desprecio de la Fortuna* (composed between 1498 and 1500), he served the Count of Ureña, from the powerful Téllez-Girón family, for 29 years.[58] From the prologues and dedications to his works (to the damsels of the Isabeline court in *Arnalte y Lucenda*, to the Alcaide de los Donzeles in *Cárcel*, to Isabel's female entourage again in his *Sermón*), and his role as one of the foremost *cancionero* poets, we know that he moved in a courtly environment: "[B]ien podríamos esbozar," Parrilla states, "el perfil de un escritor cortesano introducido en el círculo isabelino [...]" ("Introducción," ed. *Cárcel* 37-38) ["We can very well sketch the profile of a courtly writer, established in the Isabeline circle"]. The rhetorical brilliance of his texts makes it likely that he was socialized in the university milieu.[59] Most importantly, in *Cárcel*

---

[57] Cortijo Ocaña ("Introducción") has made a case for the role of the *ars dictaminis*, an instrumental aspect in the early stages of bureaucratization, and the emergence of sentimental and celestinesque discourses.

[58] See Parrilla ("Introducción," ed. *Cárcel* 37-38).

[59] Regarding San Pedro's biography see Parrilla's introduction to her edition of *Cárcel* (37-44), Whinnom's introduction to volume one of San Pedro's *Obras completas*, and the monograph on San Pedro by the same author. San Pedro's Jewish ancestry or *converso* status has been much debated (Whinnom, *Diego de San Pedro* 17-28); see also Rohland de Langbehn's discussion of "El problema de los conversos y la novela sentimental." In a now-classic article, Francisco Márquez Villanueva, for instance, bases his reading of *Cárcel* as "political novel" on San Pedro's "unquestionable" *converso* status (193); see also Weissberger's considerably more nuanced political reading ("The Politics of *Cárcel de Amor*"). For Nepaulsingh the author's presumed crypto-Judaism is the key to an understanding of the text (174-229). Although, in my opinion, Whinnom is correct in asserting that there is no explicit textual evidence to identify San Pedro as a *converso*, the role of subjectivity in his œuvre in general, El Auctor's remarkable personality and his self-fashioning in *Cárcel* point to the impact of Jewish culture on Castilian letters in general. The most striking medieval example of 'modern' structures of subjectivity is unquestionably Shem Tov de Carrión's *Proverbios morales*; see Gumbrecht's *'Eine' Geschichte der spanischen Literatur* (105-09) and Jacques Joset.

de amor, he presents the *image* of a *letrado*, representing, in Rohland de Langbehn's words, "die nicht-höfische Tendenz des Buches" (*Zur Interpretation der Romane des Diego de San Pedro* 185) ["the book's non-courtly tendency"].

The illustrator's representation of El Auctor as a 'clerk' is backed up by textual evidence. He is a man of letters, not of arms. His relationship to the noble Leriano is best described as a secretary. Without belonging to courtly society, he inserts himself smoothly into the Macedonian court,[60] becomes Leriano's confidant and manages his affairs. Taking into account that a certain "emptiness and uniformity" would have perfectly functioned as an "interchangeable and shifting site [...] of self-projection" (Camille, "Mimetic Identification and Passion Devotion" 198), it is remarkable that the narrator is a complex character. Following Rohland de Langbehn's appraisal,[61] James Mandrell contrasts El Auctor's personal development and sophistication with the "psychological simplicity" (100) of the other characters in the novel.[62] Similarly, Alfonso Rey points out that Arnalte, the protagonist of San Pedro's other sentimental romance, outshines Leriano's psychological complexity and viability. Rey argues that *Arnalte y Lucenda* – not unlike the anonymous *Lazarillo de Tormes* –[63] can be described as novelistic discourse, while *Cárcel de amor* is essentially indebted to a courtly perspective, drawing on medieval literary conventions that allow "dos perspectivas diferentes [...] concentradas en una misma figura que habla en primera persona" (98) ["two different perspectives concentrated in one and the same character who speaks in the first person"], that is, El Auctor's strictly limited perspective as witness and omniscient first-person narrator.[64] Battesti Pelegrin, on the other hand, discerns a progres-

---

[60] See Mandrell (106), Wardropper ("Allegory and the role of El Auctor"), and Whinnom (*Diego de San Pedro* 106-08).

[61] See Rohland de Langbehn (*Zur Interpretation der Romane des Diego de San Pedro* 144). Probably the most hyperbolic praise of El Auctor is Maureen Ihrie's, who sees a "great resemblance to Mercury, god of rhetoric" (10).

[62] Although focused on *Siervo libre de amor*, Weissberger's "'Habla el Auctor'" (212-14) has been and still is an important stimulus for the discussion on San Pedro's El Auctor.

[63] See Rey (98). Regarding the parallels between *Cárcel* and *Lazarillo*, see Folger ("'Besando las manos de Vuestra Merced'") and the epilogue of the present study.

[64] Miñana reviews the appraisals of San Pedro's 'problems' in establishing a participant narrator with a coherently limited perspective. In my opinion, too

sion from an initial "total assimilation" ("'Je' lyrique, 'je' narratif dans la *Cárcel de amor*" 16-17) between El Auctor and Leriano, eventually producing a distanced, objective narrator. Going in the same direction, Mandrell carefully studies the narrative dynamics and traces the development of the narrator. Elaborating on Peter N. Dunn's idea that San Pedro "discovered how to do an allegory of authorship" (198), he reads *Cárcel* as a *mise en scène* of sorts of the establishment of a gradually achieved "mastery of various systems of signs [...]. The misreadings constitute a record, the traces of a developing analytic ability and ultimately of discursive authority" (Mandrell 101).

Analyzing San Pedro's framing technique, Rogelio Miñana recently recovered an important facet to the role of El Auctor, namely his function for and his relation to Leriano. He argues that the "superimposition" of author and character has the effect of confounding frame and story, bolstering the narrator's authority and gradually turning El Auctor into the "emotional protagonist" of *Cárcel* (142).

Hence Gerli is certainly right in observing that

> *Cárcel de Amor* is, in the final analysis, more the story of El Auctor's entanglement and the chronicle of his affective reactions than the story of Leriano and Laureola. ("Toward a Poetics of Spanish Sentimental Fiction" 475)

The actual protagonist of *Cárcel* is not the suffering and passive hero Leriano, but El Auctor, who is "the only one," as Dunn points out, "among all these love-bound, honor-bound, obedient or fearful characters, who is free to create his own role. In that sense, of course, he is the real author's surrogate [...]" ("Narrator as Character in the *Cárcel de Amor*" 198). El Auctor performs an act of authorial self-fashioning. In other words, in the development of the El Auctor character, *Cárcel de amor* describes the creation of a masculine 'speaking 'I'" in the very process of writing.

It is instructive to contrast El Auctor, the *letrado*, and Juan Manuel, a 14th-century author whose *œuvre* stands out in Castil-

---

much importance has been attributed to the presumed violation of the principle of verisimilitude. The criteria of verisimilitude were being re-negotiated in San Pedro's time. Moreover, most instances of omniscient narration could be plausibly explained as information El Auctor gathered or guessed *post factum*.

ian medieval literature precisely because of his notion of authorship.[65] Juan Manuel, a nephew of Alfonso the Wise, belonged to the Castilian Royal family. Best known for his *El Conde Lucanor*, Juan Manuel is the author of numerous works, among them the so-called *Libro enfinido*. The author addresses this work to his son: "tracta de cosas que yo mismo prové en mí mismo et en mi fazienda, et bi que contençió a otros; de las que fiz et vi fazer et me fallé dellas bien, [...] son las cosas que yo prové et bi" (116-17) ["it is about things I experienced regarding myself and my house and what I saw happen to others, and about what I did and saw others do and which I approved. These are the things that I experienced and saw"]. He explains that the work is called the "Infinite Book" because he will continue it in the future. As Gumbrecht observes,[66] the text's structure resembles modern diaries: personal experiences written down on a regular basis. Yet the *Libro enfinido* is no ethopoetic writing in the modern sense. Juan Manuel's experiences are inseparably tied to his "fazienda," his household. The book does not recount personal experiences, but a series of commonplaces ratified by the I. The text is about public conduct, the administration of the household, political affairs, and the administration of friendship.[67]

One of the offices he writes about is the *portero*:

> Sabet que uno de los omnes que forçadamente mucho an de saber de [la] fazienda, [et] de los fechos de los sennores; et de sus cuerpos, et de sus mugeres, et de sus fijos; et de sus privanças, et de sus poridades, et de sus plazeres, et deleytes; o de qualquier cosa que los sennores fagan, o a los sennores acaescan [...] son los porteros. (136)
> [You should know that one of the men who must necessarily know much about the house, and the affairs of the masters, and about their bodies, and about their women, and his children, and his secrets, and his amusement and pleasures, and all the other things the masters do or which happen to them (...) are *porteros* (sic).]

---

[65] See Leonardo Funes's recent article on Juan Manuel's notion and construction of authorship: "Excentricidad y descentramiento en la figura autoral de don Juan Manuel".

[66] Gumbrecht (*'Eine' Geschichte der spanischen Literatur* 92).

[67] It should be noted that Juan Manuel's 'personal' references are references to other texts he has written.

So there is the notion of the private, which is a sphere of bodily pleasure, desires and secrets, but it must be shielded by a *portero* from the view of the others: "What people manifest and articulate is what counts about them, not what is hidden and unexpressed. Performance is a reliable measure of who one actually is" (Crane 176). The private is literally 'secret,' the part of life that must be separated from the self,[68] the part that must not be spoken of and written about. The self who is writing and being written in the *Libro enfenido* is not an interior self, but a public self defined by its performance and the resulting *existimatio*. Juan Manuel belongs to an aristocratic elite whose writing practices are part of a performance of nobility.[69] In other words, the authorial 'I' exists prior to the writing process.

El Auctor, on the other hand, is not defined by *hazienda* but, initially at least, by his service to a noble master and, more and more, by his very own writing. El Auctor makes his 'secret life' as a secretary public. It is the very essence of his sense of self. El Auctor is an overdetermined character: he's not only instrumental as a mediator in, and impresario of, the constitution of 'traditional' courtly subjectivity (through the image of Leriano which he provides), but the very *image* of a new subject that is constituted by a new dispositive of subjectification. Much of the semantic potential of the *auctor* is realized in the figure of El Auctor: he is, like the 16th-century *autores de comedia*, a "stage manager, director, and producer for a troupe of actors" (Egginton 395-96), that is, the "impresario, producer, *and* production" of a courtly spectacle (Starn 217).[70] He is an author in a sense that approaches our modern understanding (the creator and owner of a text), and, assuming the script that his own text provides, he becomes an actor who represents – functions as 'surrogate' – of a certain Diego de San Pedro.[71]

In order to appreciate San Pedro's achievement in creating an

---

[68] See Gumbrecht ('*Eine*' *Geschichte der spanischen Literatur* 96).
[69] Particularly in 15th-century Castille, members of the so-called *nobleza nueva* engaged in writing genealogical treatises, the most powerful tool in asserting aristocratic rank (Folger, *Generaciones y semblanzas*).
[70] It is worth noting that the *autor de comedia* was subjected to the licensing practices of a bureaucratic institution, namely, the Consejo de Castilla; see Egginton (*How the World Became a Stage* 406).
[71] See Dunn ("Narrator as Character in the *Cárcel de Amor*" 198).

intradiegetic first person narrator, who is not the protagonist of the love story yet doubles him, it is instructive to take a look at earlier specimens of sentimental fiction, namely Juan Rodríguez del Padrón's *Siervo libre de amor* and *Sátira de infelice e felice vida* written by Dom Pedro, Condestável de Portugal. Both texts are autobiographical letters focused on disastrous love affairs, pathologic cases of *amor hereos*, addressed to a confidant/superior.[72] On one hand, this is, *in nuce*, the structure and story of *Cárcel de amor*, whence these texts belong to a genealogy of *Cárcel*, demonstrating that San Pedro's *Cárcel* must be seen against the background of a broad literary discourse, and is significant for the 15th century as a whole. On the other, the limitations of these texts demonstrate San Pedro's boldness and ingenuity in overcoming them.

Dom Pedro authored his *Sátira de infelice e felice vida* around 1453, dedicating it to his sister, Queen Isabel of Portugal.[73] The first-person narrator presents himself as a prisoner of a figurative "carçel" of amatory service. In a monologue, he attributes his woes to Fortuna. Discretion appears, advising him to relinquish his desperate quest. Apparently convinced, the speaker falls silent and goes for a ride. He arrives at lush grove, where he meets a group of noble damsels, the "colegio de las virtudes" (53) ["council of virtues"]. Prudentia, "señora e prinçesa de aquellas" (50) ["their mistress and princess"], explains that her mission is to vindicate Pedro's blameless beloved from his revilements. She argues that Dom Pedro should welcome his fate because he fell in love with the perfect woman. He objects that she cannot be perfect, since she does not show pity for his sufferings. The accused Pietas tries to rebut his charges, but fails to convince

---

[72] See Folger (*Images in Mind* 82-146).

[73] *Sátira* has not attracted considerable critical interest; I review studies on the text in *Images in Mind* (132-34); see also Eukene Lacarra Lanz ("Los discursos científico y amoroso en la *Sátira*"), Louise M. Haywood ("'La escura selva'"), and Michael Agnew's recent article. In a seminal study Gerli pleaded for a "revaluation" of *Sátira*, emphasizing Dom Pedro's "fundamental subversion of the medieval narrative esthetic" ("Toward a Revaluation of the Condestable of Portugal's *Sátira de infelice e felice vida*" 115). Serés, on the other hand, traces *Sátira*'s debt to medieval modes of literature ("Ficción sentimental y humanismo"). Dom Pedro framed his *Sátira* with a sprawling gloss; a discussion of this important issue would go beyond the scope of this study; Brownlee (*The Severed Word* 106-27) and Lacarra ("Los discursos científico y amoroso en la *Sátira*") have analyzed the tension between main text and glosses.

him. He interprets the disappearance of the Virtues as proof of his victory in the debate. More desperate than ever, sword in hand, he curses the day he fell in love. The story ends with the narrator's contemplation "sy era mejor prestamente morir o asperar la dubdosa respuesta" (174) ["whether it was better to die quickly or wait for the uncertain answer"].

It is obviously Dom Pedro's intention to stress his status as an abject lover as far as possible, that is, being on the verge of suicide, which he naturally cannot recount as an autobiographical narrator. The lover's abjection is instrumental in making his redemption and self-affirmation all the more powerful. In the all-but suicidal ending this redemption is encapsulated in the hope for a "respuesta." Oddly, Dom Pedro does not expect this response from his unnamed beloved – who has rejected him, and whom the narrator has definitely forsaken – but from his sister, Isabel de Portugal, the addressee of his missive. There is an obvious doubling between the beloved of the narrator of *Sátira* and the Princess, whom the author addresses in terms clearly reminiscent of courtly, passionate love ("amor inmutable"; 8 ["unchanging love"]).

> Que no solo las leyes de naturaleza, mas aun las del amor que ante me avia la exçellençia vuestra en mi mas bara fortuna, aveys assy perfecta e complidamente guardado, que no solo por palabra e por escripto yo lo remerçio continuamente a la vuestra perfecçion, mas aun en las mis entrañas esta sellado e esculpido vuestro serviçio se anteponer a toda otra cosa mundana. (3)
> [You have not only perfectly obeyed the laws of nature but also the laws of love with which your excellence has provided me in my most fickle fortune. Therefore I not only requite it to your excellence in spoken and written words; even in my entrails/interior it is embossed and engraved that your service is more important than any other wordly matter.]

This doubling of *belle dame sans merci* and loving sister mirrors the disjunctive doubling of author and narrator. While the narrator is abject (rejected by his beloved), the author receives the affirmation of his status as a writer ("por escripto"). Accordingly, in the prologue, he states that Isabel has the necessary "discreçion" ["prudence"] and sufficient "ingenio" to protect his works against detractors and appreciate his achievement as a *poet*.

Sátira is, indeed, a writing of the self of a peculiar kind: "yo començe de escrivir, e, escriviendo, declarar mi apassionada vida" (4) ["I began to write and, writing, to lay bare my passion-ridden life"]. Instead of courtly performance as an abject lover, he 'feigns' his *vida* without being subjected to the gazes of the courtly public.[74] He writes about his unrequited love and the subsequent annihilation as a courtly subject, expressedly condemning his own "loca thema e desigual tristeza" (5) ["crazy imprudence and excessive sadness"] and praising the female sex: "el femineo linage propuse loar" (5) ["I proposed to praise the female sex"]. He forges a chronicle of his passion, which also documents the virtue of his lady. This dual 'biographical' aspect, he continues, explains the title's "de infelice e felice vida" (4-5) ["about (my) unhappy and happy life"]. Moreover, the rationale of the text is to make the 'unhappy life' of Dom Pedro as a passionate lover the foundation of the 'happy life' of Dom Pedro the author.[75] He solicits the reaffirming gaze of the person whom he constructs as an ersatz of his beloved. He is not 'really' suffering from love-sickness and its fatal consequences, but writing about it as if he 'really' were, he reroutes his passion in order to garner the com-passion of the female other, figured by his own sister, whose sisterly love is equally re-cathected. Thus the speaking masculine 'I' is concurrently established with the narration, and *Sátira*, the written artifact, is a record and protocol of this act of courtly self-fashioning.

Siervo libre de amor, written roughly a decade earlier (ca. 1439-1441) than *Sátira de infelice e felice vida*,[76] has, as the presumed prototype of sentimental fiction, attracted considerable critical interest.[77] The importance of subjectivity in Juan Ro-

---

[74] According to Brian Stock, the 'prototype' and great hero in the history of modern subjectivity, Petrarch, established himself as a writing subject by supplanting the "real" religious community by a "putative reading public of a lay author" (727).

[75] In his designation of *Sátira* as a vehicle for praise and vituperation, he concurs with Mena's and Santillana's notion of the term; see Gerli ("Toward a Revaluation of the Condestable of Portugal's *Sátira de infelice e felice vida*" 109) and Serés ("Ficción sentimental y humanismo" 35-37). Regarding the duality of *laus* and *vituperium* as the fundamental principle of medieval hermeneutics, or "ethical reading," see John Dagenais.

[76] Vera Castro Lingl has shown that *Sátira* is indebted to *Siervo* in terms of structure and content.

[77] Regarding scholarship on *Siervo* see Folger (*Images in Mind* 82-132) and,

dríguez del Padrón's work has been pointed out by Barbara Weissberger in her 1980 article titled "'Habla el Auctor': *L'Elegia di Madonna Fiammetta* as a Source for the *Siervo libre de amor.*" According to Weissberger, "Padrón seeks to express [...] subjectivity, or the point of view of inwardness" (205). Her study has the merit of not positing simply a nascent 'modern subjectivity,' but defining instead subjectivity "in the Stoic sense of being subjected (*subiectus*) to love, the agent for fortune" (205). It is not possible here to pursue all the lines of investigation Weissberger's study opened, nor to do justice to the complex figuration of subjectivity in the text.[78] I propose instead to trace the workings of the technology of the self Diego de San Pedro would exploit, perfect and surpass two generations later,[79] particularly addressing the question of whether subjectivity in *Siervo* can really be understood in terms of inwardness.

The incipit of the only extant manuscript of *Siervo libre de amor* identifies the author Juan Rodríguez del Padrón (also known as Juan Rodríguez de la Cámara), like Diego de San Pedro, as the "criado" (10, fol. 129ᵛ) of a powerful magnate, in this case, the Cardenal Juan de Cervantes.[80] The following "tractado" ["treatise"], as the *accessus* calls it,[81] is directed to Gonzalo de Medina, his "immediate ecclesiastical superior" (Gerli, "*Siervo li-*

---

for older scholarship, Whinnom's checklist (*The Spanish Sentimental Romance* 24-32). I will discuss studies published after 2003 here to the extent as they are relevant to my argument. A further indication for a renewed interest in Rodríguez del Padrón's work is Enric Dolz's recent online edition and the edition Antonio Cortijo Ocaña is preparing for Cátedra.

[78] In the prologue, for instance, the author describes his amatory relation with a series of polysemous terms of 'looking' and 'being looked at' which would deserve a detailed analysis in terms of gaze theory.

[79] Weissberger explicitly draws a line connecting *Siervo* and *Cárcel*: "In fact, the *Cárcel de Amor* is on one important level a fictionalization of the limits of traditional *auctoritas* to the new kind of *tractado* initiated by Rodríguez del Padrón" ("'Habla el Auctor'"213).

[80] All quotes are taken from Enric Dolz's online edition. I refer to the page numbers of the PDF-version, indicating the folio number in MS. 6052 of the Biblioteca Nacional in Madrid. Regarding the limited and uncertain biographical information about Rodríguez del Padrón, the Cardenal Cervantes, and Gonzalo de Medina, see Dolz i Ferrer ("Juan Rodríguez del Padrón"). For many years our poet was a *familiar* of the prelate and belonged to his court-like entourage. His actual function in the Cardenal's household cannot be determined.

[81] Regarding the term *tratado* and its relation to the *accessus* tradition see Dagenais ("Juan Rodríguez del Padrón's Translation of the Latin *Bursarii*"); see also Whinnom ("*Autor* and *tratado* in the Fifteenth Century").

bre de amor and the penitential tradition" 95). As a matter of fact, *Siervo* is a letter in which the author proposes to recount to his friend Gonzalo de Medina ("dos amigos eguales en bien amar"; 10, fol. 129ᵛ ["two friends equals in loving well"]) how he fared in an unhappy love affair ("en señal de amistad te escrivo de amor" ["I write to you about love as a token of friendship"]), advising him to perseverate in his own 'good love' ("por mí jusgues a ti amador"; 12, fol. 129ᵛ) ["because of me you may see yourself as a lover"] and providing him with the weapons to resist the power of passionate love ("armas te dizen contra el amor"; 12, fol. 129ᵛ ["they 'tell' (give) you weapons against love"]). Relating *Siervo* to the medieval *ars dictaminis* and the work of Boncompagno de Silva in particular, Antonio Cortijo Ocaña has emphasized the epistolary nature of the text and the central importance of the topic of true friendship. *Siervo* is essentially a letter to a friend which can be read, with Foucault, as

> un entraînement de soi-même par l'écriture, à travers les conseils et les avis qu'on donne à l'autre: elle constitue aussi une certaine manière de se manifester à soi-même et aux autres. [...] Écrire, c'est donc 'se montrer', se faire voir, faire apparaître son propre visage auprès de l'autre. ("L'écriture de soi" 425)
> [a 'self-conditioning' through writing and the advice and admonitions given to somebody else: it constitutes a certain way to manifest oneself to oneself and to others. (...) Writing, then, is a 'showing oneself', making oneself seen, make one's own face appear to the other.]

Like in *Cárcel de amor*, writing becomes a substitute for 'being seen' in a face-to-face situation, a practice of the self that creates an appearance designed by the author. The topic of the letter, a case of passionate, nearly fatal love, is perfectly suited as a vehicle for a fashioning of the self, because sickness (writing about bodily and mental afflictions) is one of the important topics in the epistolary *écriture de soi*. The self-surveillance of the suffering individual makes body and mind into an object of observation, which is transformed into discourse and 'shaped' in the process.[82]

---

[82] See Foucault ("L'écriture de soi" 427).

Like in *Cárcel*, self-constitution in *Siervo* is parasitic in relation to performative, aristocratic, courtly self-fashioning. After the introduction,[83] the first-person narrator, who, like San Pedro's El Auctor, is a *persona* of the author in the 'frame story' and a character in the framed narration,[84] tells his friend about the beginnings of his passion, in the form of a debate between his mental faculties. After the *philocaptio*, his first attempts to establish a relationship are promising. But he makes the mistake of confiding in a friend and employing him as a go-between. The friend betrays him, courting the lady himself. The rejection of the author-*persona* is the end of the love story and marks the beginning of the actual drama. The disappointed lover falls into a "solitaria e dolorosa contemplaçión" (18, fol. 132^r) ["solitary and painful contemplation"],[85] that is, a debate with his faculties on which course to follow. Desperation prevails and the author-*persona* seeks death. This thought evokes the memory of the story of the "digno de perpetua membrança Ardanlier" (32, fol. 134^r) ["Ardanlier, worthy of perpetual remembrance"]. The intercalated so-called *Estoria de dos amadores* [*Story of Two Lovers*] is a miniature chivalric romance.[86] Against the wishes of their parents, the noble Liessa and Prince Ardanlier fall in love and flee in order to satisfy their desire. In a journey through Europe, Ardanlier proves himself a chivalric champion. Among the many women who fall in love with him is Yrena, daughter of the French king. After many adventures, Ardanlier and Liessa arrive in the Galician city of

---

[83] Elsewhere I explain the reasons to believe that the introduction is actually an *accessus* added later to Rodríguez del Padrón's text; see Folger (*Images in Mind* 106-11). Cortijo Ocaña proposes looking at the beginning of the work as a "*glosa o postscriptum*" ("*De amicitia, amore et rationis discretione*" 36).

[84] See Miñana (134, note 4).

[85] Louise M. Haywood has associated this "contemplation" with the *dorveille*, a trance-like stasis which initiates an exploration of mental states through allegory ("'La escura selva'").

[86] Obviously, the nature and function of the *Estoria de dos amadores* is addressed in the majority of studies on *Siervo*. Gregory Peter Andrachuk, among others, focuses on the intercalated story ("The Function of the *Estoria de dos amadores*"). Some critics, however, consider the tale poorly integrated; see, for instance, María Rosa Lida de Malkiel ("Juan Rodríguez del Padrón" 323); César Hernández Alonso ("Introducción" 54; '*Siervo libre de amor*' *de Juan Rodríguez del Padrón* 16). In his recent study on the influence of Enea Silvio Piccolomini's *Historia de duobus amantibus* in Spain, Jaime Leaños claims not only that the title of the *Estoria* is derived from Piccolomini's work (155), but also that *Siervo* is an "imitation" of the Italian's work. This certainly does not do justice to the complex matrix of the text.

Padrón, where a secret palace is carved in a rock. There they live happily until King Creos, Ardanlier's vengeful father, finds the entrance to the subterranean palace and kills the pregnant Liessa. When Ardanlier returns, he discovers his dead lover and commits suicide. Yrena travels to Galicia and orders the construction of a lavish tomb for the two lovers. After Yrena's death, the palace becomes enchanted and can only be conquered by the most loyal of lovers. After many years, Macías, the archetypical martyr of love and poet,[87] penetrates the tomb and the spell is broken. The tomb/palace opens miraculously three times a year and becomes the center of a pilgrimage of love.

The *Estoria de dos amadores* and Ardanlier are inverted images of Siervo's situation and his personality. While Ardanlier's love is requited and consummated, Siervo is an abject lover. While Ardanlier asserts and, at the same, relinquishes his status as a subject through suicide, a radical act of self-determination, the author-*persona* decides, upon awaking, not to follow the path of desperation and end his life, but to fashion himself in the image of Ardanlier and Macías, the emblematic lover-poet, his presumed ancestor. In the words of Weissberger:

> The fictional Auctor who would surpass Macías in amorous sorrows is thus conflated with the real author who imitates the lyrics in which Macías expresses that sorrow and who creates Ardanlier, the secular saint and ultimate authority for the entire complex structure. ("*'Habla el Auctor'*" 235)

The *Estoria de dos amadores* is a vision of wish-fulfillment that enables Siervo,[88] by imaginatively emulating Ardanlier, to fantasize mutual passionate love. It is a parasitic assertion of a performative chivalric and courtly identity of a nobleman of highest rank, and, at the same time, a fantasy of sexual fulfillment. Even the *other*'s suicide – as an act of self-determination and ultimate proof of being a perfect, loyal lover – contributes to shaping his self in a favorable way.[89]

---

[87] See Carlos Martínez Barbeito.

[88] See Weissberger ("'Habla el auctor'" 231).

[89] In a recent article, Victoria Rivera-Cordero argues that the *Estoria* is instrumental in shaping the *autor-persona* as agent (in Paul Smith's sense) in a process of curative "escritura auto-consciente" (277); see also Enric Dolz i Ferrer ("El simbolismo de los colores" 130-32).

Rodríguez del Padrón's point of departure for the description of his *caso* is the game of courtly love, describing, in the first part, failed amatory self-fashioning through performance and service. Showing how he transformed himself with the help of the *Estoria de dos amadores* and the 'role model' and alter ego Ardanlier,[90] he modeled self-fashioning by means of writing practices and literature.[91] As a chronicle of failed love and salvation through supplanting performance by fiction, *Siervo libre de amor* provides his confidant, Gonzalo de Medina, with the promised weapons against love and its inherent danger of effemination and eventual self-annihilation.[92]

Thus the *Estoria de dos amadores* is a vehicle for 'living out' amatory self-fashioning, imaginatively, in private without being exposed to the potentially deprecating gazes of the public. There is, like in *Cárcel de amor*, something parasitic and subversive about this mode of subjectification: parasitic because it makes it possible for the *criado* ['vassal'] to profit from the joys and sufferings of the prince who dies *in his place*; subversive because as the writer of the text he asserts his authority over his noble cast.[93] Thus *Siervo libre de amor* does not simply reject amatory self-fashioning, but makes a plea for using literature and epistolary practice as an ersatz for performance.

In the remainder of the text, Rodríguez del Padrón elaborates on this self-transformation via literature. In search of *entendimiento*, the Siervo finally reaches the shore of the sea and awaits the arrival of a black ship with seven maidens and a "señora mastresa una dueña ançiana vestida de negro" (40, fol. 141ᵛ) ["lady preceptor/mistress, an old lady, wearing black]. This *maestra* is Synderesis, who, "por algunos reparos, refrescos, afferes, en ardit y deffensa de sus enemigos" (40, fol. 141ᵛ) ["for some remedies, refreshments, and affairs, in the attempt to outsmart and stave off her enemies"], approaches the freed Siervo

---

[90] See Weissberger ("'Habla el Auctor'" 230).

[91] Carla de Nigris sees in *Siervo* a "ricerca de sé" (14) ["exploration of the self"] in which the very writing process establishes the restoration of a self destablized by *amor hereos*.

[92] Regarding the relation between novelistic discourse and its therapeutic aspect, see Irene Albers.

[93] Weissberger makes this observation regarding Boccaccio's *Fiammetta* and the protagonist/writer ("'Habla el Auctor'" 223).

and requests a report on his adventures. Synderesis is a complex character who has provoked many interpretations; as Conscience, Prudence, Penitence, Gonzalo de Medina, even as the Arthurian fairy Morgaine.[94] In theology Synderesis is the mental *habitus* that enables man to discern good from evil.[95] The end of *Siervo libre de amor*,[96] then, is a restoration of the *habitus* previously hampered by *amor hereos*, and Siervo's autobiography is, in this sense, a tale of reintegration into society.

This view is bolstered if we take into account another facet of Synderesis: as *magistra* she is, among other things, Memory.[97] The Siervo's story is absorbed by the collective memory, which stands in for memories shared by individuals. Thus the recounting of the story, the letter writing, has the function of "faire apparaître son propre visage auprès de l'autre" (Foucault, "L'écriture de soi" 425) ["making oneself seen, making one's own face appear to the other"], initiating, like the erection of the lover's tomb in Padrón, a cult of *perpetua membrança*. Since memory is nothing but a contemplation of mental images, the fantasy that nurtures Siervo's self-fashioning is a re-integration into the scopic visual field.

A strong current in *Siervo* scholarship interprets the work as a chronicle of conversion, mirroring Rodríguez del Padrón's decision to join a religious order.[98] However, in the introduction to *Siervo*, that is, the letter *sensu stricto*, to Gonzalo de Medina, the

---

[94] Elsewhere I discuss the interpretations of the Synderesis character in detail; see Folger (*Images in Mind* 127).

[95] See Philippe Delhaye (112-14).

[96] The *accessus* states that "el siguiente tratado es departido en tres partes prinçipales" (10, fol. 129ᵛ) ["the following 'treatise' is divided into three principal parts"]. This pronouncement has inspired a series of critics, for instance Andrachuk ("On the Missing Third Part of *Siervo libre de amor*"), to cast doubt on the completeness of the text; I discuss critical opinions on this topic in *Images in Mind* (106-32). In my opinion, the importance of the *accessus* as an interpretive clue has been exaggerated (Folger, *Images in Mind* 107-111). The author provides a perfect closure for his text.

[97] See Folger (*Images in Mind* 131).

[98] Drawing on a comparison with Guillaume de Deguilevilles's *Le Rommant des trois pèlerinages*, probably a source used by the author, Gerli makes a strong case for a missing third part that would have contained the Siervo's religious conversion. I explain my reasons for rejecting his thesis in *Images in Mind* (95-106). Eukene Lacarra Lanz has recently continued the discussion of whether *Siervo* can be read as a "spiritual autobiography" ("*Siervo libre de amor*, ¿Autobiografía espiritual?").

author-persona presents himself as a lover who has lost the favor of his lady and the hope for sexual gratification, having achieved a higher state of love, voluntarily pursuing his amatory service:

> Esfuérçate en pensar lo que creo pensarás: yo aver sido bien affortunado, aunque agora me vees en contrallo; e por amar alcançar lo que mayores de mí deseavan, que perdí por amor la prinçipal causa de mi perdiçión. (12, fol. 130^r)
> [Strive to think what I think you are thinking: that I have been fortunate, although you see me now in the opposite state; and that, as a lover, I have achieved more than greater men than I aspired, because I lost for/through love the principal cause of my doom.][99]

Of course, the possibility cannot be excluded that the author is referring here to the 'good love' of God. Nevertheless, there are persistent indications in the discussion of the author-*persona*'s mental faculties that steadfastness in love, without hope of its return, is the noblest form of earthly love.[100] Moreover, the *Estoria de dos amadores* celebrates amatory fidelity beyond death, whence it can be inferred that the introduction's ambiguity serves to exalt the spiritual dignity of 'pure' courtly love.

The reintegration, then, which the author stages with his encounter with Synderesis and the folding back to the primal scene of writing (through Synderesis's request for his story), is a reintegration (and redemption) as a hero of love: he will be admired as a martyr of love who has freed himself from debasing lust, accepted amatory servitude without hope of reward. In sum, he has made his name as a *Siervo libre de amor*. Most importantly, Synderesis is a figure for the recipient of the story, Gonzalo de Medina.[101] The story the Siervo delivers to Synderesis is the story he tells Medina, and the last sentence of the text will be followed by the first. In other words, the end of the story establishes a cyclic closing in which the restitution of mental health, the culmination of the self-fashioning as a hero of unrequited love, and as the

---

[99] In his mind-boggling *canción* (song) "El mayor bien de quereros," Diego de San Pedro takes up the theme of the 'loss of losing oneself.' I think that in both cases wordly amorous pain is positively revalorized.
[100] See Folger (*Images in Mind* 106-46).
[101] See De Nigris (13).

subject of enunciation, culminate, coincide and begin with the writing process.

There is evidence that Rodríguez del Padrón's self-fashioning was successful. In the anonymous *Vida del trovador Juan Rodríguez del Padrón*,[102] a fictitious biography extrapolated principally from his *Siervo libre de amor*.[103] In this *Vida*, Rodríguez del Padrón, the humble *criado* of Cardenal Cervantes, the 'inferior' of the Judge of Mondoñedo,[104] is imagined as, transformed into, a member of the highest Catalan nobility, the epitome of the courtly lover-poet and martyr of love.

We find essential aspects of the techniques of the self that Rodríguez del Padrón used in *Siervo* perfected in *Cárcel*: the parasitic relation of writerly/readerly self-fashioning to courtly performativity, the dissolution of the face-to-face situation, the doubling of narrator and hero, the use of *retablos* as identificatory tools, and the superimposition of author-*persona* and character. This last aspect, the frame-story structure, is instrumental in both texts, but a closer look at San Pedro's narrative technique shows that the essential difference is that *Cárcel* is much more than just a step in the evolution of the genre of sentimental fiction. In *Siervo* the self-fashioning process of the Autor (re-)establishes, with the cyclic closure, a courtly subject. San Pedro's El Auctor, on the other hand, asserts a new form of subjectivity, with an altered relation to authority and to techniques of public governance (bureaucracy) and governance of the self (*assujettisement*).[105]

Unlike Juan de Flores, who signals to the readers of *Grimalte y Gradissa* the discontinuity between himself and the first-person narrator, San Pedro presents *Cárcel de amor* as an autobiographical report commissioned by a male authority figure ("virtuoso señor"; 3) ["virtuous lord"]. Since the reader first meets the narra-

---

[102] The authenticity of the *Vida* published by Pedro José Pidal in 1839 was disputed until the recent discovery of two extant manuscripts; see Whinnom ("The marquis de Pidal vindicated") and Michel Garcia.

[103] See Marcelino Menéndez Pelayo (19). Nicolás Antonio, in his *Bibliotheca Hispana Vetus*, and Fernando de Lucena, the 15th-century translator of *Triunfo de las donas*, regarded the legendary liaison of Rodríguez del Padrón and the queen as a historical fact; see Hernández Alonso ("Introducción" 14).

[104] See Rodríguez del Padrón (10, f. 129ᵛ).

[105] Jonathan Goldberg's *Writing Matter* discusses the forging of the subject through hand writing in conjunction with an implementation and ratification of a political regime in Early Modern England.

tor on his way back from a military campaign, he supposes that he accompanies a knightly subject. However, soon afterwards, El Auctor identifies with Leriano and assumes – in the parasitic mode I have described earlier – a courtly identity by subjecting himself to the service of the nobleman Leriano. This paradoxical empowerment through subjection is doubled by asserting his masculinity as a *letrado*, not by domination over women, but as being the "opposite of a beast, and [in the University milieu] dominance over other men came through rationality" (Karras 12).[106] In the rest of the novel El Auctor proves a loyal secretary to his noble master, and, at the same time, he is a kind of mastermind of Leriano's course of action. It is not Leriano who stages his own performance, but his double, El Auctor, who is the "impresario" (Starn 217) of the spectacle. Developing in the course of the narration, he accrues authoritative mastery, as Mandrell has shown:

> As the end of the story approaches, the points of view converge until the object of narration, the subject of the past, is brought up to date, that is, until his perspective merges with that of the narrator and unity is in this way restored to the speaking subject. (102)

However, Mandrell's emphasis on this merging must not obfuscate the performative aspect of the narrative process: with the last sentence, "besando las manos de vuestra merced" (San Pedro 79), El Auctor is *transformed* – as Siervo is transformed into the ideal lover-poet Rodríguez del Padrón – into the author Diego de San Pedro, who presents his report to his master. It is, as it were, an Augustinian 'conversion' of the 'self as character' into the 'self as author,' the structural precondition of autobiography in our modern understanding.[107] This moment is crucial on several accounts. It is the end of a twofold process of subjectification that requires involvement and detachment. From the 'real world' of the military campaigns in the Spanish South, El Auctor is drawn into the 'imaginary world' of Macedonia, where he identifies with

---

[106] Karras points out that "one type of masculinity may predominate at one moment and another type at another, but competing ideas always coexist – even within a single subculture or the mind of a particular individual" (151).

[107] See John Freccero (17).

a knightly subject, Leriano, culminating in the death scene in which Leriano's and El Auctor's gazes meet. This culmination of the identification coincides, however, with the annihilation of El Auctor's double. Unlike Leriano, who is tied (literally in the opening icon) to his *alter ego*, El Auctor is able to 'let go' and leave Macedonia for Peñafiel, the scene of writing, the realm of the Symbolic. In Peñafiel, in an act of auto-affection, the author San Pedro identifies with the *persona*, El Auctor, whom he created and who gained more and more shape in the 'auto-biographical' writing process. Although Rohland de Langbehn is certainly right that *Cárcel de amor* is not an autobiography in the narrow sense of the term, and San Pedro presents El Auctor as a "dichterisches Ich" (*Zur Interpretation der Romane des Diego de San Pedro* 146) ["poetic 'I'"], the text performs an auto-*poesis* of sorts: The reader witnesses the 'education' of a writer, based on new concepts of writing, authorship and subjectivity.

In the old model, as Cynthia Hahn points out,[108] the book could be a metaphor for the self because particular experiences were gradually assimilated to a whole (a set of *habitus*); the self appears as a compiler, a patch-work 'I' of laboriously collected 'alien thoughts.'[109] The material practice of writing can be auxiliary in this process but it is not instrumental.[110] San Pedro's writing about himself, however, is a Foucaultian "entraînement de soi par soi" ["a conditioning of the self by the self"] (Foucault, "L'écriture de soi" 417), not based on "routine bookkeeping" (Dünne, "Herborisieren und Selbstpraxis" 133) but on the bold self-invention of an *auctor sui*. While the courtly subject exists because it sees and is seen (and estimated), and the Cartesian subject because it thinks (or doubts), the 'weak' authorial subject's *cogito* is: "I write about myself, therefore I am" (Spadaccini and Talens 31).

---

[108] See Hahn (188).

[109] Referring to Boccaccio's *Fiammetta*, Weissberger speaks of "the highly literary nature of her subjectivity" ("'Habla de auctor'" 220) and argues that his "subjection" to literary tradition is canceled by the "absolute control" she exerts as an author (223).

[110] Focusing on the metaphor of the "Book of the Heart," Eric Jager argues that "during the Middle Ages [the] subject was conceived in essentially scribal terms" (22). This argument rests on the mistaken premise that the heart was universally accepted as the material site of the self (as *hegemonikon*), and fails to acknowledge the heart's central role in a more comprehensive "pneumophantasmology"; see Agamben (*Stanze*).

Paradoxically, this self-assertion as a writing subject is predicated on the renunciation of authority in another doubling or fold: the climatic moment of the 'authorial education' reenacts, as it were, El Auctor's subjection to Leriano; San Pedro kisses the hand of Diego de Hernández, a powerful courtier (*Alcaide de los donceles*). It is a scene of a metonymic inversion of the process of authorization: the *story teller's mouth* touches the nobleman's hand, turning his own hand into a *writing hand*.[111] He subjects himself to the power of a court functionary, accepting his preordained role as subordinate official – and authorized writer. The denouement reveals *Cárcel de amor* as an ethopoetic text, a writing that transforms the truth (of fiction) in *ethos*.[112]

The kiss seals a process of subjection which is constitutive of subjectivity. The final libidinal investment of the male subject is not in another female but another powerful male; the relation to women (and their subjection) has been marginalized or deferred in the course of the narration.[113] The setting is no longer the phantasmatic other-world of the Sierra Morena haunted by the *imagen femenil* and Desire, but the homo-social milieu of Peñafiel. El Auctor has traveled from a diffuse space (an unnamed dark valley in the mountains) to a concrete place: the castle of Peñafiel, seat of the powerful Girón family. *Cárcel* is, as Ulrich Winter observes,[114] staged as oral narration: San Pedro reports to Diego de Hernández while the publication of the text in printed form is in the future. In the diegetic world (or extra-diegetic, as Winter has it), San Pedro pleads for authority while in the paratextual prologue he presents this authority as a *fait accompli*. Hence, Winter is correct in claiming that authorial self-constitution in *Cárcel* oscillates between a *strategic* "einen Subjektort voraussetzenden und ihn konsolidierenden Verhandeln" (Winter 324) ["negotiation which presupposes and consolidates a locus of subjectivity"] and a *tactical* appropriation of this locus.[115]

---

[111] See Goldberg.
[112] See Foucault ("L'écriture de soi" 418).
[113] "The subjection of women was always a part of masculinity, but not always its purpose or its central feature" (Karras, 11).
[114] See Winter (330).
[115] His frame of reference is Michel de Certeau's theory of strategies and tactics (*Arts de faire* 59-60, which corresponds to pp. 35-37 of Steven Rendall's translation, *The Practice of Everyday Life*). Elsewhere I use Certeau's notion to describe subjectification through interpellation; see Folger ("Alfonso Borregán writes himself"; *Writing as Poaching*, chapter 1).

When *Cárcel* was written, the dominant mode of masculinity and subjectivity was still the knightly, and the protagonist Leriano is both exemplar of the knightly subject and a specter that haunted courtly self-fashioning. With El Auctor, San Pedro skillfully grafted upon his tale of male subjectivity and its ultimate failure another successful story of male self-fashioning and the tactical staking out of a locus of authority. Focusing on the intradiegetic protagonist Leriano and his amatory woes, Bruce Wardropper has associated *Cárcel de amor* with the nostalgia of the "Waning of the Middle Ages";[116] focusing on El Auctor, his 'authorial education' which culminates in the fashioning of the writerly subject, it becomes plain that San Pedro's masterpiece is starkly original and 'post-medieval.' In this text, San Pedro modeled a new form of literary identification based on representation rather than reenactment, performing in this writing process a subtle fashioning of the self which is subject and subjected.

Burke and Starn show that, in the aristocratic sphere, the subjectification through a scopic regime or "courtly arts of seeing and being seen" (Starn 213-14)[117] had their place in Early Modern elite cultures. Wolfgang Matzat argues that, in the *novela pastoral*, the "espacio interior de los afectos" ("Amor y subjetividad" 896) ["interior space of the affects"] is counterbalanced, in a way reminiscent of the performative mode of 15th-century *poesía cancioneril*, by the representation of the passion in an exterior space. This interplay establishes an "Identitätszentrum" (Matzat, "Frühneuzeitliche Subjektivität und das literarische Imaginäre" 358) ["center of identity"]. Notwithstanding the persistence of the 'traditional' performative mode and the emergence of new literary forms which transport it, *Cárcel* shows that new forms of subjectification emerged which were parasitically related to elite subjectivity, that is, in terms of a self-subjecti(ficati)on of individuals belonging to other social strata. San Pedro asserts himself as an author, but his authority is derivative, ultimately bestowed upon him by a member of the aristocratic elite. This is not literature as the expression of an autonomous subject. We see, instead, an individual being summoned by an authority to write about his life in the service of authority (as secretary, chronicler, writer,

---

[116] See Wardropper ("El mundo sentimental de la *Cárcel de amor*" 168-69).
[117] See Burke (*Vision, the Gaze, and the Function of the Senses* 26-27).

functionary), in the hope of garnering further mercies. This is the realm of bureaucracy which is, as Gumbrecht has shown, epistemologically congruous with print culture and the transition from co-presentist medieval interaction to modern 'communication.'[118]

San Pedro's *Cárcel* does not mark a clear break with an outdated episteme. In 1496, Fadrique Alemán printed Diego de San Pedro's *Cárcel* together with a 'tratado' by Nicolás Núñez, a man also known as a *cancionero* poet.[119] Núñez was the first known 'discontent' reader of *Cárcel*,[120] apparently disturbed by the pathetic death of the male protagonist. He conceived of a supplement to *Cárcel* in which El Auctor, after Leriano's death and his return to Peñafiel, has a dream vision which stages a postmortem encounter between a weak, mournful and repentant Laureola and a Leriano who has fully regained his male agency. Núñez perceived the unsettling gender implications of San Pedro's *Cárcel de amor* and used literary imagination as a means to remedy this crisis. He undoubtedly contributed to the editorial success of *Cárcel*, known to most early modern readers as a compound of the original text and his own *tratado*,[121] but apparently failed to see the 'visionary' aspects of San Pedro's text. While Núñez's work attests to the persistence of traditional forms of courtly subjectification (and literature), the transcendence of San Pedro's brief *magnum opus* lies in its repercussions in a spectacularly innovative, if not inaugural, text of the Golden Age of Spanish literature: Lazarillo's *Vida*.

---

[118] See Gumbrecht ("Garcilaso de la Vega, el Inca"). Gumbrecht's terminology is derived from Luhmann. In a series of publications Gumbrecht has studied aspects of this process, which he considers constitutive of modern subjectivity and literature.

[119] Elsewhere ("Cárceles de amor") I analyze Núñez's continuation and its gender implications in detail.

[120] See Parrilla ("'Acrescentar lo que de suyo está crescido'" 242).

[121] See Ivy A. Corfis (21-47). Whinnom edited the Spanish *editio princeps* of Núñez's *tratado* (*Dos opúsculos isabelinos* 51-92). He was the first modern editor to publish San Pedro's text together with Núñez's in his English translation of *Cárcel*. This procedure was followed in Parrilla's recent edition of *Cárcel*.

CONCLUSION

"VUESTRA MERCED ESCRIBE SE LE ESCRIBA [...]"

DIEGO de San Pedro wrote his *Cárcel de amor* "a pedimiento" (3) ["at the request" (3)] of a high-ranking personality, as the rubric to his "tractado" explains. In the very last words of the text, this personality, Diego de Hernández, reappears as "vuestra merced" (79) ["your lordship" (82)]. The fact that *Cárcel* is formally a letter, commissioned by "Vuestra Merced," has occasionally earned San Pedro's *ficción sentimental* a passing mention in the exuberant list[1] of possible models, influences, predecessors, and sources of the acclaimed first 'modern novel':[2] *La vida de Lazarillo de Tormes, y de sus fortunas y adversidades*,[3] published roughly two generations after *Cárcel*.[4] To my knowledge, nobody has system-

---

[1] See, for instance, Lázaro Carreter (42).

[2] The inaugurating modernity of *Lazarillo* is a commonplace among critics of Hispanic literature; in 1931, Marcel Bataillon spoke of a "commencement absolu" (5) ["absolute beginning"]. See also, for instance, Francisco Rico ("Introducción" 47): "[L]a suprema originalidad del *Lazarillo* está en haber urdido una extensa narración en prosa con sostenido diseño realista" ["the supreme originality of the *Lazarillo* is having plotted an extensive prose narration with a sustained realist design"]. While most of these appraisals base themselves on the problematic criterion of representational and psychological realism, John Beverley relates the text to Lukács's notion of the modern novel as the 'biography' of an alienated subject (47-53).

[3] In 1586 Abell Ieffes printed an English translation by David Rowland of Anglesey with the title *The Pleasaunt Historie of Lazarillo Tormes a Spaniarde, wherin is conteined his marvelous deedes and life. With the strange aduentures happened to him in the seruice of sundrie Masters.* The most comprehensive compendium of studies on the *Lazarillo* is Alberto Martino's. In this conclusion, I will discuss only the scholarship necessary to illustrate my point.

[4] In 1554, *Lazarillo* was published in four different editions in Burgos, Medina del Campo, Antwerp, and Alcalá de Henares; see Cañas Murillo. None of them is the *editio princeps*. Regarding the editorial history, see Martino (I, 2-45).

atically traced the parallels between *Cárcel* and *Lazarillo* – too huge appears the gap that separates the lofty, lachrymose and 'unrealistic' tale of a disastrous love affair and the ironic, irreverent, and all-too quotidian life-account of the Toledan town crier. Indeed, it is impossible, or unconvincing at least, to make a case for *Cárcel de amor* as a source, influence or model for *Lazarillo*. I think, however, that both texts share crucial characteristics and, more importantly, that these characteristics are predicated on a shared matrix – the matrix of modern forms of subjectivity and literature.[5]

In a historical perspective, *Cárcel de amor* seems to point to the love literature of the Golden Age. Petrarchist poetry and the pastoral novel imbued with Neo-Platonic ideas leap to mind. Passionate love, and literary forms dealing with it, certainly continued to be important technologies of the self in the Early Modern Period. Nonetheless, I think that the main interest of *Cárcel de amor* is that it explores new ways of subjectification in literature. The reason is that San Pedro's sentimental fiction is, in spite of its medieval tarnish and seemingly escapist tinge, indexical of a profound change in governance.[6] The Isabeline epoch saw the culmination of a shift from the exercise in power essentially based on immediate contact between subject and superior, to a system in which bureaucracy mediated governance, in many instances implying the dissolution of face-to-face situations. Writing professionals, *letrados*, commoners like Juan de Flores and Diego de San Pedro, were the protagonists of the bureaucratization of state affairs. Naturally, this process found its most pronounced manifestation in colonial affairs. Naturally, because from the beginning the Spanish Kings prevented the establishment of largely inde-

---

[5] I provide a detailed analysis of *Lazarillo*'s relation to early modern bureaucracy and its interpellative function in *Writing as Poaching* (chapter 3); my article "The picaresque subject writes" is a short preliminary version of this argument. Elsewhere I also relate *Cárcel* and *Lazarillo*, particularly regarding the emergence of 'autobiographic' discourse; see Folger ("'Besando las manos de vuestra merced'").

[6] Regarding the evolution of public offices in 15th-century Castile see, for instance, Emma Montanos Ferrín and José María García Marín (*El oficio público en Castilla. La burocracia castellana bajo los Austrias*), and the contributions in *Orígenes de la monarquía española: propaganda y legitimación (ca. 1400-1520)* (ed. José Manuel Nieto Soria). Most studies of late medieval/early modern governmentality focus on the legal and institutional aspects in the narrow sense, unfortunately, paying little attention to bureaucracy as a practice.

pendent local elites in the newly conquered territories, striving to maintain a firm grip on government.

Hence the gulf separating the authorities in Castile and their subjects overseas necessarily entailed a deferral of communication: a system of reports (*relaciones, informaciones, memoriales*) and written orders (*cédulas, pragmáticas*) supplanted the traditional governmental practice of super*vision* by superiors. The Crown was very well aware that it was impossible to assert authority in the 'traditional' way; the remedy was the establishment of a bureaucracy of astounding dimensions and measures to control the subjects in the colonies. Works like Juan Rodríguez Freyle's *Carnero*,[7] a chronicle of the first 100 years of colonial rule in the New Kingdom of Granada, document the Sisyphean attempts to assert control through bureaucracy; the modern reader does not know whether to admire this paper regime, or the thousands of ways in which energy was unleashed to subvert it.

With the Archivo de Indias we have a monument of the masses of texts produced by colonial bureaucracy,[8] and the equally monumental legal compilation *Recopilación de las leyes de Indias* [*Compilation of Laws of the Indies*] indicates how tightly the writing process was regulated.[9] One of the major branches of this bureaucracy was the administration of an economy of *mercedes* [privileges/grants]. Those men who had served the crown (soldiers, settlers, and not least, state functionaries) and wanted to be recompensated had to file so-called *relaciones de méritos y servicios* [Reports on Merits and Rendered Services] and send it to the Consejo de Indias [Council of the Indies].[10] This council was the

---

[7] See my "Cien años de burocracia," in which I discuss pertinent scholarship.

[8] Regarding colonial bureaucracy see, among others, Ernst Schäfer, Magali Sarfatti, John H. Parry, John Leddy Phelan, and Horst Pietschmann.

[9] The 1681 *Recopilación* is a monumental yet selective compilation of the colonial 'laws' promulgated since the times of Catholic Kings; see Juan Manzano Manzano's introduction. I am not referring in this instance to censorship properly speaking, which hampered literary production throughout the colonial period; see Maya Smith Ramos.

[10] Regarding the economy of *mercedes*, see Folger ("Alfonso Borregán writes himself"; *Writing as Poaching*, particularly chapter 1). Although, as Murdo MacLeod points out, "*relaciones de méritos y servicios* are [...] evidently one of the major genres of writing and publishing in colonial Spanish America" (25), and passing references abound in studies on colonial matters of great variety, MacLeod's and John F. Chuchiak IV's articles are the only systematic studies on these texts. Both scholars focus on their value as 'sources,' while I strive, in the

decisive institution in colonial matters, although ultimately all decisions were reserved to the source of all authority, the Spanish King. *Relaciones de méritos y servicios* were 'autobiographical' reports, *curricula vitae* of sorts, focusing on the supplicant's gestation as a functionary and events in which the applicant had participated. This is basically the matrix of San Pedro's *Cárcel de amor*: Summoned by an authority (Vuestra Merced), El Auctor reports on memorable events (the love story and also a profound political crisis), and subtly assumes, in and through the writing process, the role of the protagonist himself, emphasizing his loyal service as counsellor-secretary of the hapless nobleman.

The early modern economy of *mercedes* is not only an interesting facet of political history but, in my opinion, also of monumental importance for the history of subjectivity. Foucault and many scholars in his suite have emphasized the importance of "pastoral power,"[11] confessional discourse which forced individuals, men and women from all social strata, to monitor themselves and produce stories of their lives, for the genesis of modern forms of subjectivity. It is less well-known that bureaucracy, too, produced masses of 'biographies,' forcing the subject of his Majesty to assume an *image*.[12] Bureaucratically produced *curricula vitae* can be described in terms of interpellation, in the sense given to the term by Louis Althusser. For Althusser, "*l'idéologie est une «représentation» du rapport imaginaire des individus à leurs conditions réelles d'existence*" (296; italics in the original) ["ideology is a 'representation' of the imaginary relation individuals entertain with their real conditions of existence"],[13] a representation that is part of the process of reproducing these condi-

---

studies mentioned above, to tease out their epistemological underpinning and its implications for subjectivity and modern forms of literature.

[11] "Pastoral Power and Political Reason" (originally a talk delivered in 1979) is arguably Foucault's most concise outline of this concept.

[12] Regarding 19th-century Germany, the connection between bureaucracy and subjectivity has been made by Friedrich Kittler.

[13] The essay was originally published in the review *La pensée* (1970) and subsequently revised. I use the 1995 re-publication of the extended version. Althusser has been, and is, rejected by orthodox Lacanians. See, for instance, Joe Valente's caustic rebuttal of "Marxism's Lacan." More balanced and instructive appraisals are provided by John Ellis and Rosalind Coward and, more recently, Michael Payne. Regarding the notion of interpellation in particular, see Slavoj Žižek (352-56) and Benjamin Scharmacher's recent monograph.

tions. Interpellation is a 'hailing' ("«hé, vous, là-bas!»"; 305; ["hey, you there!"]) which, in the words of John Mowitt,

> incites human beings to identify their self-experience with the image of that experience that comes for them in the discourses emanating from the ideological state apparatuses. [...] The identification with an image of one's self is constitutive of that self. (xiv)

Interpellation as an empowering and subjugating process also entails, according to Althusser, an "assujettissement au Sujet" (310),[14] a specular relation to an absolute, unique Subject. In the case of *relaciones de méritos y servicios*, the bureaucratic dispositive invited the subject to present itself, in its written curriculum vitae, as a perfect subject of his majesty (the stand-in for Althusser's *Sujet*), and thus identify with 'prescribed' ideological images. The necessary precondition of this process of interpellation is, of course, identification in the psychoanalytic sense, the sort of identification San Pedro probes and/or mirrors in *Cárcel de amor*. The parallels with *Cárcel* are suggestive: Although El Auctor (and his readers) identifies with the noble Leriano, he ultimately assumes the image of a *criado* of Vuestra Merced in the concluding portion. He reports to an authority figure, accepting the 'officially' proffered self-image of a servant of Vuestra Merced. The hand kiss is, at the same time, a token of a libidinally charged interpellation and of the ratification of the image of a loyal official and writer that the author had projected in his text. *Cárcel* indicates that interpellation implies submission *and* self-empowerment. San Pedro appropriates the interpellative process – possibly creating a simulacrum of it – to fashion himself as an author, "impresario, producer, *and* production" (Starn 217) of fiction. The same imbrication of interpellation and the toppling of the prescribed self-image is constitutive for Lázaro de Tormes's *Vida*.

So far I have only talked about interpellation through bureaucracy in the colonial context. However, the economy of *mercedes* predates the colonial expansion in the narrow sense of the

---

[14] "Submission to the Subject" is probably the best translation, although it must be noted that the French term implies the empowering aspect of this process, that is, the becoming subject.

term.[15] While the *Consejo de Indias*, as the supreme organ in the administration of colonial matters, assumed the function of deciding who deserved which *mercedes* or public offices, in Castile a special institution was created: the Consejo de Cámara de Castilla.[16] The fact that it was found necessary to create an institution on the highest level of governmental hierarchy (analogous to the councils of State, War, Finances, etc.) indicates the key role of the distribution of *gracia* and *merced* in the Early Modern Spanish state. From the 15th century until the second decade of the 16th century, the King was assisted in the task of guaranteeing distributive justice – traditionally one of his most important duties[17] – by a group of councillors from the Consejo Real. In 1518, their activity was institutionalized with the founding of the Consejo de la Cámara, or Consejo de Cámara de Castilla, and its confirmation in 1523.[18]

Due to the scarcity of studies on this state organ, it is difficult to reconstruct its workings. It is clear, however, that it was an institution of astounding dimensions, which had an impact on the lives of most subjects (as supplicants or witnesses) of the Castilian Monarch.[19] Similar to the Consejo de Indias, the Consejo de Cá-

---

[15] See chapter 3.4. of my *Writing as Poaching*. Salustiano de Dios addresses the issue from the perspective of the history of institutions and law (*Gracia, merced y patronazgo real*).

[16] Surprisingly, this important institution is far from being satisfactorily studied. De Dios ("El ejercicio de la gracia regia en Castilla entre 1250 y 1530", *Gracia, merced y patronazgo real*) has studied the 13th-century roots and institutional aspects of the emergence of the Consejo de Cámara, relating it to the evolution of the royal *cancillería* or *chancillería*, the Royal *cámara* and the *audiencias* in the 15th century. See also José Antonio Escudero.

[17] Elsewhere I show that the rationale of Fernán Pérez de Guzmán's *Generaciones y semblanzas* is to provide a *registro o memorial* of deserving aristocratic families (Folger, *Generaciones y semblanzas*).

[18] This institutionalization in 1518/1523 was recorded by 17th-century scholars. Salustiano de Dios claims that this information is apocryphal, arguing that the Consejo de la Cámara did not properly exist before the reform of 1588. Regarding the decisive period between 1516 and 1530 see de Dios (*Gracia, merced y patronazgo real* 155-90). Escudero ("El consejo de Cámara de Castilla y la reforma de 1588"), on the other hand, holds that the traditional timeline is plausible.

[19] In 1658, Alonso Núñez de Castro claims, in a book with the title *Libro histórico político: solo Madrid es Corte y el cortesano en Madrid*, that the Consejo de Cámara dispatched more than seventy thousand *consultas* per year; see Escudero ("El consejo de Cámara de Castilla y la reforma de 1588" 476). This number was, in all likelihood, a gross exaggeration, but it nevertheless supplies proof that the Consejo de Cámara was an apparatus for the recruiting of state officials

mara based its decisions on *relaciones de méritos y servicios* of sorts, prompting individuals to write *curricula*, imagine and fashion themselves as perfect subjects of the Crown. One of them was Lázaro de Tormes. This is, as we will see, the explicit premise of the autobiographical narration. This pervasive economy of *mercedes* has not been included among the multifarious 'sources' of autobiographic and novelistic discourse (the Inquisition, humanist epistolary discourse, transformation literature in the vein of Apuleius and Lucian, etc.).

The reason is, I think, that too much attention has been paid to the narrator's presumed abject status at the moment when he is writing. There is evidence that the office of *pregonero* is not "vil y baxo" ["vile and base"] as most critics assume;[20] it was a coveted position that could bring its tenant a fair income and even social standing. At any rate, if we consider Lazarillo's miserable childhood and adolescence, there can be no doubt that this made his career. In his last *tratado*, Lázaro tells his reader(s) that he works for the Archpriest of Toledo and that his mentor has arranged a marriage with a servant of his. There have been rumours that this was a fishy *ménage à trois*, but Lázaro assures us that he has quelled these rumours and that he has reached the "cumbre de toda buena fortuna" (135) ["peak of good fortune"].[21] Due to the focus on this episode, only a few scholars have realized that the *caso* [case] Lázaro proposed to clarify is his rise to

---

of impressive dimensions. Considering that the applications often involved a considerable number of *testigos* [witnesses], we can surmise that a substantial portion of the population was, in one way or another, involved in the economy of *mercedes*. Lazarillo's Escudero, who desperately aspires to an office in the service of a magnate, is emblematic of the early modern Spaniards' obsession with *mercedes*.

[20] This qualification stems form the *Diccionario de Autoridades* (Real Academia Española). Referring to Philippe Berger, Martino points out that in a 1558 document from Valencia, we know of the existence of a *pregonero* who possessed a library with thirty-two volumes (including Petrarch's *De remediis*), and who was married to the daughter of a wealthy merchant (I, 395). Martino lists further arguments and documents that indicate that the *pregonero* could be a person of considerable social standing. Woods' characterization is appropriate: Lázaro is "a big fish in a small and slightly muddy pond" (586).

[21] Gleefully, Lázaro sums up his efforts to suppress the slander: "Desta manera no me dicen nada, y yo tengo paz en mi casa" (135) ["So from thence forward, they neuer durst moue any such matter unto me, & I had peace always in my house"; if not indicated otherwise, all translations are Rowland's; the English text does not have page numbers].

the "peak of good fortune," or, in the words of García de la Concha, the "ostentation" of a successful life.[22] This life account is essentially a curriculum of "the seruice of sundrie Masters" – as we read on the title page of David Rowland of Anglesey's 1586 translation. Lazarillo, born 'nowhere' in the river Tormes, and struggling for survival as a boy, achieves a coveted "oficio real" ["Royal office"] (*Lazarillo* 128) as the town crier of Toledo. This is the actual climax of the last *tratado* and *Vida* in general.

Although it is unclear whether Lázaro had to produce a *relación de méritos y servicios* to get this job in the first place, and that it is possibly part of the novel's pervasive irony that a humble subject like him writes a *relación* of his life,[23] one may also see in the text an intentional parody of the 'real-life' interpellation of state officials. In the beginning of his account, the narrator pretends to write about his 'case' because an unidentified authority, addressed as Vuestra Merced, has requested this report. The parallels with *Cárcel de amor* are obvious, as is the 'progress' in terms of narrative techniques and the status of the writing subject. Both Lázaro and El Auctor write *curricula* of sorts, presenting themselves as subjects, conforming with the parameters of ideological interpellation: they present themselves as humble yet deserving servants of Vuestra Merced. In both cases this becomes the 'pretext' for authorial self-fashioning. The concluding lines of *Cárcel* are reminiscent of the 'courtly,' oral presentation of fictional texts and approving gazes by a courtly community. It is, however, essentially a simulacrum of this communicative situation. I have argued that his 'writerly' education gradually transforms El Auctor into an image of the writer as author, and that this authorial self-fashioning is ratified by Vuestra Merced. This sentimental

---

[22] See Víctor García de la Concha (71-91). Domingo Ynduráin ("El renacimiento de Lázaro") and M. J. Woods are two more voices who see Lázaro's *Vida* as a success story.

[23] The actual range of the Consejo's responsibilities is difficult to determine because they include a "sinfín de cosas"; see de Dios ("El ejercicio de la gracia regia en Castilla entre 1250 y 1530" 344). Moreover, due to the local nature of Castilian law in many respects, it is impossible to determine the actual procedure for the appoint of Toledo's *pregoneros*. Although I tend to think that the Toledan *pregonero* was actually appointed by the city council, it should be noted that the office required a literate tenant, and, given the pervasiveness of written applications (including a curriculum vitae), 16th-century readers would consider it plausible that the applicant for even a lowly office would write a *relación de méritos y servicios* of sorts.

fiction, however, does not primarily address a clearly delimited courtly community, soliciting their approving gazes. *Cárcel*, as a text conceived for the letter press, addresses a diffuse readership, 'private' readers who are separated from the author. Although the text is dedicated to a specific individual, Diego Fernández (who may really have commissioned the text), this individual is actually supplanted by a reading public whose *imagined* gazes ratify the author's self-fashioning. Vuestra Merced becomes a mere stand-in for Althusser's absolute *Sujet*.

The 'imaginary' nature of Vuestra Merced is part of the reason that Lázaro chooses not to identify his narratee.[24] While in *Cárcel* self-fashioning and interpellation are parasitic in relation to courtly literature and performativity, Lazarillo is a straightforward response to interpellation by Vuestra Merced. In the late 15th century San Pedro had to write a simulacrum of an oral delivery; Lazarillo's prologue, on the other hand, marks the *Vida* as part and parcel of an 'epistolary' exchange: "Vuestra Merced escribe se le escriba" ["Your Lordship writes that I may write to you"].[25] Most importantly, Lázaro spectacularly unfolds the potential for novelistic discourse and authorly self-fashioning inherent in interpellation.[26] El Auctor's 'biography' is a graft, as it were, to the amorous/chivalric tale; only in the concluding portion does the 'real' life of the commoner *letrado* take shape. *Lazarillo* is the autobiography of an individual born into a world where everyday life means a struggle for subsistence. He recounts his ascent to a modest yet comfortable life as a 'royal official.' In the prologue, however, this 'infamous subject' proudly displays humanist erudition and asserts the worth of his 'life':[27] "parescióme no tomalle por el medio, sino del principio, porque se tenga entera noticia de mi persona" (10-11) ["I haue thought good not to begin the midst of my life, but first to tel you of my birth, that al me\<n\> may haue ful knowledge of my person"; Rowland's translation, no pagination]. Of course, this prologue blends the voices of the first-person narrator of the *Vida* and the unknown humanist who

---

[24] See Folger (*Writing as Poaching*, chapter 3.7.).

[25] Rowland translates rather freely: "you haue commanded me to write the matter at length".

[26] Regarding the fictional kernel in bureaucratically generated 'autobiographies,' see Bernhard Siegert and Folger ("Alfonso Borregán writes himself").

[27] See Foucault's famous essay "La vie des hommes infâmes".

actually wrote the text, but it is precisely the game of literature that makes it possible to project this self-image and have it validated by a reading public. *Lazarillo* shows that compliance with interpellation can be a literary ruse, and that the function of literature is to interpellate (readers and writers) and, at the same time, to provide avenues for escaping interpellation.

This potential of literature in our understanding is embryonic in San Pedro's *Cárcel de amor*. More than half a century ago, Walter Pabst argued that Leriano never leaves his prison because he is suffering his amorous torment at each and every moment of the narration.[28] Leriano's alter ego, El Auctor, however, escapes from the Prison of Love, fashioning himself as an author. In this respect, *Cárcel* foreshadows the possibility of writing, two generations later, the autobiography of an infamous subject, *La vida de Lazarillo de Tormes, y de sus fortunas y adversidades*, in which passionate love is totally absent and courtly, amorous service merely a matter of ridicule.[29]

---

[28] See Pabst (45).

[29] Of course, I am talking about the Escudero's pathetic, frustrated attempt as a 'courtly lover,' and Lázaro's very pragmatic marital arrangement.

TEXTS CITED

Aers, David. "A Whisper in the Ear of Early Modernists; or, Reflections on Literary Critics Writing the 'History of the Subject'." *Culture and History, 1350-1600: Essays on English Communities, Identities, and Writing*. Ed. David Aers. Detroit: Wayne State UP, 1992. 177-202.

Agamben, Giorgio. *Das Offene: Der Mensch und das Tier*. [*L'aperto: L'uomo e l'animale*. Turin: Bollati Boringhieri, 2002]. Trans. Davide Guiriato. Frankfurt am Main: Suhrkamp, 2003.

———. *Stanze: La parola e il fantasma nella cultura occidentale*. Torino: Einaudi, 1977.

Agnew, Michael. "The Comedieta' of the *Sátira*: Dom Pedro de Portugal's Monkeys in the Margins." *Modern Language Notes* 118 (2003): 298-317.

Alcázar López, Pablo y José A. González Núñez. Introducción. *La historia de Grisel y Mirabella, edición facsímil sobre la de Juan de Cromberger de 1529*. By Juan de Flores. Versión e introducción de Pablo Alcázar López y José A. González Núñez. Los libros del curioso impertinente, serie clásica 1. Granada: Don Quijote, 1983.

Althoff, Gert. "Gefühle in der öffentlichen Kommunikation des Mittelalters." *Emotionalität: Zur Geschichte der Gefühle*. Ed. Claudia Benthien and Ingrid Kasten. Literatur Kultur Geschlecht, kleine Reihe 16. Köln; Weimar; Wien: Böhlau, 2000. 82-99.

Althusser, Louis. "Idéologie et appareils idéologiques d'état (notes pour une recherche)." *Sur la réproduction*. Paris: Presses Universitaires de France, 1995. 269-314.

Alminyana i Vallés, Josep. *El crit de la llengua*. Vol. 2: Lluïs de Fenollet. Valencia: Lo Rat Penat, 1999. 5.07.2008. <http://www.loratpenat.org/biblioteca/_CRIT_2.pdf>.

Amasuno Sárraga, Marcelino V. "Calisto, entre *amor hereos* y una terapia eficaz." *Dicenda* 18 (2000): 11-49.

———. "La enfermedad de Melibea: dos perspectivas médicas de la *ægritudo amoris* en *Celestina*." *Revista de Filología Española* 81 (2001): 5-47.

———. "Hacia un contexto médico para *Celestina*: sobre *amor hereos* y su terapia." *Celestinesca* 24 (2000): 135-69.

Andrachuk, Gregory Peter. "The Function of the *Estoria de dos amadores* within the *Siervo libre de amor*." *Revista Canadiense de Estudios Hispánicos* 2 (1977): 27-38.

———. "On the Missing Third Part of *Siervo libre de amor*." *Hispanic Review* 45 (1977): 171-80.

Antonucci, Fausta. *El salvaje en la comedia del Siglo de Oro: Historia de un tema de Lope a Calderón*. Números Anejos del RILCE 16. Pamplona: RILCE, Universidad de Pamplona; Toulouse: LESO, Université de Toulouse, 1995.

Aristotle. *De memoria et reminiscentia*. Trans. Richard Sorabij. *On Memory*. Providence, RI: Brown UP, 1972. 47-62.

———. *Problemas*. [*Problemata*]. Ed. and trans. Ester Sánchez Millán. Biblioteca Clásica Gredos 320. Madrid: Gredos, 2004.

Avalle-Arce, Juan Bautista. Don Quijote *como forma de vida*. Madrid: Fundación Juan March, 1976.

Bataillon, Marcel. *Le roman picaresque*. Paris: La Renaissance du livre, 1931.

Battesti Pelegrin, Jeanne. "'Je' lyrique, 'je' narratif dans la *Cárcel de amor* (à propos du personnage de Leriano)." *Cahiers d'Études Romanes* 11 (1986): 7-19.

———. "La poésie *cancioneril* ou l'anti-autobiographie?" *L'autobiographie dans le monde hispanique*. Aix-en-Provence: Publications de l'Université de Provence, 1980. 95-113.

Beecher, Donald A. and Massimo Ciavolella. Introduction. *A Treatise on Lovesickness*. By Jacques Ferrand. Trans. and ed. Donald A. Beecher and Massimo Ciavolella. Syracuse, NY: Syracuse UP, 1990. 1-202.

Belmar Marchante, Mª Ángeles. "La tensión de la dicotomía del personaje actor, como acción amorosa y del autor-narrador como ocultamiento: Ardanlier, Arnalte, Leriano." *Medioevo y literatura: Actas del V Congreso de la Asociación Hispánica de Literatura Medieval*. Vol. I. Ed. Juan de Paredes. Granada: Universidad de Granada, 1995. 311-20.

Benvenuto, Bice and Roger Kennedy. *The Works of Jacques Lacan: An Introduction*. London: Free Associations Books, 1986.

Berger, Philippe. *Libro y lectura en la Valencia del Renacimiento*. Valencia: Institució Valenciana d'Estudis i Investigació, 1987.

Bernheimer, Richard. *Wild Men in the Middle Ages: A Study in Art, Sentiment, and Demonology*. Cambridge, MA: Harvard UP, 1952.

Besó Portalés, César. "La ficción sentimental: Apuntes para una caracterización." *Espéculo* 27 (2004). 12 July 2007. <www.ucm.es/info/especulo/numero27/fsentime.html>.

Beverley, John R. "On the Concept of the Spanish Literary Baroque." *Culture and Control in Counter-Reformation Spain*. Ed. Anne J. Cruz and Mary Elizabeth Perry. Hispanic Issues 7. Minneapolis; Oxford: U of Minnesota P, 1992. 216-30.

Beysterveldt, Antony van. "La nueva teoría del amor en las novelas de Diego de San Pedro." *Cuadernos Hispanoamericanos* 349 (1979): 70-83.

Biernoff, Suzannah. *Sight and Embodiment in the Middle Ages*. New York: Palgrave Macmillan, 2002.

Blasius, Mark. Introductory Note. "About the Beginning of the Hermeneutics of the Self: Two Lectures at Dartmouth." By Michel Foucault. *Political Theory* 21 (1993): 198-200.

Blay Manzanera, Vicenta. "El discurso femenino en los cancioneros de los siglos XV y XVI." *Actas del XIII Congreso de la Asociación Internacional de Hispanistas, Madrid 6-11 de Julio de 1998*. Ed. Florencio Sevilla and Carlos Alvar. Vol. 1. Madrid: Castalia, 2000. 48-58.

———. "El varón que finge voz de mujer en las composiciones de cancionero." *Cultural Contexts/ Female Voices*. Ed. Louise M. Haywood. Papers of the Medieval Hispanic Research Seminar 27. London: Department of Hispanic Studies, Queen Mary & Westfield College, 2000. 9-26.

Boccaccio, Giovanni. *Libro de Fiameta*. Ed. Lia Mendia Vozzo. Collana di testi e studi ispanici I, Testi critici 4. Pisa: Giardini, 1983.

Bourdieu, Pierre. *Outline of a Theory of Practice*. Trans. Richard Nice. Cambridge Studies in Social and Cultural Anthropology 16. 16th ed. Cambridge: Cambridge UP, 2002.

Brownlee, Marina Scordilis. "The Counterfeit Muse: Ovid, Boccaccio, Juan de Flores." *Discourse of Authority in Medieval and Renaissance Literature*. Ed. Kevin Brownlee and Walter Stephens. Hanover, NH: UP of New England for Dartmouth College, 1989. 109-127.

———. *The Cultural Labyrinth of María de Zayas*. Philadelphia: U of Pennsylvania P, 2000.

———. "Imprisoned Discourse in the *Cárcel de amor*." *Romanic Review* 78 (1987): 188-201.

———. *The Severed Word: Ovid's* Heroides *and the* Novela Sentimental. Princeton: Princeton UP, 1990.

Bryson, Norman. *Vision and Painting: The Logic of the Gaze*. New Haven; London: Yale UP, 1983.

Bumke, Joachim. "Emotion und Körperzeichen: Beobachtungen zum *Willehalm* Wolframs von Eschenbach." *Das Mittelalter* 8:1 (2003): 13-32.

Bundy, Murray Wright. *The Theory of Imagination in Classical and Mediaeval Thought*. University of Illinois Studies in Language and Literature 12, 2-3. Urbana: U of Illinois P, 1927.

Burckhardt, Jacob. *The Civilization of the Renaissance in Italy*. Trans. S. G. C. Middlemore. London: Penguin Books, 1990.

Burke, James F. *Desire Against the Law: The Juxtaposition of Contraries in Early Medieval Spanish Literature*. Stanford: Stanford UP, 1998.

———. "The Insouciant Reader and the Failure of Memory in *Celestina*." *Crítica Hispánica* 15:1 (1993): 35-46.

———. *Vision, the Gaze, and the Function of the Senses in* Celestina. University Park, PA: Pennsylvania State UP, 2000.

Burke, Peter. "Representations of the Self from Petrarch to Descartes." *Rewriting the Self: Histories from the Renaissance to the Present*. Ed. Roy Porter. London; New York: Routledge, 1999. 17-28.

Butler, Judith. *Gender Trouble: Feminism and the Subversion of Identity*. New York; London: Routledge, 1999.

Bynum, Caroline Walker. "The Female Body and Religious Practice in the Later Middle Ages." *Fragmentation and Redemption: Essays on Gender and the Human Body in Medieval Religion*. New York: Zone Books, 1991. 181-238.

———. "Did the Twelfth Century Discover the Individual?" *Journal of Ecclesiastical History* 31 (1980): 1-17.

———. *Metamorphosis and Identity*. New York: Zone Books, 2001.

Cadden, Joan. *Meanings of Sex Difference in the Middle Ages: Medicine, Science and Culture*. Cambridge: Cambridge UP, 1993.

Camille, Michael. "Before the gaze: the internal senses and late medieval practices of seeing." *Visuality Before and Beyond the Renaissance: Seeing as Others Saw*. Ed. Robert S. Nelson. Cambridge: Cambridge UP, 2000. 197-223.

———. "Hybridity, Monstrosity, and Bestiality in the *Roman de Fauvel*." *Fauvel Studies: Allegory, Chronicle, Music, and Image in Paris, Bibliothèque nationale de France, MS français 146*. Ed. Margaret Bent and Andrew Wathey. Oxford: Clarendon Press; New York: Oxford UP, 1998. 161-74.

———. "Mimetic Identification and Passion Devotion in the Later Middle Ages: A Double-Sided Panel by Meister Francke." *The Broken Body: Passion Devotion in the Later Middle Ages*. Ed. Alisdair MacDonald and Rita Schlussemann. Groeningen: Egbert Forsten, 1998. 183-210.

Campbell, Kimberlee A. "The Reiterated Self: Temporality and Ritual Renewal in *Hervis de Metz*." *Transtextualities: Of Cycles and Cyclicity in Medieval*

French Literature. Ed. Sara Sturm-Maddox and Donald Maddox. Medieval and Renaissance Texts & Studies 149. Binghamton, NY: Center for Medieval and Early Renaissance Studies, 1996. 157-77.

Cancionero de Estúñiga. Ed. Nicasio Salvador Miguel. Colección clásicos 33. Madrid: Alhambra, 1987.

Canet Vallés, José Luis. "El proceso del enamoramiento como elemento estructurante de la ficción sentimental." *Historias y ficciones: Coloquio sobre la literatura del siglo XV.* Ed. Rafael Beltrán, et al. València: Universitat de València, 1992. 227-39.

Cañas Murillo, Jesús. *Una edición recién descubierta de Lazarillo de Tormes, Medina del Campo, 1554.* Mérida: Junta de Extremadura, 1996.

Carruthers, Mary J. *The Book of Memory. A Study of Memory in Medieval Culture.* Cambridge: Cambridge UP, 1990.

———. *The Craft of Thought: Meditation, Rhetoric, and the Making of Images, 400-1200.* Cambridge; New York: Cambridge UP, 1998.

Cascardi, Anthony J. "The Subject of Control." *Culture and Control in Counter-Reformation Spain.* Ed. Anne J. Cruz and Mary Elizabeth Perry. Hispanic Issues 7. Minneapolis; Oxford: U of Minnesota P, 1992. 231-54.

Castro Lingl, Vera. "The Constable of Portugal's *Sátira de infelice e felice vida*: A Reworking of Rodríguez del Padrón's *Siervo libre de amor.*" *Revista de Estudios Hispánicos* 32 (1998): 76-100.

Cátedra, Pedro M. *Amor y pedagogía en la Edad Media: estudio de doctrina amorosa y práctica literaria.* Salamanca: Universidad de Salamanca, 1989.

Caviness, Madeline H. *Visualizing Women in the Middle Ages: Sight, Spectacle, and Scopic Economy.* Philadelphia: U of Pennsylvania P, 2001.

Cerquiglini, Jacqueline. *'Un engin si soutil': Guillaume de Machaut et l'écriture au XIV*e *siècle.* Genève; Paris: Slatkine, 1985.

Certeau, Michel de. *L'invention du quotidien.* Vol. 1: *Arts de faire.* Ed. Luce Giard. Paris: Gallimard, 1990.

———. *The Practice of Everyday Life.* Trans. Steven Rendall. Berkeley: U of California P, 1988.

Checa, Jorge. "*Grisel y Mirabella* de Juan de Flores: rebeldía y violencia como síntomas de crisis." *Revista Canadiense de Estudios Hispánicos* 12 (1988): 369-82.

Chomsky, Noam. *Cartesian Linguistics: A Chapter in the History of Rationalist Thought.* New York: Harper & Row, 1966.

Chorpenning, Joseph F. "Rhetoric and feminism in the *Cárcel de Amor.*" *Bulletin of Hispanic Studies* 54 (1977): 1-8.

Chuchiak IV, John F. "Toward a regional definition of idolatry: Reexamining idolatry trials in the '*relaciones de méritos*' and their role in defining the concept of '*idolatría*' in colonial Yucatán, 1570-1780." *Journal of Early Modern History* 6:2 (2002): 140-67.

Cocozzella, Peter. "Pere Torroella: Pan-Hispanic Poet of the Catalan Pre-Renaissance." *Hispanófila* 86 (1986): 1-14.

Constantinus Africanus. *De Coitu.* See Delany.

Corfis, Ivy A. "Catalogue of editions." *Cárcel de amor.* By Diego de San Pedro. Ed. Ivy A. Corfis. London: Tamesis, 1987. 16-50.

Cortijo Ocaña, Antonio. "*De amicitia, amore et rationis discretione.* Breves notas a propósito de Boncompagno da Signa y el *Siervo libre de amor.*" *Revista de poética medieval* 16 (2006): 23-52.

——— (ed.). "Critical Cluster on Sentimental Romance." *La corónica* 29:1 (2000): 5-229.

———. *La evolución genérica de la ficción sentimental de los siglos XV y XVI: género literario y contexto social.* Colección Támesis, Serie A: Monografías 184. London: Tamesis, 2001.

Cortijo Ocaña, Antonio. "La ficción sentimental: ¿un género imposible?" *La corónica* 29:1 (2000): 5-13.

———. Introducción. *El tratado del amor carnal o Rueda de Venus: Motivos literarios en la tradición sentimental y celestinesca (ss. XIII-XV)*. By Boncompagno da Silva. Ed. and trans. Antonio Cortijo Ocaña. Anejos de RILCE 43. Pamplona: EUNSA, 2002. 11-66.

———. "Notas sobre el Tostado *De amore*." *La corónica* 33:1 (2004): 67-83.

Costa Lima, Luiz. *Die Kontrolle des Imaginären: Vernunft und Imagination in der Moderne*. [*O controle do imaginário*]. Trans. Armin Biermann. Frankfurt am Main: Suhrkamp, 1990.

Couliano, Ioan P. *Eros and Magic in the Renaissance*. Trans. Margaret Cook. Chicago: U of Chicago P, 1987.

Coward, Rosalind and John Ellis. *Language and Materialism: Developments in Semiology and the Theory of the Subject*. London; Henley; Boston: Routledge & Kegan Paul, 1977.

Crane, Susan A. *The Performance of the Self: Ritual, Clothing, and Identity During the Hundred Years War*. Philadelphia: U of Pennsylvania P, 2002.

Crohns, Hjalmar. "Zur Geschichte der Liebe als 'Krankheit'." *Archiv für Kulturgeschichte* 3 (1905): 66-86.

Cruz, Anne J. and Mary Elizabeth Perry, ed. *Culture and Control in Counter-Reformation Spain*. Hispanic Issues 7. Minneapolis; Oxford: U of Minnesota P, 1992.

Cruz, Jaqueline. "Estrategias de ocultación y autoafirmación en *El sueño* de Sor Juana." *Revista Canadiense de Estudios Hispánicos* 19:3 (1995): 533-41.

Dagenais, John. *The Ethics of Reading in Manuscript Culture: Glossing the* Libro de buen amor. Princeton: Princeton UP, 1994.

Dangler, Jean. *Making Difference in Medieval and Early Modern Iberia*. Notre Dame: U of Notre Dame P, 2005.

Davis, Natalie Zemon. "Boundaries and the Sense of Self in Sixteenth-Century France." *Reconstructing Individualism: Autonomy, Individuality, and the Self in Western Thought*. Thomas C. Heller, Morton Sosna, and David E. Wellbery. Stanford: Stanford UP, 1986. 53-63.

de Dios, Salustiano. *Gracia, merced y patronazgo real*. Madrid: Centro de Estudios Políticos y Constitucionales, 1993.

de Grazia, Margareta. "World Pictures, Modern Periods, and the Early Stage." *A New History of Early English Drama*. Ed. John D. Cox and David Scott Kastan. New York: Columbia UP, 1997. 7-21.

Delany, Paul. "Constantinus Africanus' *De Coitu*: A Translation." *Chaucer Review* 4 (1969): 55-65.

Deleuze, Gilles. *Foucault*. Paris: Les Éditions de Minuit, 1986.

———. *Le pli: Leibniz et le baroque*. Paris: Les Éditions de Minuit, 1986.

Delhaye, Philippe. *The Christian Conscience*. Trans. Charles Underhill Quinn. New York: Desclee, 1968.

de Nigris, Carla. Introduzione. *Schiavo d'amore (Siervo libre de amor)*. By Juan Rodríguez del Padrón. Ed. and trans. Carla de Nigris. Milano; Trento: Luni, 1999. 7-52.

Deyermond, Alan. "El heredero anhelado, condenado y perdonado." *Tradiciones y puntos de vista en la ficción sentimental*. México: Universidad Nacional Autónoma de México, 1993. 105-18.

———. "El hombre salvaje en la novela sentimental." *Tradiciones y puntos de vista en la ficción sentimental*. México: Universidad Nacional Autónoma de México, 1993. 17-42 [originally published in *Filología* 10 (1964): 97-111].

Deyermond, Alan. "The Woodcuts of Diego de San Pedro's *Cárcel de Amor*, 1492-1496." *Bulletin Hispanique* 2 (2002): 511-28.
Dolz i Ferrer, Enric. "Juan Rodríguez del Padrón, Juan de Cervantes y Gonzalo de Medina. Apuntes biográficos." *Lemir* 9 (2005). 2 Aug. 2007 <http://parnaseo.uv.es/Lemir/Revista/Revista9/Dolz/Dolz.pdf>.
———. "El simbolismo de los colores y la estructura del *Siervo libre de amor*." *La corónica* 35:1 (2006): 109-36.
———. "El vocabulario del alma en el *Siervo libre de amor*." *Revista de poética medieval* 16 (2006): 79-122.
Dunn, Peter N. "Narrator as Character in the *Cárcel de Amor*." *Modern Language Notes* 94 (1979): 187-99.
Dünne, Jörg. *Asketisches Schreiben: Rousseau und Flaubert als Paradigmen literarischer Selbstpraxis in der Moderne*. Romanica Monacensia 65. Tübingen: Gunter Narr, 2003.
———. "Herborisieren und Selbstpraxis: Das 'schwache Subjekt' in Rousseaus *Rêveries*." *Von Rousseau zum Hypertext: Subjektivität in Theorie und Literatur der Moderne*. Ed. Paul Geyer and Claudia Jünke. Würzburg: Königshausen & Neumann, 2001. 127-49.
Egginton, William. "An Epistemology of the Stage: Theatricality and Subjectivity in Early Modern Spain." *New Literary History* 27 (1996): 391-413.
———. *How the World Became a Stage: Presence, Theatricality and the Question of Modernity*. Albany, NY: SUNY Press, 2003.
Elias, Norbert. *Über den Prozeß der Zivilisation: Soziogenetische und psychogenetische Untersuchungen*. 1939. 2 vol. Frankfurt am Main: Suhrkamp, 1997.
El Saffar, Ruth. "The 'I' of the Beholder: Self and Other in Some Golden Age Texts." *Cultural Authority in Golden Age Spain*. Ed. Marina S. Brownlee and Hans Ulrich Gumbrecht. Baltimore; London: Johns Hopkins UP, 1995. 178-205.
Escudero, José Antonio. "El consejo de Cámara de Castilla y la reforma de 1588." *Administración y estado en la España moderna*. Valladolid: Junta de Castilla y León, Consejería de Educación y Cultura, 1999. 467-82.
Ferry, Anne. *The 'Inward' Language: Sonnets of Wyatt, Sidney, Shakespeare, Donne*. Chicago; London: U of Chicago P, 1983.
Fetz, Reto Luzius, Roland Hagenbüchle and Peter Schulz, ed. *Geschichte und Vorgeschichte der Subjektivität*. 2 vol. European Cultures Studies in Literature and the Arts 11:2. Berlin, New York: 1998.
Ficino, Marsilio. *Über die Liebe oder Platons Gastmahl. [Commentarium in convivium Platonis, de amore]*. Latin-German. Ed. Paul Richard Blum. Trans. Karl Paul Hasse. Fourth revised ed. Hamburg: Felix Meiner, 1994.
Filios, Denise K. *Performing Women in the Middle Ages: Sex, Gender, and the Iberian Lyric*. New York: Palgrave Macmillan, 2005.
Fisher, Will. "The Renaissance Beard: Masculinity in Early Modern England." *Renaissance Quarterly* 54 (2001): 155-87.
Flores, Juan de. *Grimalte y Gradissa*. Ed. Pamela Waley. London: Tamesis, 1971.
———. *La historia de Grisel y Mirabella, edición facsímil sobre la de Juan de Cromberger de 1529*. Versión e introducción de Pablo Alcázar López y José A. González Núñez. Los libros del curioso impertinente, serie clásica 1. Granada: Don Quijote, 1983.
Folger, Robert. "Alonso Borregán writes himself: the colonial subject and the writing of history in *relaciones de méritos y servicios*." *Talleres de la memoria – reivindicaciones y autoridad en la historiografía indiana de los siglos XVI y XVII*. Ed. Robert Folger and Wulf Oesterreicher. P & A 5. Münster; Hamburg; London: LITVerlag, 2005. 267-93.

Folger, Robert. "'Besando las manos de vuestra merced': la emergencia del discurso novelesco en *Cárcel de amor* y *Lazarillo de Tormes*." Forthcoming in *La fractura historiográfica: las investigaciones de Edad Media y Renacimiento desde el tercer milenio: Actas del I Congreso Internacional de la Sociedad de Estudios Medievales y Renacentistas*. Salamanca: SEMYR, in press.

———. "Bestialische Leidenschaft und 'anthropologische Maschine' (*Cárcel de amor*, *Grimalte y Gradissa* und *Grisel y Mirabella*)." *Über die Grenzen des natürlichen Lebens: Formen der Inszenierung des Tier-Mensch-Maschine-Verhältnisses in der Iberoromania*. Ed. Christopher F. Laferl and Claudia Leitner. Münster: LIT-Verlag, in press.

———. "*Cárceles de amor*: 'Gender Trouble' and Male Fantasies in 15th-Century Castile." *Bulletin of Spanish Studies* 83 (2006): 617-35.

———. "Cien años de burocracia: *El carnero* de Juan Rodríguez Freyle." *Iberoromania* 58 (2003): 49-61.

———. '*Generaciones y semblanzas*': *Memory and Genealogy in Medieval Iberian Historiography*. Romanica Monacensia 68. Tübingen: Gunter Narr, 2003.

———. *Images in Mind: Lovesickness, Spanish Sentimental Fiction and* Don Quijote. North Carolina Studies in the Romance Languages and Literatures 274. Chapel Hill: U of North Carolina P, 2002.

———. "The picaresque subject writes: *Lazarillo de Tormes*." *Das Paradigma des Pikaresken/The Paradigm of the Picaresque*. Ed. Christoph Ehland and Robert Fajen. Heidelberg: Winter, 2007. 45-68.

———. "Noble subjects: interpellation in *Generaciones y semblanzas* and *Claros varones de Castilla*." *eHumanista* 4 (2004): 22-50. 21 Jun. 2008 < http://www.ehumanista.ucsb.edu/volumes/volume_04/Articles/Folger.pdf>.

———. "Passion and Persuasion: Philocaption in *La Celestina*." *La corónica* 34:1 (2005): 5-29.

———. "Liebeskrankheit und *querelle des hommes* im Spanien des 15. "Jahrhunderts." *Heiber Streit und Ralte Ordnung*. Ed. Friedericke Hassaner. Göttingen: Wallstein, 2008. 143-54.

———. *Writing as Poaching: Subject Constitution, Strategic Interpellation and Tactical Writing in Early Modern Spanish Culture*. Manuscript completed.

Fontes, Manuel da Costa. "Martínez de Toledo's 'Nightmare' and the Courtly and Oral Traditions." *Oral Tradition and Hispanic Literature: Essays in Honor of Samuel G. Armistead*. Ed. M. Caspi Mishael. New York: Garland, 1995. 189-216.

Foucault, Michel. "About the Beginning of the Hermeneutics of the Self: Two Lectures at Dartmouth." *Political Theory* 21 (1993): 198-227.

———. "Das Denken des Draußen." *Schriften zur Literatur*. Trans. Karin von Hofer and Anneliese Botond. Frankfurt am Main: Fischer, 1988. 130-56.

———. *Dispositive der Macht*. Various trans. Berlin: Merve, 1978.

———. "L'écriture de soi." *Dits et écrits*. Ed. Daniel Defert and François Ewald. Vol. 4. Paris: Gallimard, 1994. 415-30.

———. "Des espaces autres." *Dits et écrits*. Ed. Daniel Defert and François Ewald. Vol. 4. Paris: Gallimard, 1994. 752-62.

———. *The History of Sexuality*. Vol. 1: *Introduction*. Trans. Robert Hurley. New York: Vintage Books, 1990.

———. *The History of Sexuality*. Vol. 2: *The Use of Pleasure*. Trans. Robert Hurley. New York: Vintage Books, 1990.

———. *The History of Sexuality*. Vol. 3: *The Care of the Self*. Trans. Robert Hurley. New York: Vintage Books, 1990.

———. "Pastoral Power and Political Reason." *Religion and Culture*. Ed. Jeremy R. Carrette. Manchester: Manchester UP, 1999. 135-52.

Foucault, Michel. "The Subject and Power." *Critical Inquiry* 8 (1982): 777-95.
———. "La vie des hommes infâmes." *Cahiers du Chemin* 29 (1977): 12-29.
———. *Die Wahrheit und die juristischen Formen*. Trans. Michael Bischoff. Frankfurt am Main: Suhrkamp, 2003.
Fradenberg, Louise O. *City, Marriage, Tournament: Arts of Rule in Late Medieval Scotland*. Madison, WI: U of Wisconsin P, 1991.
Frank, Manfred. "Subjekt, Person, Individuum." *Die Frage nach dem Subjekt*. Ed. Manfred Frank. Frankfurt am Main: Suhrkamp, 1988. 7-28.
———. *Was ist Neostrukturalismus?* Frankfurt am Main: Suhrkamp, 1984.
Frank, Manfred and Anselm Haverkamp (ed.). *Individualität*. Poetik und Hermeneutik 13. München: Wilhelm Fink, 1988.
Fraxanet Sala, María Rosa. "Estudios sobre los grabados de la novela *La Cárcel de Amor* de Diego de San Pedro." *Estudios de iconografía medieval española*. Ed. Joaquín Yarza Luaces. Bellaterra: Universidad Autónoma de Barcelona, 1984. 430-82.
Freccero, John. "Autobiography and Narrative." *Reconstructing Individualism: Autonomy, Individuality, and the Self in Western Thought*. Thomas C. Heller, Morton Sosna, and David E. Wellbery. Stanford, CA: Stanford UP, 1986.
Friedman, John Block. *The Monstrous Races in Medieval Art and Thought*. Cambridge, MA; London: Harvard UP, 1981.
Fuhrmann, Manfred. "*Persona*, ein römischer Rollenbegriff." *Identität*. Ed. Odo Marquard and Karlheinz Stierle. Poetik und Hermeneutik 8. München: Wilhelm Fink, 1979. 83-106.
Funes, Leonardo. "Excentricidad y descentramiento en la figura autoral de don Juan Manuel." *eHumanista* 9 (2007): 1-19. 15 Jun. 2008 <http://www.ehumanista.ucsb.edu/volumes/volume_09/Articles/1%20Leonardo%20Funes%20Article.pdf>.
Garcia, Michel. "Vida de Juan Rodríguez del Padrón." *Actas del IX Congreso de la Asociación Internacional de Hispanistas (18-23 agosto 1986, Berlín)*. Ed. Sebastian Neumeister. Vol. 1. Frankfurt am Main: Vervuert, 1989. 205-213.
García Marín, José María. *La burocracia castellana bajo los Austrias*. Alcalá de Henares: Instituto Nacional de Administración Pública, 1986.
———. *El oficio público en Castilla durante la Baja Edad Media*. Alcalá de Henares: Instituto Nacional de Administración Pública, 1987.
Gerli, E. Michael. "Gender Trouble: Juan de Flores's *Triunfo de Amor*, Isabel la Católica, and the Economies of Power at Court." *Journal of Spanish Cultural Studies* 4 (2003): 169-85.
———. "Leriano's Libation: Notes on the *Cancionero* Lyric, *Ars moriendi*, and the Probable Debt to Boccaccio." *Modern Language Notes* 96 (1981): 414-20.
———. "Leriano and Lacan: The Mythological and Psychoanalytical Underpinnings of Leriano's Last Drink." *La corónica* 29:1 (2000): 113-28.
———. "Metafiction in Spanish Sentimental Romances." *The Age of the Catholic Monarchs, 1474-1516. Literary Studies in Memory of Keith Whinnom*. Ed. Alan Deyermond and Ian Macpherson. Liverpool: Liverpool UP, 1989. 57-63.
———. "The Old French Source of *Siervo libre de amor*: Guillaume de Deguilevilles's *Le Rommant des trois pèlerinages*." *Studies on the Spanish Sentimental Romance (1440-1550): Redefining a Genre*. Ed. Michael E. Gerli and Joseph J. Gwara. London: Tamesis, 1997. 3-19.
———. "*Siervo libre de amor* and the penitential tradition." *Journal of Hispanic Studies* 12 (1988): 93-102.
———. "Toward a Poetics of the Spanish Sentimental Romance." *Hispania* 72 (1989): 474-82.
———. "Toward a Revaluation of the Condestable of Portugal's *Sátira de infe-*

lice e felice vida." *Hispanic Studies in Honour of Alan D. Deyermond: A North American Tribute*. Ed. John S. Miletich. Madison, WI: Hispanic Seminary of Medieval Studies, 1986. 107-18.
Gilman, Stephen. *The Spain of Fernando de Rojas: The Intellectual and Social Landscape of* La Celestina. Princeton: Princeton UP, 1972.
Goldberg, Jonathan. *Writing Matter: From the Hands of the English Renaissance*. Stanford: Stanford UP, 1990.
Gómez Redondo, Fernando. "De la imaginación a la ficción en el *Libro de Fiameta*." *Romance Quarterly* 50 (2003): 243-57.
Granjel, Luis S. *Juan Huarte y su* Examen de Ingenios para las Ciencias. Salamanca: Real Academia de Medicina, 1988.
Green, Otis H. "El *ingenioso* hidalgo." *Hispanic Review* 25 (1957): 175-93.
Greenblatt, Stephen J. "Fiction and Friction." *Reconstructing Individualism: Autonomy, Individuality, and the Self in Western Thought*. Ed. Thomas C. Heller, Morton Sosna, and David E. Wellbery. Stanford: Stanford UP, 1986. 30-52.
———. *Renaissance Self-Fashioning from More to Shakespeare*. Chicago: U of Chicago P, 1980.
Greene, Thomas. "The Flexibility of the Self in Renaissance Literature." *The Disciplines of Criticism: Essays in Literary Theory, Interpretation, and History*. Ed. Peter Demetz, Thomas Greene and Lowry Nelson, Jr. New Haven, CT; London: Yale UP, 1968. 241-64.
Grieve, Patricia E. "Mothers and Daughters in Fifteenth-Century Spanish Sentimental Romance: Implications for *Celestina*." *Bulletin of Hispanic Studies* 67 (1990): 345-55.
———. *Desire and Death in Spanish Sentimental Romance*. Newark, DEL: Juan de la Cuesta, 1987.
Groebner, Valentin. *Der Schein der Person: Steckbrief, Ausweis und Kontrolle im Mittelalter*. München: C. H. Beck, 2004.
Grosz, Elisabeth. *Jacques Lacan: A Feminist Introduction*. New York; London: Routledge, 1990.
Gumbrecht, Hans Ulrich. "The body vs. the printing press: Media in the early modern period, mentalities in the reign of Castile, and another history of literary forms." *Sociocriticism* 1 (1985): 179-202.
———. "Garcilaso de la Vega, el Inca: Von der Geburt des Subjekts aus dem System der Bürokratie." *Gutenberg und die Neue Welt*. Ed. Friedrich Kittler, Manfred Schneider and Horst Wenzel München: Wilhelm Fink, 1994. 285-305.
———. "Lachen und Arbitrarität/Subjektivität und Ernst. Der *Libro de buen amor*, die *Celestina* und der Sinnbildungsstil der frühen Neuzeit." *Wolfram-Studien* 7 (1982): 184-213.
———. *'Eine' Geschichte der spanischen Literatur*. Frankfurt am Main: Suhrkamp, 1990.
Gwara, Joseph J. "The Identity of Juan de Flores: The Evidence of the *Crónica incompleta de los Reyes Católicos*." *Journal of Hispanic Philology* 11 (1987): 103-130 and 205-222.
———, ed. *Juan de Flores: Four Studies*. Papers of the Medieval Hispanic Research Seminar 49. London: Department of Hispanic Studies, Queen Mary, University of London, 2005.
———. "'La muger en la sardina, de rostros en la ceniza': An Old Spanish Proverb in *Grisel and Mirabella*." *Juan de Flores: Four Studies*. Ed. Joseph J. Gwara. Papers of the Medieval Hispanic Research Seminar 49. London: Department of Hispanic Studies Queen Mary, University of London, 2005. 49-73.

Hahn, Cynthia. "*Visio Dei*. Changes in Medieval Visuality." *Visuality Before and Beyond the Renaissance: Seeing as Others Saw*. Ed. Robert S. Nelson. Cambridge: Cambridge UP, 2000. 169-96.

Haidu, Peter. *The Subject Medieval/Modern: Text and Governance in the Middle Ages*. Stanford: Stanford UP, 2004.

Halka, Chester S. "*Don Quijote* in the Light of Huarte's *Examen de ingenios*: A Reexamination." *Anales Cervantinos* 19 (1981): 3-13.

Harris-Northall, Ray. *Manual of Manuscript Transcription for the Dictionary of the Old Spanish Language by David Mackenzie*. 5th ed., revised and expanded by Ray Harris-Northall. Madison, WI: Hispanic Seminary of Medieval Studies, 1997.

Harvey, Ruth E. *The Inward Wits: Psychological Theory in the Middle Ages and the Renaissance*. Warburg Institute Surveys 6. London: The Warburg Institute, University of London, 1975.

Haug, Walter. "Francesco Petrarca - Nicolaus Cusanus - Thüring von Ringoltingen. Drei Probestücke zu einer Geschichte der Individualität im 14./15. Jahrhundert." *Individualität*. Ed. Manfred Frank and Anselm Haverkamp. Poetik und Hermeneutik 13. München: Wilhelm Fink, 1988. 291-324.

Haywood, Louise M. "'La escura selva': Allegory in early sentimental romance." *Hispanic Review* 68 (2000): 415-28.

———, ed. *Cultural Contexts/ Female Voices*. Papers of the Medieval Hispanic Research Seminar 27. London: Department of Hispanic Studies, Queen Mary & Westfield College, 2000.

———. "Gradissa: A fictional female reader in/of a male author's text." *Medium Aevum* 64,1 (1995): 85-99.

Heller, Thomas C. and David E. Wellbery. Introduction. *Reconstructing Individualism: Autonomy, Individuality, and the Self in Western Thought*. By Thomas C. Heller, Morton Sosna, and David E. Wellbery, ed. Stanford: Stanford UP, 1986. 1-15.

Heller, Thomas C., Morton Sosna, and David E. Wellbery, ed. *Reconstructing Individualism: Autonomy, Individuality, and the Self in Western Thought*. Stanford: Stanford UP, 1986.

Hernández Alonso, César. Introducción. *Obras completas*. By Juan Rodríguez del Padrón. Ed. César Hernández Alonso. Madrid: Editora Nacional, 1982.

———. Siervo libre de amor *de Juan Rodríguez del Padrón*. Valladolid: Universidad de Valladolid, 1970.

Howe, Elizabeth Teresa. "A Woman Ensnared: Laureola as Victim in the *Cárcel de amor*." *Revista de Estudios Hispánicos* 21 (1987): 13-27.

Howells, Edward. "Mystical Experience and the View of the Self in Teresa of Avila and John of the Cross." *Studia Mystica* 18 (1997): 87-104.

Huarte de San Juan, Juan. *Examen de ingenios para las ciencias*. Ed. Guillermo Serés. Madrid: Cátedra, 1989.

———. *The examination of mens wits in whicch* [sic]*, by discouering the varietie of natures, is shewed for what profession each one is apt, and how far he shall profit therein*. Trans. R. C. Esquire [Richard Carew]. London: Richard Watkins, 1594. Ed. facs. Amsterdam: Theatrum Orbis Terrarum; New York: Da Capo Press, 1969.

Hugh of St. Victor. *De unione corporis et spiritus*. Ed. Jacques-Paul Migne. *Patrologia Latina* 177. Col. 285-88.

Huot, Sylvia. *From Song to Book: The Poetics of Writing in Old French Lyric and Lyrical Narrative Poetry*. Ithaca, NY; London: Cornell UP, 1987.

Husband, Timothy. *The Wild Man: Medieval Myth and Symbolism*. New York: The Metropolitan Museum of Art, 1980.

Ihrie, Maureen. "Rhetoric, didactic intent, and the *Cárcel de amor*." *Hispanófila* 30:2 (1996): 1-13.
Iriarte, M. de. *El doctor Huarte de San Juan y su* Examen de ingenios: *contribución a la historia de la psicología diferencial*. Madrid: Consejo Superior de Investigaciones Científicas, 1948.
Jacquart, Danielle and Claude Thomasset. *Sexuality and Medicine in the Middle Ages*. Cambridge: Polity Press, 1988.
Jager, Eric. "The Book of the Heart: Reading and Writing the Medieval Subject." *Speculum* 71 (1996): 1-26.
Jauß, Hans Robert. "Vom *plurale tantum* der Charaktere zum *singulare tantum* des Individuums." *Individualität*. Ed. Manfred Frank and Anselm Haverkamp. Poetik und Hermeneutik 13. München: Wilhelm Fink, 1988. 237-69.
Joset, Jacques. "Opposition et réversibilité des valeurs dans les *Proverbios morales*: approche du système de pensée de Santob de Carrión." *Hommage au Professeur Maurice Delbouille. Marche Romane*, numéro spécial (1973): 177-89.
Juan Manuel. *Libro enfinido. Cinco tratados*. Ed. Reinaldo Ayerbe-Chaux. Madison, WI: Hispanic Seminary of Medieval Studies, 1989. 115-62.
Karras, Ruth Mazo. *From Boys to Men: Formations of Masculinity in Late Medieval Europe*. Philadelphia: U of Pennsylvania P, 2003.
Kay, Sarah. *Subjectivity in Troubadour Poetry*. Cambridge, et al.: Cambridge UP, 1990.
Keßler, Eckhart. "The intellective soul." *The Cambridge History of Renaissance Philosophy*. Ed. Eckhard Keßler and Quentin Skinner. Cambridge: Cambridge UP, 1988. 485-543.
Keßler, Eckhard and Katherine Park. "The concept of psychology." *The Cambridge History of Renaissance Philosophy*. Ed. Eckhard Keßler and Quentin Skinner. Cambridge: Cambridge UP, 1988. 455-63.
Kittler, Friedrich. "Das Subjekt als Beamter." *Die Frage nach dem Subjekt*. Ed. Manfred Frank, Gérard Raulet and Willem Van Reijen. Frankfurt am Main: Suhrkamp, 1988. 401-20.
Knoespel, Kenneth J. *Narcissus and the Invention of Personal History*. New York; London: Garland, 1985.
Kobusch, Theo. "Person und Subjektivität: Die Metaphysik der Freiheit und der moderne Subjektivitätsgedanke." *Geschichte und Vorgeschichte der Subjektivität*. Vol. 2. Ed. Reto Luzius Fetz, Roland Hagenbüchle and Peter Schulz. European Cultures Studies in Literature and the Arts 11:2. Berlin, New York: 1998. 743-61.
Kolve, V. A. *Chaucer and the Imagery of Narrative: The First Five* Canterbury Tales. London: E. Arnold, 1984.
Kramer, Heinrich and Jacob Sprenger. *Mallevs maleficarvm, maleficas et earvm hæresim frameam conterens, ex variis avctoribvs compilatus*. Vol. 1. Lyon: Claude Bourgeat, 1669. Ed. facs. Bruxelles: Culture et Civilisation, 1969.
Krause, Anna. "El tractado novelístico de Diego de San Pedro." *Bulletin Hispanique* 54 (1952): 245-75.
Küpper, Joachim. *Diskurs-Renovatio bei Lope de Vega und Calderón: Untersuchungen zum spanischen Barockdrama; mit einer Skizze zur Evolution der Diskurse in Mittelalter, Rennaissance und Manierismus*. Romanica Monacensia 32. Tübingen: Narr, 1990.
———. "(H)er(e)os: Petrarcas *Canzoniere* und der medizinische Diskurs seiner Zeit." *Romanische Forschungen* (111) 1999: 178-224.
Lacan, Jacques. *Encore. Das Seminar von Jacques Lacan Buch XX (1972-1973)*. Text Jacques-Alain Miller. Trans. Norbert Haas, Vreni Haas and Hans-Joachim Metzger. Weinheim; Berlin: Quadriga, 1986.

Lacan, Jacques. *Die Ethik der Psychoanalyse. Das Seminar von Jacques Lacan Buch VII (1959-1960)*. Ed. Jacques-Alain Miller. Trans. Norbert Haas. Weinheim; Berlin: Quadriga, 1996.
———. *The Four Fundamental Principles of Psychoanalysis*. Trans. Alan Sheridan. The Seminar of Jacques Lacan. Ed. Jacques-Alain Miller. New York; London: W. W. Norton & Company, 1998.
———. "God and the Jouissance of Woman." *Feminine Sexuality: Jacques Lacan and the école freudienne*. Ed. Juliet Mitchell and Jacqueline Rose. Trans. Jacqueline Rose. New York; London: W. W. Norton & Company; New York: Pantheon Books, 1982. 138-48.
———. "The Instance of the Letter in the Unconscious." *Écrits: The First Complete Edition in English*. Trans. Bruce Fink. New York; London: W.W. Norton & Company, 2005. 412-41.
———. "The Meaning of the Phallus." *Feminine Sexuality: Jacques Lacan and the école freudienne*. Ed. Juliet Mitchell and Jacqueline Rose. Trans. Jacqueline Rose. New York; London: W.W. Norton; New York: Pantheon Books, 1982. 74-136.
———. "The Mirror Stage as Formative of the *I* Function as Revealed in Psychoanalytic Experience." *Écrits: The First Complete Edition in English*. Trans. Bruce Fink. New York; London: W.W. Norton & Company, 2005. 75-81.
———. "Some Reflections on the Ego." *International Journal of Psychoanalysis* 34 (1953): 11-17.
Lacarra Lanz, Eukene: "Los discursos científico y amoroso en la *Sátira de felice e infelice vida* del Condestable D. Pedro de Portugal." *'Never-Ending Adventure': Studies in Medieval and Early Modern Spanish Literature in Honor of Peter N. Dunn*. Ed. Edward H. Friedman and Harlan Sturm. Newark, DEL: Juan de la Cuesta, 2002. 109-28.
———. "*Siervo libre de amor*, ¿Autobiografía espiritual?" *La corónica* 29 (2000): 147-70.
Laqueur, Thomas. *Making Sex: Body and Gender from the Greeks to Freud*. Cambridge, MA: Harvard UP, 1990.
Lazarillo de Tormes. Ed. Francisco Rico. Madrid: Cátedra, 1987.
Lázaro Carreter, Fernando. Lazarillo de Tormes *en la picaresca*. Barcelona: Ariel, 1972.
Leaños, Jaime. *Piccolomini en Iberia: Influencias italianas en el génesis de la literatura sentimental española*. Scripta Humanistica 159. Potomac, MD: Scripta Humanistica, 2007.
Lida de Malkiel, María Rosa."Juan Rodríguez del Padrón: vida y obras." *Nueva Revista de Filología Hispánica* 6 (1952): 313-51.
Logan, Richard D. "A conception of the self in the later middle ages." *Journal of Medieval History* 12 (1986): 253-68.
Low, Anthony. *Aspects of Subjectivity: Society and Individuality from the Middle Ages to Shakespeare and Milton*. Pittsburgh: Duquesne UP, 2003.
Luhmann, Niklas. "The Individuality of the Individual: Historical Meanings and Contemporary Problems." *Reconstructing Individualism: Autonomy, Individuality, and the Self in Western Thought*. Thomas C. Heller, Morton Sosna, and David E. Wellbery. Stanford: Stanford UP, 1986. 313-25.
MacLeod, Murdo J. "Self-Promotion: The *Relaciones de Méritos y Servicios* and Their Historical and Political Interpretation." *Colonial Latin American Historical Review* 76,1 (1998): 25-42.
Mandrell, James. "Author and Authority in *Cárcel de amor*." *Journal of Hispanic Philology* 8 (1984): 99-122.
Mansfield, Nick. *Subjectivity: Theories of the Self from Freud to Haraway*. New York: New York UP, 2000.

Manzano Manzano, Juan. "El proceso recopilador de las leyes de Indias hasta 1681." *Recopilación de las leyes de los Reynos de las Indias.* 1681. Ed. facs. Madrid: Ediciones Cultura Hispánica, 1973.

Manzoni, T. "The cerebral ventricles, the animal spirits, and the dawn of brain localization of function." *Archives Italiennes de Biologie* 136 (1998): 103-52.

Maravall, José Antonio. "Los 'hombres de saber' o letrados y la formación de su conciencia estamental." *Estudios de historia del pensamiento español.* Vol. 1: Edad Media. 2ª ed. ampliada. Madrid: Cultura Hispánica, 1973. 355-89.

Marino, Nancy. "The *Cancionero de Valencia, Questión de Amor,* and the Last Medieval Courts of Love." *Cultural Contexts/ Female Voices.* Ed. Louise Haywood. Papers of the Medieval Hispanic Research Seminar 27. London: Department of Hispanic Studies, Queen Mary & Westfield College, 2000. 41-49.

Mariscal, George. *Contradictory Subjects: Quevedo, Cervantes, and Seventeenth Century Spanish Culture.* Ithaca, NY: Cornell UP, 1991.

Márquez Villanueva, Francisco. "*Cárcel de amor,* novela política." *Revista de Occidente* 14 (1966): 185-200.

Martin, John Jeffries. *Myths of Renaissance Individualism.* New York: Palgrave-Macmillan, 2004.

Martínez Barbeito, Carlos. *Macías el enamorado y Juan Rodríguez del Padrón: Estudio y antología.* Biblioteca de Galicia 4. Santiago de Compostela: Sociedad de Bibliófilos Gallegos, 1951.

Martínez-San Miguel, Yolanda. "Engendrando el sujeto femenino del saber o las estrategias para la construcción de una conciencia epistemológica colonial en Sor Juana." *Revista de Crítica Literaria Latinoamericana* 20 (1994): 259-80.

Martino, Alberto. *Lazarillo de Tormes e la sua ricezione in Europa (1554-1753).* 2 vol. Pisa; Roma: Istituti Editoriali e Poligrafici Internazionali, 1999.

Matulka, Barbara. *The Novels of Juan de Flores and their European Diffusion: A Study in Comparative Literature.* Comparative Literature Series. New York: The French Institute, 1931.

Matzat, Wolfgang. "Frühneuzeitliche Subjektivität und das literarische Imaginäre: Vom Schäferroman zum Don Quijote." *Welterfahrung - Selbsterfahrung: Konstitution und Verhandlung von Subjektivität in der spanischen Literatur der frühen Neuzeit.* Ed. Wolfgang Matzat and Bernhard Teuber. Tübingen: Max Niemeyer, 2000. 345-61.

Matzat, Wolfgang and Bernhard Teuber, ed. *Welterfahrung - Selbsterfahrung: Konstitution und Verhandlung von Subjektivität in der spanischen Literatur der frühen Neuzeit.* Tübingen: Max Niemeyer, 2000.

Mazur, Oleh. *The Wild Man in the Spanish Renaissance & Golden Age Theater: A Comparative Study Including the* Indio, *the* Bárbaro *and Their Counterparts in European Lores.* Diss. University of Pennsylvania, 1966. Ann Arbor, MI: University Microfilms International for Villanova University, 1980.

McKnight, Kathryn. *The Mystic of Tunja: The Writings of Madre Castillo (1671-1742).* Amherst: U of Massachusetts P, 1997.

Menéndez Pelayo, Marcelino. *Orígenes de la novela.* Vol. II: *Novelas sentimental, bizantina, histórica y pastoril.* Edición Nacional de las obras completas de Menéndez Pelayo 3. Ed. Enrique Sánchez Reyes. 2ª ed. Madrid: Consejo Superior de Investigaciones Científicas, 1961.

Miguel-Prendes, Sol. "Las cartas de la *Cárcel de amor.*" *Hispanófila* 34 (1991): 1-22.

———. "Reimagining Diego de San Pedro's Readers at Work: *Cárcel de amor.*" *La corónica* 32:2 (2004): 7-44.

Minervini, Vicenzo. "*Càrcer d'amor*: La traduzione catalana." *Càrcer d'amor/*

Carcer d'amore: Due tradizioni della 'novela' di Diego de San Pedro. By Diego de San Pedro. Ed. María Luisa Indini and Vicenzo Minervini. Fasano: Schena, 1986. 19-31.

Miñana, Rogelio. "Auctor omnisciente, auctor testigo: el marco narrativo en *Cárcel de amor.*" *La corónica* 30:1 (2001): 133-48.

Miquel y Planas, R. Noticia preliminar. *Lo carcer d'amor: Novela del XVen segle composta per Diego de San Pedro y traduhida al catalá per Bernardí Vallmanya.* By Diego de San Pedro. Ed. R. Miquel y Planas. 2ª ed. Barcelona: Johan Oliva, 1912.

Montanos Ferrín, Emma. *España en la configuración histórico-jurídica de Europa.* Vol. 2: La época nueva: siglos XII al XV. Roma: Il Cigno Galileo Galilei, 1999.

Montaña de Monserrate, Bernardino. *Libro de la Anothomia del hombre.* [Valladolid: Sebastián Martínez Añode] 1551. Ed facs. Valencia: Librerias París-Valencia, 1998 [the text was also edited as: *Libro de la Anathomia del hombre*: Madrid BN R-3398. 1551. Ed. Mirta Alejandra Balestra and Patricia Gubitosi. Textos y Concordancias Electrónicas del *Corpus Médico Español.* Ed. (CD-Rom) Mª Teresa Herrera and Mª Estela González de Fauve. Madison, WI: Hispanic Seminary of Medieval Studies, 1997].

Moos, Peter von. "Das mittelalterliche Kleid als Identitätssymbol und Identifikationsmittel." *Unverwechselbarkeit: Persönliche Identität und Identifikation in der vormodernen Gesellschaft.* Ed. Peter von Moos. Norm und Struktur: Studien zum sozialen Wandel in Mittelalter und Früher Neuzeit 23. Köln, Weimar, Wien: Böhlau, 2004. 123-46.

———. "Persönliche Identität und Identifikation vor der Moderne: Zum Wechselspiel von sozialer Zuschreibung und Selbstbeschreibung." *Unverwechselbarkeit: Persönliche Identität und Identifikation in der vormodernen Gesellschaft.* Ed. Peter von Moos. Norm und Struktur: Studien zum sozialen Wandel in Mittelalter und Früher Neuzeit 23. Köln, Weimar, Wien: Böhlau, 2004. 1-42.

———, ed. *Unverwechselbarkeit: Persönliche Identität und Identifikation in der vormodernen Gesellschaft.* Norm und Struktur: Studien zum sozialen Wandel in Mittelalter und Früher Neuzeit 23. Köln, Weimar, Wien: Böhlau, 2004.

Morros Mestres, Bienvenido. *Otra lectura del* Quijote: *Don Quijote y el elogio de la castidad.* Madrid: Cátedra, 2005.

Mowitt, John. Foreword. *Discerning the Subject.* By Paul Smith. Theory and History of Literature 55. Minneapolis: U of Minnesota P, 1988.

Myles, Robert. *Chaucerian Realism.* Chaucer Studies 20. Woodbridge, Suffolk: D.S. Brewer, 1994.

Nelson, Robert S. "Descartes's cow and other domestications of the visual." *Visuality Before and Beyond the Renaissance: Seeing as Others Saw.* Ed. Robert S. Nelson. Cambridge: Cambridge UP, 2000. 1-21.

Nepaulsingh, Colbert I. *Towards a History of Literary Composition in Medieval Spain.* University of Toronto Romance Series 54. Toronto: U of Toronto P, 1986.

Nieto Soria, José Manuel, ed. *Orígenes de la monarquía española: propaganda y legitimación (ca. 1400-1520).* Madrid: Dykinson, 1999.

Núñez, Nicolás. See San Pedro, Diego de.

Orth, Myra Dickman. "*The Prison of Love*: A Medieval Romance in the French Renaissance and its Illustration (B.N. MS fr. 2150)." *Journal of the Warburg and Courtauld Institutes* 46 (1983): 211-21.

Pabst, Walter. "Die Selbstbestrafung auf dem Stein." *Der Vergleich: Literatur- und spachwissenschaftliche Interpretationen. Festgabe für Hellmuth Petriconi zum 1. April 1955.* Ed. Rudolf Grossmann, Walter Pabst and Edmund Schramm. Hamburg: Cram; De Gruyter, 1955. 33-49.

Parrilla, Carmen. "'Acrescentar lo que de suyo está crescido': el cumplimiento de Nicolás Núñez." *Historias y ficciones: coloquio sobre la literatura del siglo XV.* Ed. Rafael Beltrán, José Luis Canet, José Luis Sirera. València: Departament de Filologia Espanyola, Universitat de València, 1992. 241-53.

———. "Un cronista olvidado: Juan de Flores, autor de la *Crónica incompleta de los Reyes Católicos.*" *The Age of the Catholic Monarchs, 1474-1516: Literary Studies in Memory of Keith Whinnom.* Ed. Alan Deyermond and Ian Macpherson. Liverpool: Liverpool UP, 1989. 123-33.

———. "La ficción sentimental y sus lectores." *Ínsula* 675 (2003): 21-24.

———. Introducción. *Grimalte y Gradisa.* By Juan de Flores. Ed. Carmen Parrilla García. Santiago de Compostela: Universidade de Santiago de Compostela, Servicio de Publicacións e Intercambio Científico, 1988.

———. Prólogo. *Cárcel de amor, con la continuación de Nicolás Núñez.* By Diego de San Pedro and Nicolás Núñez. Ed. Carmen Parrilla. Barcelona: Crítica, 1995.

Parry, John H. *The Audiencia of New Galicia in the Sixteenth Century: A Study in Spanish Colonial Government.* 1948. Repr. Cambridge: Cambridge UP, 1968.

Patterson, Lee. *Chaucer and the Subject of History.* Madison, WI: U of Wisconsin P, 1991.

———. "Making Identities in Fifteenth-Century England: Henry V and John Lydgate." *New Historical Literary Study: Essays on Reproducing Texts, Representing History.* Ed. Jeffrey N. Cox and Larry J. Reynolds. Princeton, NJ: Princeton UP, 1993. 68-107.

———. "On the Margin: Postmodernism, Ironic History, and Medieval Studies." *Speculum* 65 (1990): 87-108.

Payne, Michael. *Reading Knowledge: An Introduction to Barthes, Foucault, and Althusser.* Oxford: Blackwell Publishers, 1997.

Pedro, Constable of Portugal. *Sátira de infelice e felice vida. Obras completas do condestável dom Pedro.* Ed. Luis Adão Fonseca. Lisboa: Fundação Calouste Gulbenkian, 1975. 1-175.

Penzkofer, Gerhard. "Innovation und Introspektion in *Cárcel de Amor* von Diego de San Pedro." *Welterfahrung – Selbsterfahrung: Konstitution und Verhandlung von Subjektivität in der spanischen Literatur der frühen Neuzeit.* Ed. Wolfgang Matzat and Bernhard Teuber. Tübingen: Max Niemeyer, 2000. 246-65.

Pérez Priego, Miguel Ángel. "Espectáculos y textos teatrales en Castilla a fines de la Edad Media." *Epos* 5 (1989): 141-63.

Pérouse, Gabriel-André. "Les femmes et l'*Examen des Esprits* du Dr Huarte (1575)." *Les représentations de l'Autre du Moyen Âge au XVIIe siècle: Mélanges en l'honneur de Kazimierz Kupisz.* Saint-Étienne: Publications de l'Université de Saint-Étienne, 1995. 273-83.

Phelan, John Leddy. "Authority and Flexibility in the Spanish Imperial Bureaucracy." *Administrative Science Quarterly* 5 (1960): 47-65.

Phillips, William D. "The University Graduates in Castilian Royal Service in the Fifteenth Century." *Estudios en homenaje a Don Claudio Sánchez de Albornoz en sus 90 años.* Vol. 4. Buenos Aires: Ministerio de Educación y Justicia; Universidad de Buenos Aires, Facultad de Filosofía y Letras, 1986. 475-90.

Pico della Mirandola. *Oratio de dignitate hominis.* [Ed. Giovan Francesco Pico. Bologna: Benedetto Faelli, 1496]. Transcription, notes, trans. and ed. facs. Brown University and Università di Bologna. 23 Jun. 2008. <http://www.brown.edu/Departments/Italian_Studies/pico/>.

Pietschmann, Horst. *Die staatliche Organisation des kolonialen Iberoamerika.* Stuttgart: Klett-Cotta, 1980.

Poppenberg, Gerhard. "*Antiperistasis*: Zur Dynamik der Subjektkonstitution in der spanischen Spiritualität des Siglo de Oro." *Welterfahrung - Selbsterfahrung: Konstitution und Verhandlung von Subjektivität in der spanischen Literatur der frühen Neuzeit.* Ed. Wolfgang Matzat and Bernhard Teuber. Tübingen: Max Niemeyer, 2000. 151-77.

Porter, Roy. Introduction. *Rewriting the Self: Histories from the Renaissance to the Present.* Ed. Roy Porter. London; New York: Routledge, 1999. 1-14.

Pott, Hans-Georg. "Das 'Subjekt' bei Niklas Luhmann." *Von Rousseau zum Hypertext: Subjektivität in Theorie und Literatur der Moderne.* Ed. Paul Geyer and Claudia Jünke. Würzburg: Königshausen & Neumann, 2001. 65-75.

Quintiliana Raso, María Concepción. "La nobleza." *Orígenes de la monarquía española: Propaganda y legitimación (ca. 1400-1520).* Ed. José Manuel Nieto Soria. Madrid: Dykinson, 1999. 63-103.

Rabaté, Jean-Michel, ed. *The Cambridge Companion to Lacan.* Cambridge: Cambridge UP, 2003.

Read, Malcolm. *Juan Huarte de San Juan.* Twayne's World Authors Series 619. Boston: Twayne, 1981.

Real Academia Española. *Diccionario de Autoridades.* 1726-1737. Ed. facs. 3 vol. Biblioteca Románica Hispánica V, Diccionarios 3. Madrid: Gredos, 1990.

Recopilación de las leyes de los Reynos de las Indias. 1681. Ed. facs. Estudio preliminar Juan Manzano Manzano. Madrid: Ediciones Cultura Hispánica, 1973.

Reisch, Gregor. *Margarita philosophica.* Freiburg im Breisgau: Schott, 1503.

———. *Margarita philosophica nova.* Basel: Furter, 1517.

Rey, Alfonso. "La primera persona narrativa en Diego de San Pedro." *Bulletin of Hispanic Studies* 58 (1981): 95-102.

Richthofen, Erich von. "Petrarca, Dante y Andreas Capellanus: Fuentes inadvertidas de *La Cárcel de Amor.*" *Revista Canadiense de Estudios Hispánicos* 1 (1976): 30-38.

Rivera-Cordero, Victoria. "Enfermedad, creación poética y autoconciencia en *Siervo libre de amor.*" *La corónica* 35:2 (2007): 273-89.

Rocca, Julius. *Galen on the Brain: Anatomical Knowledge and Physiological Speculation in the Second Century AD.* Studies in Ancient Medicine 26. Leiden; Boston: Brill, 2003.

Rodríguez del Padrón, Juan. *Siervo libre de amor.* Ed. Enric Dolz. *Anexos de la Revista Lemir* (2004). 2 Aug. 2007. <http://parnaseo.uv.es/Lemir/Textos/Siervo/Index.htm>.

Roffé, Mercedes. *La cuestión del género en Grisel y Mirabella de Juan de Flores.* Newark, DEL: Juan de la Cuesta, 1996.

———. "*Grisel y Mirabella*: a la luz del debate medieval." *Cincinnati Romance Review* 14 (1995): 8-15.

Rogers, Robert. *A Psychoanalytic Study of the Double in Literature.* Detroit: Wayne State University P, 1970.

Rohland de Langbehn, Regula. "El problema de los conversos y la novela sentimental." *The Age of the Catholic Monarchs, 1474-1516: Literary Studies in Memory of Keith Whinnom.* Ed. Alan D. Deyermond and Ian Macpherson. Liverpool: Liverpool UP, 1989. 134-43.

———. "Una lanza por el género sentimental ... ¿ficción o novela?" *La corónica* 31:1 (2002): 137-41.

———. [here as Langbehn-Rohland, Regula]. *Zur Interpretation der Romane des Diego de San Pedro.* Studia Romanica 18. Heidelberg: C. Winter, 1970.

Roubaud, Sylvia. "Le 'yo' – auteur et personnage – du roman sentimental: quelques exemples." *Écrire sur soi en Espagne: Modèles & Écarts (Actes du*

IIIe Colloque International d'Aix-en-Provence (4-5-6 décembre 1986)). Aix-en-Provence: Université de Provence, 1988. 25-43.
Roudinesco, Elisabeth. "The mirror stage: an obliterated archive." *The Cambridge Companion to Lacan*. Ed. Jean-Michel Rabaté. Cambridge: Cambridge UP, 2003. 25-34.
Rouse, Joseph. "Power/Knowledge." *The Cambridge Companion to Foucault*. Ed. Gary Gutting. Cambridge: Cambridge UP, 1994. 92-114.
Rowland of Anglesey, David, trans. *The Pleasaunt Historie of Lazarillo Tormes a Spaniarde, wherin is conteined his marvelous deedes and life. With the strange aduentures happened to him in the seruice of sundrie Masters*. London: Abell Ieffes, 1586.
Rubin, Miri. "The Eucharist and the Construction of Medieval Identities." *Culture and History 1350-1600: Essays on English Communities, Identities, and Writing*. Ed. David Aers. Detroit: Wayne State UP, 1992. 43-63.
Ruiz García, Elisa. "El poder de la escritura y la escritura del poder." *Orígenes de la monarquía española: propaganda y legitimación (ca. 1400-1520)*. Ed. José Manuel Nieto Soria. Madrid: Dykinson, 1999. 275-313.
Sabean, David Warren. "The Production of the Self during the Age of Confessionalism." *Central European History* 29 (1996): 1-18.
Saenger, Paul. *Space Between Words: The Origins of Silent Reading*. Stanford: U of Stanford P, 1997.
Salillas, Rafael. *Un gran inspirador de Cervantes: El doctor Juan Huarte y su Examen de ingenios*. Madrid: Eduardo Arias, 1905.
Salvador Miguel, Nicasio. "La tradición animalística en las *Coplas de las calidades de las donas*." *El Crotalón* 2 (1985): 217-220.
San Pedro, Diego de. *Lo carcer d'amor*. Trans. Bernardi Vallmanya. 1493 [Barcelona: Johan Rosenbach]. Ed. facs. Barcelona: Societat Catalana de Bibliófils, 1906.

———. *Lo carcer d'amor*. Ed. facs. Lambert Mata. Histories d'altre temps III. Vilanova; La Beltrú: Johan Oliva, 1906.

———. *Lo carcer d'amor: Novela del XVen segle composta per Diego de San Pedro y traduhida al català per Bernardí Vallmanya*. Ed. R. Miquel y Planas. Histories d'altre temps III. Barcelona: Fidel Girò, 1907.

———. *Lo carcer d'amor: Novela del XVen segle composta per Diego de San Pedro y traduhida al català per Bernardí Vallmanya*. Ed. R. Miquel y Planas. Histories d'altre temps III. 2ª ed. Barcelona: Fidel Girò, 1912.

———. "El mayor bien de quereros." *Cancionero general, recopilado por Hernando del Castillo (Valencia, 1511)*. Ed. facs. Antonio Rodríguez Moñino. Madrid: Real Academia Española, 1958. fol. 124ᵛ.
San Pedro, Diego de and Nicolás Núñez. *Cárcel de amor, con la continuación de Nicolás Núñez*. Ed. Carmen Parrilla. Barcelona: Crítica, 1995.

———. *Prison of Love (1492) together with the continuation by Nicolás Núñez (1496)*. Ed. and trans. Keith Whinnom. Edinburgh: Edinburgh UP, 1979.
Sarfatti, Magali. *Spanish Bureaucratic Patrimonialism in America*. Berkeley: Institute of International Studies, 1966.
Sawday, Jonathan. "Self and Selfhood in the Seventeenth Century." *Rewriting the Self: Histories from the Renaissance to the Present*. Ed. Roy Porter. London; New York: Routledge, 1999. 29-48.
Schäfer, Ernesto [Ernst]. *El consejo real y supremo de las Indias: Su historia, organización y labor administrativa hasta la terminación de la Casa de Austrias*. Vol. 1: Historia y organización del Consejo y de la Casa de Contratación de las Indias. 1935. Reprint: Nendeln (Liechtenstein): Kraus, 1975.
Scharmacher, Benjamin. *Wie die Menschen Subjekte werden: Einführung in Althussers Theorie der Anrufung*. Marburg: Tectum, 2004.

Schneider, Ulrich Johannes. *Die Vergangenheit des Geistes: Eine Archäologie der Philosophiegeschichte.* Frankfurt am Main: Suhrkamp, 1990.
Schnell, Rüdiger. Causa amoris: *Liebeskonzeption und Liebesdarstellung in der mittelalterlichen Literatur.* Bibliotheca Germanica 27. Bern: Francke, 1985.
Sears, Theresa Ann. "Prisoners of Love: Love, Destiny, and Narrative Control in *Le Chevalier de la Charette* and *Cárcel de amor.*" *Fifteenth-Century Studies* 15 (1989): 269-82.
Serés, Guillermo. "Ficción sentimental y humanismo: La *Sátira* de don Pedro de Portugal." *Bulletin Hispanique* 93:1 (1991): 31-60.
———. Introducción. *Examen de ingenios para las ciencias.* By Juan Huarte de San Juan. Ed. Guillermo Serés. Madrid: Cátedra, 1989.
———. *La transformación de los amantes: Imágenes del amor de la Antigüedad al Siglo de Oro.* Barcelona: Crítica, 1996.
Serres, Michel. *The Parasite.* Trans. Lawrence R. Schehr. Baltimore: Johns Hopkins UP, 1982.
Severin, Dorothy Sherman. "Audience and Interpretation: Gradisa the Cruel and Fiometa the Rejected in Juan de Flores's *prosimetrum Grimalte y Gradisa.*" *Cultural Contexts/ Female Voices.* Ed. Louise Haywood. London: Department of Hispanic Studies, Queen Mary & Westfield College, 2000. 63-71.
———. "Diego de San Pedro from Manuscript to Print: The Curious Case of *La pasión trobada, Las siete angustias,* and *Arnalte y Lucenda.*" *La corónica* 29:1 (2000): 187-91.
———. *Del manuscrito a la imprenta en la época de Isabel la Católica.* Estudios de Literatura 86. Kassel: Reichenberger, 2004.
———. *Religious Parody and the Spanish Sentimental Romance.* Newark, DEL: Juan de La Cuesta, 2005.
Sharrer, Harvey L. "La *Cárcel de amor* de Diego de San Pedro: La confluencia de lo sagrado y lo profano en 'la imagen femenil entallada en una piedra muy clara'." *Actas del III Congreso de la Asociación Hispánica de Literatura Medieval.* Ed. María Isabel Toro Pascua. Tom. 2. Salamanca: Biblioteca Española del Siglo XV, Departamento de Literatura Española e Hispanoamericana, 1994. 983-96.
Siegert, Bernhard. "*Pasajeros a Indias*: Biographical Writing between the Old World and the New." *Talleres de la memoria – reivindicaciones y autoridad en la historiografía indiana de los siglos XVI y XVII.* Ed. Robert Folger y Wulf Oesterreicher. P & A 5. Münster: LITVerlag, 2005. 295-306.
Smith, Paul. *Discerning the Subject.* Foreword by John Mowitt. Theory and History of Literature 55. Minneapolis: U of Minnesota P, 1988.
Smith, Paul Julian. *Writing in the Margin: Spanish Literature of the Golden Age.* Oxford: Clarendon P, 1988.
Smith, Roger. "Self-Reflection and the Self." *Rewriting the Self: Histories from the Renaissance to the Present.* Ed. Roy Porter. London; New York: Routledge, 1999. 49-57.
Smith Ramos, Maya (ed.). *Censura y teatro novohispano (1539-1822). Ensayos y antología de documentos.* México, DF: Consejo Nacional para la Cultura y las Artes-Instituto Nacional de Bellas Artes-Centro Nacional de Investigación e Información Teatral Rodolfo Usigli, 1998.
Soufas, Teresa Scott. *Melancholy and the Secular Mind in Spanish Golden Age Literature.* Columbia, MI: U of Missouri P, 1990.
Spadaccini, Nicolas and Jenaro Talens. "The Construction of the Self: Notes on Autobiography in Early Modern Spain." *Autobiography in Early Modern Spain.* Ed. Nicholas Spadaccini and Jenaro Talens. Hispanic Issues. Minneapolis: The Prisma Institute, 1988. 9-40.

Starn, Randolph. "Seeing Culture in a Room for a Renaissance Prince." *The New Cultural History*. Ed. Lynn Hunt. Berkeley: U of California P, 1989. 205-32.
Stierle, Karlheinz. *Francesco Petrarca: Ein Intellektueller im Europa des 14. Jahrhunderts.* München: Carl Hanser, 2003.
Stock, Brian. "Reading, Writing, and the Self: Petrarch and His Forerunners." *New Literary History* 26 (1995): 717-30.
Stroud, Matthew D. "The Desiring Subject and the Promise of Salvation: A Lacanian Study of Sor Juana's *El divino Narciso.*" *Hispania* 76,2 (1993): 204-12.
Sturges, Robert S. *The Critical Reception of Machaut's* Voir-Dit *and the History of Literary History.*" *French Forum* 17:2 (1992): 133-51.
Summers, David. *The Judgement of Sense: Renaissance Naturalism and the Rise of Aesthetics*. Cambridge: Cambridge UP, 1987.
Suntrup, Rudolf and Jan R. Veenstra, ed. *Self-Fashioning/Personendarstellung*. Frankfurt am Main et al.: Peter Lang, 2002.
Surtz, Ronald E. *Writing Women in Late Medieval and Early Modern Spain: The Mothers of Saint Teresa of Avila*. Philadelphia: U of Pennsylvania P, 1995.
Talens, Jenaro. *La escritura como teatralidad: acerca de Juan Ruiz, Santillana, Cervantes y el marco narrativo en la novela corta castellana del siglo XVII.* Valencia: Universidad de Valencia, 1977.
Tallis, Frank. *Love Sick: Love as a Mental Illness*. New York: Thunder Mouth's Press, 2005.
Tarp, Helen Cathleen. "Legal Fictions: Literature and Law in *Grisel y Mirabella.*" *eHumanista* 7 (2006): 95-114. 23 Jun. 2008 <http://www.ehumanista.ucsb.edu/volumes/volume_07/Articles/7%20Tarp.pdf>.
Taylor, Charles. *Sources of the Self: The Making of the Modern Identity*. Cambridge: Harvard UP, 1989.
Teuber, Bernhard. "*Per speculum in aenigmate*: Medialität und Anthropologie des Spiegels vom Mittelalter zur frühen Neuzeit." *Vom Flugblatt zum Feuilleton: Mediengebrauch und ästhetische Anthropologie in historischer Perspektive*. Ed. Bernhard Teuber and Wolfram Nitsch. Tübingen: Narr, 2002. 13-33.
———. "*Vivir quiero conmigo*: Verhandlungen mit sich und dem anderen in der ethopoetischen Lyrik des Fray Luis de León und des Francisco Aldana." *Welterfahrung – Selbsterfahrung: Konstitution und Verhandlung von Subjektivität in der spanischen Literatur der frühen Neuzeit*. Ed. Wolfgang Matzat and Bernhard Teuber. Tübingen: Max Niemeyer, 2000. 179-206.
Thiemann, Susanne. "*Sex trouble*: Die bärtige Frau bei José de Ribera, Luis Vélez de Guevara und Huarte de San Juan." *Geschlechtervariationen: Gender-Konzepte im Übergang zur Neuzeit*. Ed. Judith Klinger and Susanne Thiemann. Potsdamer Studien zur Frauen- and Geschlechterforschung, Neue Folge 1. Potsdam: Universitätsverlag Potsdam, 2006. 48-82.
Thomas Aquinas. *In Aristotelis libros De sensu et sensato, De memoria et reminiscentia commentarium*. Ed. Raymund M. Spiazzi. Roma: Marietti, 1949.
———. *Commento al* Corpus Paulinum *(Expositio et lectura super epistolas Pauli Apostoli.* Vol. 2: Prima lettera ai Corinzi. Trans. Battista Mondin. Bologna: Edizioni Studio Domenicano, 2005.
———. *On the First Epistle to the Corinthians*. Trans. Fabian Larcher, O. P. (paragraphs 987-1046 trans. by Daniel Keating). Ed. Aquinas Center for Theological Renewal. 12 Jul. 2007 <http://www.aquinas.avemaria.edu/Aquinas-Corinthians.pdf>.
———. *A Commentary on Aristotle's* De anima. [*Sentencia libri De anima*]. Trans. Robert Pasnau. Yale Library of Medieval Philosophy. New Haven, CT: Yale UP, 1999.
Torrellas, Pedro. "Coplas fechas por mosén PEDRO TORRELLAS de las calidades

de las donas." *Cancionero de Estúñiga*. Ed. Nicasio Salvador Miguel. Colección clásicos 33. Madrid: Alhambra, 1987. 647-56 [n. CLXI].
Valente, Joe. "Lacan's Marxism and Marxism's Lacan." *The Cambridge Companion to Lacan*. Ed. Jean-Michel Rabaté. Cambridge: Cambridge UP, 2003. 153-72.
Valvassori, Mita. "La *Estoria muy verdadera de dos amantes* y el *Libro de Fiameta*." *Revista de poética medieval* 16 (2006): 179-200.
Veenstra, Jan R. "Self-Fashioning and Pragmatic Introspection: Reconsidering the Soul in the Renaissance (Some Remarks on Pico, Pomponazzi and Macchiavelli)." *Self-Fashioning/Personendarstellung*. Ed. Rudolf Suntrup and Jan R. Veenstra. Frankfurt am Main et al.: Peter Lang, 2002. 285-308.
Vitz, Evelyn Birge. "Inside/Outside: Guillaume's Roman de la Rose and Medieval Selfhood." *Medieval Narrative and Modern Narratology: Subjects and Objects of Desire*. New York: New York UP, 1989. 64-95.
Vollendorf, Lisa. *Reclaiming the Body: María de Zayas's Early Modern Feminism*. North Carolina Studies in the Romance Languages and Literatures 270. Chapel Hill: U of North Carolina P, 2001.
Wack, Mary Frances. *Lovesickness in the Middle Ages: The* Viaticum *and its Commentaries*. Philadelphia: U of Pennsylvania P, 1990.
Walde Moheno, Lillian von der. *Amor e ilegalidad:* Grisel e Mirabella *de Juan de Flores*. Mexico: Universidad Nacional Autónoma de México, El Colegio de México, 1996.
———. "El episodio final de *Grisel y Mirabella*." *La corónica* 20:2 (1992): 18-31.
———. "La experimentación literaria del siglo XV: a propósito de *Grimalte y Gradisa*." *Juan de Flores: Four Studies*. Ed. Joseph J. Gwara. Papers of the Medieval Hispanic Research Seminar 49. London: Department of Hispanic Studies Queen Mary, University of London, 2005. 75-89.
Waley, Pamela. "*Cárcel de amor* and *Grisel y Mirabella*: A Question of Priority." *Bulletin of Hispanic Studies* 50 (1973): 340-56.
———. Introduction. *Grimalte y Gradissa*. By Juan de Flores. Ed. Pamela Waley. London: Tamesis, 1971.
Walthaus, Rina. "Espacio y alienación en *Grimalte y Gradissa* de Juan de Flores." *Scriptura* (Lleida) 13 (1997): 5-18.
Wardropper, Bruce W. "Allegory and the role of *El Autor* in the *Cárcel de amor*." *Philological Quarterly* 31 (1952): 39-44.
———. "El mundo sentimental de la *Cárcel de amor*." *Revista de Filología Española* 37 (1953): 168-93.
Weinrich, Harald. *Das Ingenium Don Quijotes. Ein Beitrag zur literarischen Charakterkunde*. Forschungen zur Romanischen Philologie 1. Münster: Aschendorf, 1956.
Weiss, Julian. "Álvaro de Luna, Juan de Mena and the Power of Courtly Love." *Modern Language Notes* 106 (1991): 241-256.
Weissberger, Barbara F. "'¡A tierra, puto!' Alfonso de Palencia's Discourse of Effeminacy." *Queer Iberia: Sexualities, Cultures and Crossings from the Middle Ages to the Renaissance*. Ed. Josiah Blackmore and Gregory S. Hutcheson. Durham, NC; London: Duke UP, 1999. 291-324.
———. "Authority Figures in *Siervo libre de amor* and *Grisel y Mirabella*." *Revista de Estudios Hispánicos* 9 (1982): 255-62.
———. "Authors, Characters and Readers in *Grimalte y Gradissa*." *Studies in Honor of Stephen Gilman*. Ed. Ronald E. Surtz and Nora Weinerth. Newark, DEL: Juan de la Cuesta, 1983. 61-76.
———. "'Habla el Auctor': *L'Elegia di Madonna Fiammetta* as a Source for the *Siervo libre de amor*." *Journal of Hispanic Philology* 4 (1980): 203-36.

Weissberger, Barbara F. "Isabel's 'Nuevas leyes': Monarchic Law and Justice in *Triunfo de amor.*" *Juan de Flores: Four Studies.* Ed. Joseph J. Gwara. Papers of the Medieval Hispanic Research Seminar 49. London: Department of Hispanic Studies Queen Mary, University of London, 2005. 91-110.

———. *Isabel Rules: Constructing Queenship, Wielding Power.* Minneapolis, MN; London: U of Minnesota P, 2004.

———. "The Politics of *Cárcel de Amor.*" *Revista de Estudios Hispánicos* 26 (1992): 307-26.

———. "Role-Reversal and Festivity in the Romances of Juan de Flores." *Journal of Hispanic Philology* 13 (1988-89): 197-213.

Whinnom, Keith. "*Autor* and *tratado* in the Fifteenth Century: Semantic Latinism or Etymological Trap?" *Bulletin of Hispanic Studies* 59 (1982): 211-18.

———. "Cardona, the Crucifixion and Leriano's Last Drink." *Studies on the Spanish Sentimental Romance (1440-1550): Redefining a Genre.* Ed. Michael E. Gerli and Joseph J. Gwara. London: Tamesis, 1997. 207-13.

———. *Diego de San Pedro.* Twayne's World Author Series 310. New York: Twayne, 1974.

———. *Dos opúsculos isabelinos:* La coronación de la señora Gracisla *(BN ms. 22020) y Nicolás Núñez,* Cárcel de Amor. Ed. Keith Whinnom. University of Exeter Hispanic Texts 22. Exeter: University of Exeter, 1979.

———. Introducción. *Obras completas I.* By Diego de San Pedro. Ed. Keith Whinnom. 2ª ed. Madrid: Castalia: 1985.

———. "The marquis de Pidal vindicated: the fictional biography of Juan Rodríguez del Padrón." *La corónica* 13 (1984): 142-44.

———. *La poesía amatoria cancioneril en la época de los Reyes Católicos.* Durham: U of Durham, 1981.

———. *The Spanish Sentimental Romance 1440-1550: A Critical Bibliography.* Research Bibliographies & Checklists 41 London: Grant & Cutler, 1983.

White, Hayden. "The Forms of Wildness: Archaeology of an Idea." *The Wild Man Within: An Image of Western Thought from the Renaissance to Romanticism.* Ed. Edward Dudley and Maximilian E. Novak. Pittsburgh: U of Pittsburgh P, 1972. 3-38.

Winter, Ulrich. "Subjektivierung im Schreiben und Erzählen." *Welterfahrung – Selbsterfahrung: Konstitution und Verhandlung von Subjektivität in der spanischen Literatur der frühen Neuzeit.* Ed. Wolfgang Matzat and Bernhard Teuber. Tübingen: Max Niemeyer, 2000. 321-43.

Wolfson, Harry Austryn. "The internal senses in Latin, Arabic and Hebrew Philosophic Texts." *Harvard Theological Review* 28 (1935): 69-133.

Woods, M. J. "Pitfalls for the Moralizer in *Lazarillo de Tormes.*" *Modern Language Review* 76 (1979): 580-98.

Yamamoto, Dorothy. *The Boundaries of the Human in Medieval English Literature.* Oxford; New York: Oxford UP, 2000.

Ynduráin, Domingo. "El renacimiento de Lázaro." *Hispania* 75 (1992): 474-83.

———. "En torno al *Examen de ingenios* de Huarte de San Juan." *Boletín de la Real Academia Española* 79 (1999): 7-54.

Zink, Michel. *La subjectivité littéraire autour du siècle de saint Louis.* Paris: Presses Universitaires de France, 1985.

Žižek, Slavoj. *Die Tücke des Subjekts.* [*The Ticklish Subject: The Absent Centre of Political Ontology.* 1999]. Trans. Eva Gilmer, Andreas Hofbauer, Hans Hildebrandt and Anne von der Heiden. Frankfurt am Main: Suhrkamp, 2001.

Zumthor, Paul. *Essai de poétique médiévale.* Paris: Seuil, 1972.

GENERAL INDEX

Note: Modern authors are included only when their work has received substantive discussion in the text or notes. Names of authors are not registered if they appear merely as bibliographic references. If a term appears on one page in the main text and in footnotes, only the page number is indicated.

(*vis*) *aestimativa* (mental faculty of the sensitive soul) 46, 48-49, 64, 107; *entendimiento* 107-08, 110, 145
Agamben, Giorgio 39, 43 n. 47, 63 n. 110, 64, 66, 74, 99, 102, 122 n. 27
Albertus Magnus 46 n. 58
Alemán, Fadrique 153
Alexander of Hales 34 n. 32
Alfarabi 46 n. 58
Alfonso the Wise 136
Alonso de Córdoba 129
Althusser, Louis 28, 157-58
amor hereos (lovesickness) 15, 18, 62-71, 74, 94, 109-111; re-semantization of lovesickness 66-67; obsessing *phantasma/imago* 64-68, 74, 82, 95-96, 113
anima rationalis (rational soul) 46 n. 55, 48-49, 107
anthropological machine (Agamben) 99, 122 n. 27
Antonio, Nicolás 148 n. 103
appetitus (*concupiscibilis* and *irrascibilis*) 48, 64, 90
Aristotle 43-48, 106
Arnaut, Daniel 114 n. 3
ars moriendi 86-87
Augustine of Hippo 36, 55, 149
Averroes 46 n. 58, 66, 108
Avicenna 46 n. 58

Bacon, Roger 45
Baena, Juan Alonso 59-60, 67 n. 116
Biernoff, Suzannah 39-40, 44 n. 48, 48, 52, 69, 78 n. 149, 91

Boccaccio, Giovanni, *Fiammetta* 44 n. 51, 69 n. 123, 92, 145 n. 93, 150 n. 109
body, 35-36, 40-41, 43, 87-88, 90-92; limits of 52-54
Boncompagno de Silva 26 n. 26, 142
Borregán, Alfonso 130 n. 50
Brazaida (Briseida, Cressida) 98-102
Burckhardt, Jacob 29, 42-43
bureaucracy 30, 32 n. 26, 132-34, 153, 156-60
Burke, James F. 44, 50-51, 53-54, 69, 83 n. 160
Burton, Robert 63

caloric identity 16, 42, 71-92; and sex change 90-91, 110
Camili, Camillo 105 n. 224
Carew, Richard 105 n. 224, 106
Cervantes, Miguel de, *Don Quijote* 37, 105, 132 n. 55
choric phantasmatic field/regime 15, 18, 32-33, 44-45, 49-52, 57-58, 64, 79, 93, 101, 122, 126
(*vis*) *cogitativa* 49
Columbus, Christopher 22
Consejo de Cámara de Castilla 159-60
Constantine the African 62 n. 103, 63, 90 n. 181
corps morcelé (Lacan) 96-97

Dante Alighieri 66, 74, n. 139
Deleuze, Gilles 28, 42, 57, 78-79, 82, 115

Delicado, Francisco, *La lozana andaluza* 2 n. 7
Descartes, René 27-29, 36, 56
double/*doppelgänger* 78, Wild Man and knight as *doppelgänger* 76-78, 81-82, 94-95; 122-23 'clerk' and knight as *doppelgänger* 18, 117-20, 123, 135

Egginton, William 30-35, 37, 124-25
enargeia ('vivid' representation/evocation) 121
existimatio ('esteem', 'value') 52, 56, 58, 62, 91, 101, 137
extramission see *intromission*

faculty psychology 17, 41- 62, 104-11; workings of the interior or senses in the animal soul (*anima sensitiva*) 46, 107; *intentiones* ('attitudes', 'intensities') 46-47, 46 n. 59, 64, 101
Fernández de Córdoba, Diego (*alcaide de los donzeles*) 127, 151, 162
Ficino, Marsilio 52 n. 76, 65-66
Flores, Juan de 106, 111, 128-29, 155; *Grimalte y Gradissa* 15, 92-96; 120 n. 21, 128-29, 148; *Grisel y Mirabella* 15, 92, 96-103
Foucault, Michel 22-23, 26, 28 n. 18, 30, 53, 55, 67, 78 n. 149, 142, 146, 150, 157
Francis of Assisi 78 n. 149
Franke, Meister 117
Freigius, Johannes Thomas 43 n. 45
Freud, Sigmund 21, 28, 74, 102, 120 n. 20

Galen 43, 45, 45 n. 54, 89; humorology 104, 106-08
Greenblatt, Stephen 15 n 4, 34, 61, 90
Guillaume de Deguileville 146 n. 98
Gumbrecht, Hans-Ulrich 37-38, 61-62, 69, 113, 125, 127, 129 n. 43, 153

Heidegger, Martin 31, 39
hexis/habitus 15, 18, 41, 53-57, 59, 82, 94, 126-27, 146, 150; disruption through *amor hereos* 15, 18 67-69, 71, 102-02, 117; as the skin or vestiment of the self 70-71
Huarte de San Juan, Juan, *Examen de ingenios* 16, 50 n. 66, 64 n. 112, 88-90, 104-111; on women 109-111

Hugh of St. Victor 70
humanity, loss of 68, 94-95, 98-102
Hume, David 28

identification: psychological 31, 41-42, 115-21, 126, 132 n. 55, 150, 157; through *imitatio Christi* and passion devotion 18, 69, 116-17, in passionate love 15, 18, 83, 116-18; locus of identification 18, 117, 120 n. 21, 122, 134; readerly identification 23, 32, 96 n. 196, 120-26
Ieffes, Abell 154 n. 3
imaginatio (mental faculty of the sensitive soul) 46, 64, 107
imitatio, aemulatio (of exemplary figures) 68-69
imitatio Christi 69, 116
ingenium 106-107, 110
interpellation (Althusser) 23, 157-58, 162
intromission/extramission 44-46, 51-52, 78 n. 149
inwardness (of the self) 27, 29, 54-55, 78-79, 114-15

Jerome (Saint) 91
Juan Manuel 135-37
Juana Inés de la Cruz (Sor) 20, 39

Kant, Immanuel 28
Kramer (Institoris), Heinrich, Sprenger, Jacob, *Malleus maleficarum* 63 n. 110

Lacan, Jacques 21, 28, 33, 39-41, 51, 69, 71-72, 82, 87-88, 96-97, 113-15, 124
Laqueur, Thomas 89-90
Lazarillo de Tormes 17, 132 n. 55, 134, 154-63
Leonardo da Vinci 71 n. 130
letrado ('clerk') 112, 130, 132-35, 149, 155, 162
Locke, John 36
López de Ayala, Pero 19
López de Mendoza, Íñigo (Marqués de Santillana) 38 n. 40
Lucena, Juan de 148 n. 103
Luhmann, Niklas 30, 34
lyric poetry/*poesía cancioneril* 58 n. 94, 59-62, 70 n. 126, 113, 116; *gaya ciencia* 60

Machaut, Guillaume de 112
machina mentis (mind machine) 13 n. 1
Martínez de Toledo, Alfonso, *El Corbacho* 68 n. 120, 102 n. 218
masculinity 16, 18, 50, 58-59, 81-87, 91, 96, 149, 152
melancholy (black bile): adust melancholy 64, 94, 108-09; Freudian melancholy 102
Melanchthon, Philipp 108
memoria (mental faculty of the sensitive soul) 46, 107, 109
Miguel Prendes, Sol 26 n. 15, 116, 125, 130
Montaigne, Michel de 36, 90
Montaña de Monserrate, Bernardino 46 n. 60

Name-of-the-Father (Lacan) 72
Nebrija, Antonio de 22
Núñez, Nicolás, Continuation of *Cárcel* 86, 116 n. 7, 131, 153
Núñez de Castro, Alonso 159 n. 19

one-sex model 16, 89-91, 103, 104-111

Paré, Ambroise 90
passio (Passion) 48, vision as 52
passionate love according to Lacan 40-41; emasculation of the male subject 16, 18, 83-92, 101-02, 109-11, 113; 125; 'feigning' of passionate love 60-61, 67-68
Pedro, Condestável de Portugal, *Sátira de infelice e felice vida* 16, 25, 138-40
Pedro I of Castile 19
Pérez de Guzmán, Fernán 130 n. 50, 159 n. 17
periodization (Medieval vs. Early Modern Period) 19-20, 31, 36-39, 42-43
Petrarca, Francesco 36, 43, 117, 140 n. 74
Petrus Aureoli 56
Phallus according to Lacan 71-72; Laureola's *imago* as the phallus 74-79; loss of phallus in *Grisel y Mirabella* 101-02
philocaptio 63 n. 110, 64, 143
Piccolomini, Enea Silvio 26 n. 13, 143 n. 86
Pico della Mirandola, Giovanni 60 n. 98

Plato 29
Pliny the Younger 90 n. 181
pneuma see *spiritus*
prohairesis (moral choice) 48
Pulgar, Hernando del 130 n. 50

Recopilación de las leyes de Indias 156
Reisch, Gregor 47, 107
relaciones de méritos y servicios (service records) 156-58, 161
Ribera, Suero de 61
Rodríguez Freyle, Juan 156
Rodríguez del Padrón, *Siervo libre de amor* 16, 25 116 n. 9, 140-49
Rojas, Fernando de, *La Celestina* 17, 20, n. 7, 37, 132 n. 55
Rosenbach woodcut of the initial encounter in *Cárcel de amor* 13, 14 n. 2, 22, 24-25, 42, 71, 73-82, 95 n. 194, 112, 117, 121-23, 132
Rousseau, Jean-Jacques 36
Rowland of Anglesey, David 154 n. 3, 160 n. 21, 161-62
Ruiz Juan, *Libro de buen amor* 19

San Pedro, Diego de 106, 111, 133-34; *converso* status 133 n. 59; *Cárcel de amor* 13-16, 22-24, 27, 42, 72-87, 94-96, 103-04, 154-56; editorial history 22, 24-25; readers of 85, 128-31; 85-86 n. 170; constitution of male subject 16-17, 73-87; 112-53; narrative structure 113 n. 1, 118, 120-22, 128-30, 137-38, 148-49; role of El Auctor 16, 18, 115-18, 120-26, 132-53; construction of authorship 16-17, 135-53; *Arnalte y Lucenda* 84 n. 165, 129 n. 45, 133-34
self-fashioning 16, 50, 67-68, 126-28, 135, 142-44, 147-48; according to Stephen Greenblatt 15 n 4, 34; 61; writing of the self 16, 17-18, 26-27; 138-53; 161; *cura sui* 53
sentimental romance (sentimental fiction) genre 25-26; and *Voir Dit* 112; readers of 116-17, 125-31; and printing 125-30
silent reading 125-26, 130
species, *imagines* 44-46, 50-53, 64; thinking in images 49
spiritus or *pneuma* 43, 48, 64, 66

subjectivity 15, 27-42; female subjectivity 20-21, 102-03, 109-11, 131; Cartesian subjectivity 18, 27-29, 31, 35-36, 39, 56, 150; neo-structuralist criticism of 28-29; in the History of Ideas 29-30; in system theory 30; as 'theatricality' 30-32, 124-25; according to Lacan 33, 39-41, 51, 69, 71-72, 112-13; as agency 35-36, and body 35-36, 39-41; and faculty psychology 42-62, 71-92; dispersed subject 15, 18, 42, 55-56, 83; weak subjectivity/subjectivity as a fold 15, 18, 42, 57-58, 78 n. 151, 79, 87, 114, 126-27, 151; and performance 15, 18, 55, 58-62, 68, 101, 124, 137; and *amor hereos* 15, 18, 62-71, 82-83, 96; through literature, reading and writing practices 16, 18, 115, 120-26, 131-53, 161-63
Synderesis 146-47

tactical writing 17
Taylor, Charles 28-30, 34, 36 n. 34, 56
Teresa de Ávila 20
Thomas Aquinas 46 n. 58, 49
Torrellas, Pedro (Pere Toroella) 61 n. 102, 89 n. 178, 98-102
transformation of lovers 44 n. 51, 69-70
Triste deleytaçión 25

Vallmanya, Bernardí 24, 73
Vida del trobador Juan Rodríguez del Padrón 148

Wild Man in *Cárcel de amor* 73-82, 99, 122; in *Grimalte y Gradissa* 94-96; in *Grisel y Mirabella* 99-103; and virility 76, 79-80
William of Conches 52 n. 73, 46 n. 56

Zayas, María de 20.

NORTH CAROLINA STUDIES IN THE ROMANCE LANGUAGES AND LITERATURES

I.S.B.N. Prefix 0-8078-

Recent Titles

TRANSPOSING ART INTO TEXTS IN FRENCH ROMANTIC LITERATURE, by Henry F. Majewski. 2002. (No. 273). -9277-7.

IMAGES IN MIND: LOVESICKNESS, SPANISH SENTIMENTAL FICTION AND *DON QUIJOTE*, by Robert Folger. 2002. (No. 274). -9278-5.

INDISCERNIBLE COUNTERPARTS: THE INVENTION OF THE TEXT IN FRENCH CLASSICAL DRAMA, by Christopher Braider. 2002. (No. 275). -9279-3.

SAVAGE SIGHT/CONSTRUCTED NOISE. POETIC ADAPTATIONS OF PAINTERLY TECHNIQUES IN THE FRENCH AND AMERICAN AVANT-GARDES, by David LeHardy Sweet. 2003. (No. 276). -9281-5.

AN EARLY BOURGEOIS LITERATURE IN GOLDEN AGE SPAIN. *LAZARILLO DE TORMES, GUZMÁN DE ALFARACHE* AND BALTASAR GRACIÁN, by Francisco J. Sánchez. 2003. (No. 277). -9280-7.

METAFACT: ESSAYISTIC SCIENCE IN EIGHTEENTH-CENTURY FRANCE, by Lars O. Erickson. 2004. (No. 278). -9282-3.

THE INVENTION OF THE EYEWITNESS. A HISTORY OF TESTIMONY IN FRANCE, by Andrea Frisch. 2004. (No. 279). -9283-1.

SUBJECT TO CHANGE: THE LESSONS OF LATIN AMERICAN WOMEN'S *TESTIMONIO* FOR TRUTH, FICTION, AND THEORY, by Joanna R. Bartow. 2005. (No. 280). -9284-X.

QUESTIONING RACINIAN TRAGEDY, by John Campbell. 2005. (No. 281). -9285-8.

THE POLITICS OF FARCE IN CONTEMPORARY SPANISH AMERICAN THEATRE, by Priscilla Meléndez. 2006. (No. 282). -9286-6.

MODERATING MASCULINITY IN EARLY MODERN CULTURE, by Todd W. Reeser. 2006. (No. 283). -9287-4.

PORNOBOSCODIDASCALUS LATINUS (1624). KASPAR BARTH'S NEO-LATIN TRANSLATION OF *CELESTINA*, by Enrique Fernández. 2006. (No. 284). -9288-2.

JACQUES ROUBAUD AND THE INVENTION OF MEMORY, by Jean-Jacques F. Poucel. 2006. (No. 285). -9289-0.

THE "I" OF HISTORY. SELF-FASHIONING AND NATIONAL CONSCIOUSNESS IN JULES MICHELET, by Vivian Kogan. 2006. (No. 286). -9290-4.

BUCOLIC METAPHORS: HISTORY, SUBJECTIVITY, AND GENDER IN THE EARLY MODERN SPANISH PASTORAL, by Rosilie Hernández-Pecoraro. 2006. (No. 287). -9291-2.

UNA ARMONÍA DE CAPRICHOS: EL DISCURSO DE RESPUESTA EN LA PROSA DE RUBÉN DARÍO, por Francisco Solares-Larrare. 2007. (No. 288). -9292-0.

READING THE *EXEMPLUM* RIGHT: FIXING THE MEANING OF *EL CONDE LUCANOR*, by Jonathan Burgoyne. 2007. (No. 289). -9293-9.

MONSTRUOS QUE HABLAN: EL DISCURSO DE LA MONSTRUOSIDAD EN CERVANTES, por Rogelio Miñana. 2007. (No. 290). -9294-7.

BAJO EL CIELO PERUANO: THE DEVOUT WORLD OF PERALTA BARNUEVO, by David F. Slade and Jerry M. Williams. 2008. (No. 291). -9295-4.

ESCAPE FROM THE PRISON OF LOVE: CALORIC IDENTITIES AND WRITING SUBJECTS IN FIFTEENTH-CENTURY SPAIN, by Robert Folger. 2009. (No. 292). -9296-1.

When ordering please cite the *ISBN Prefix* plus the last four digits for each title.

Send orders to: University of North Carolina Press
P.O. Box 2288
Chapel Hill, NC 27515-2288
U.S.A.
www.uncpress.unc.edu
FAX: 919 966-3829

www.ingramcontent.com/pod-product-compliance
Lightning Source LLC
Chambersburg PA
CBHW020738230426
43665CB00009B/485